Marx and Justice
PHILOSOPHY AND SOCIETY
General Editor: Marshall Cohen

Also in this series:

Marx and Justice

Marx and Justice
The Radical Critique of Liberalism

ALLEN E. BUCHANAN

ROWMAN & ALLANHELD
Totowa, New Jersey

ROWMAN & ALLANHELD PUBLISHERS

Copyright © 1982 by Rowman and Littlefield

First published in the United States 1982 by Rowman and Littlefield,
81 Adams Drive, Totowa, New Jersey 07512.

Library of Congress Cataloging in Publication Data

Buchanan, Allen E., 1948–
  Marx and justice.

  (Philosophy and society)
  Includes index.
  1. Marx, Karl, 1818–1883. 2. Liberalism.
3. Justice.   4. Civil rights.   I. Title.
II. Series.
HX39.5.B79   1982   335.4'01   81-23436
ISBN 0-8476-7039-2   AACR2

83 84 85 86 87 10 9 8 7 6 5 4 3 2

Printed in the United States of America

for Deborah, Lucy, Steve, and Jack

Contents

Acknowledgments

Whatever is valuable in this book owes much to a number of people whose work on Marx and on justice I have profited from or who have generously commented on my own efforts. It was the scope and power of John Rawls' book *A Theory of Justice* which stimulated me to explore the role of juridical conceptions in social theories, while it was Allen Wood's article "The Marxian Critique of Justice" which focused my attempts to grapple with the intimidating corpus of Marx's works. Though I criticize Rawls' theory and Wood's interpretation of Marx in what follows, I am indebted to them both.

When this book was almost completed I was fortunate enough to study G. A. Cohen's book, *Marx's Theory of History,* which has set a new standard for both Marxian social theory and Marx scholarship. Since my main concern in this book is with Marx's social criticism rather than with his model of historical explanation, references to Cohen's work are rather infrequent. It was, however, what I took to be the inadequacy of Cohen's account of Marx's notion of progress in the succession of socio-economic forms from capitalism to communism which prompted me to recast the chapter on Marx's evaluative perspective in its present form. In addition, the final chapter of this book examines Marx's prediction that democratic control of natural and social resources will result in a great increase in harmony and productivity, and it is the lack of a systematic defense of this crucial prediction that makes Cohen's defense of Marx seriously incomplete.

I also wish to thank the following colleagues and students for helping me refine my thoughts on Marx and on juridical theories: Annette Baier, David Brink, Norman Dahl, Stephen Darwall, Gordon Graham, Jim Hill, Conrad Johnson, Michael Morris, Stephen Munzer, James Nickel, Michael Root, Rolf Sartorius, Eugenia Toma, and Mark Toma. Special thanks are due to William Leon McBride and Kai Nielsen who provided helpful comments on each chapter.

I gratefully acknowledge the generous support which the following institutions and foundations provided for my research: The University of Minnesota Graduate School; The Liberty Fund, Incorporated; The Reason Foundation; and the Institute for Humane Studies.

Finally, I would like to thank Vicki Field, Ruth Anne Ruud and Lisa Strombeck for their patient and accurate service in preparing this manuscript for publication.

Preface

Among analytic philosophers in the past few years, there has been a growing commitment to taking Marx seriously. Since the publication in 1971 of John Rawls' book *A Theory of Justice*, there has also been a growing commitment to taking problems of justice seriously. These two refreshing developments should intersect in penetrating mutual criticism. Marx's radical critique is a challenge to all theories of justice, while the sophistication of recent theories raises the possibility that they escape some of Marx's most basic criticisms.

The aim of this book is two-fold: to reconstruct and assess Marx's thought on justice in all its rich complexity, and then to apply his reconstructed position to some of the best contemporary thinking about justice. These two tasks are not independent, because an accurate assessment of Marx's position will depend in part upon an estimate of its effectiveness against opposing views.

Brevity in a title is a virtue, but it tends to mislead. By Marx's views on justice I mean not only his treatment of *distributive* justice, understood rather narrowly as the just distribution of material goods, and his brief but provocative comments on criminal justice, so far as the latter includes the notion of just punishment, but also what may be called civil and political justice. The breadth of the subject may be best appreciated if it is framed in terms of *rights*. Much must be said about various conceptions of rights as we proceed with the task of reconstruction, but for now we need only note that Marx criticized not only rights to a share of wealth but also a whole range of rights of political participation, as well as various civil rights, such as the right to freedom from arbitrary arrest and seizure, the right to free speech, and the right to freedom of religion.

The originality and power of Marx's thoughts on conceptions of justice and rights of the various sorts listed above—what I shall henceforth call *juridical conceptions*—can best be appreciated if we approach his works with this question clearly before us: What roles do juridical conceptions play in social theory? Two broad distinctions will prove fruitful in what follows.

First, we may distinguish between *explanatory* and *critical* uses of juridical concepts. A social theory employs juridical conceptions ex-

xi

planatorily if it uses notions of rights or justice to *describe* and *explain* social institutions or their development over time. Juridical conceptions function critically in a social theory when they serve as criteria or principles for *assessing* social institutions or the conduct which those institutions structure. The critical use of juridical conceptions will typically have normative import: the charge that certain institutions are unjust or violate rights can be used to motivate us to reform or overthrow those institutions.

Second, we may distinguish between juridical conceptions which are *internal* and those which are *external*, relative to a given society. Internal juridical conceptions are those which are at least in part embodied in the basic institutional structure and which predominate in the consciousness of the members of the society in question. Thus when we examine juridical criticisms of a certain society we may ask whether or not the juridical conceptions those criticisms invoke are internal to that society. Similarly, the juridical conceptions used to explain institutional phenomena in a given society may be just those conceptions which are codified in the laws and constitutional forms of the society and which structure the sense of justice of its members, or they may be imported from elsewhere. Once this distinction is admitted, we can no longer assume that the proper assessment or explanation of a set of social institutions is to be framed in the juridical conceptions employed by those who participate in those institutions, any more than a post-Freudian psychologist can assume that a person's testimony about his reasons for acting is unassailable.

Since, as I shall argue later, the interest of Marx's views on juridical conceptions lies as much in the roles these notions do *not* play in his social theory as in the ones they do, my strategy is to approach the subject indirectly. In Chapter 1, I offer an interpretation of some of the elements of Hegel's political philosophy which were most influential on the development of Marx's thought and which provided material for his first systematic social criticism. I argue that Hegel's *Philosophy of Right* is an attempt to ascertain the scope and limits of juridical thinking and juridical practice and that Marx's critique is the radicalized descendant of Hegel's position. Where Hegel wished to circumscribe the institutional and conceptual domain of the juridical, Marx ultimately left no room for it.

In Chapter 2, I articulate Marx's basic evaluative perspective—the vantage point from which he launched his radical criticisms of capitalism and which grounds his judgment that the emergence of communism is not only change but progress. Two main conclusions are reached: first, that the coherence of Marx's basic evaluative perspective depends not upon his early normative concept of human nature but upon the adequacy of his materialist theory of consciousness; and second, that his evaluative perspective is essentially non-juridical and external in the sense explained above.

Chapter 3 provides an analysis of Marx's theory of exploitation,

defends that theory against several widespread but unsound criticisms, and develops connections between the theory of exploitation,
Marx's account of alienation, and the basic evaluative perspective
examined in the preceding chapter. I argue that both Marx's critics and
his defenders have failed to appreciate the complexity of his theory of
exploitation because they have concentrated exclusively on his analysis of exploitation in wage-labor, neglecting other exploitative relationships in capitalism, and failed to develop the connection between
exploitation and alienation. Most of the material in this chapter is
adapted from an earlier essay, "Exploitation, Alienation, and Injustice" (*Canadian Journal of Philosophy*, vol. IX, no. 1, 1979).

Chapter 4, "The Marxian Critique of Justice and Rights," is a revised
and significantly expanded version of a long essay of the same title
(forthcoming in a Supplementary Volume of the *Canadian Journal of
Philosophy* on Marx). It develops the distinctions sketched above and
shows that, for Marx, juridical concepts play neither a major explanatory nor a major critical role, and reinforces the conclusion of Chapter 2
that his most fundamental criticisms of capitalism presuppose a perspective which is both non-juridical and external. It is also argued that
the radical character of Marx's critique of juridical theory and practice
can only be fully appreciated if we understand his views on the sources
of conflict in what Hume and others call the circumstances of justice.

Chapter 5 explores Marx's theory of revolutionary motivation. I
argue that Marx's attempt to construct a non-juridical theory of the
motivational roots of successful proletarian revolution is seriously
defective and that certain central features of Marx's social theory may
present obstacles to remedying its defects. The material of this chapter
is adapted from my essay, "Revolutionary Motivation and Rationality"
(*Philosophy and Public Affairs*, vol. 9, no. 1, 1979; reprinted in *Marx,
History, and Justice*, edited by M. Cohen, T. Nagel, and T. Scanlon,
Princeton University Press, 1980).

In Chapter 6, I first present what I believe is the best available theory
of justice, John Rawls' theory, and I then examine the most serious
Marxian objections to it. The assumption underlying this strategy is
that one way of assessing Marx's critique of juridical conceptions is to
test its effectiveness against an impressive example of juridical theorizing. The summary of Rawls' theory is based in part upon my essay,
"Rawls' Theory of Justice; An Introduction" (in *John Rawls' Theory of
Social Justice*, edited by G. Blocker and E. Smith, Ohio University Press,
1980). Considerable space is devoted to presenting the main elements
of Rawls' theory for two reasons. First, that theory is extremely complex; second, many Marxian critiques of Rawls have been based at least
in part on misinterpretations. My exposition of Rawls' system should
be of considerable interest, since it is based not only on *A Theory of
Justice* but also upon published and unpublished papers Rawls has
written since the appearance of the book. My aim in this chapter is to
provide both the best available exposition of Rawls' theory in a rela-

tively brief compass and the most comprehensive available examination of Marxian objections to Rawls. By examining these Marxian objections to Rawls, the virtues and defects of both theories become clearer.

The seventh and final chapter continues the assessment of Marx's views. I argue that some of Marx's most provocative and original views are based on an inadequate understanding of the sources of interpersonal conflict and of the roles which juridical conceptions may play and that they presuppose the success of a theory of democratic social coordination which Marx did not provide. I conclude, nevertheless, that Marx's thought provides the most systematic and troubling challenge to two dogmas of traditional and contemporary political philosophy: the thesis that justice is the first virtue of social institutions and the thesis that respect for persons as right-holders is the first virtue of individuals.

In developing my reconstruction, I have quoted Marx frequently and sometimes at considerable length in an effort to reduce the dangers of interpreting his words out of context. My choice of translations was based in each case on the criterion of accuracy and availability. In the relatively few instances where an issue of substance turns upon a translation that might be subject to controversy, I have provided my own translation and supplied the German, from the standard *Marx-Engels Werke* edition (East Berlin).

Both prudence and intellectual honesty dictate that I emphasize that it is a *reconstruction* of Marx's thought on juridical conceptions and juridical institutions which I present and assess. Marx wrote for over 30 years, producing a vast, undisciplined array of published and unpublished manuscripts, letters, and notebooks on a remarkably wide range of topics, directed to diverse audiences from barely literate workers to academic economists. He produced no systematic treatise on the state or on juridical theory and practice. While I believe that my reconstruction does the best job of explaining the most significant passages bearing on the subject, I am well aware that the textual evidence I adduce is often indirect and that its weight is cumulative rather than decisive at every point. For this reason I frequently refer to a particular view as *Marxian* rather than as Marx's, signaling that I am concerned not only with what Marx actually said but with the most interesting ideas that can be developed consistently from what he actually said.

Though I have taken Marx's critique of juridical conceptions and institutions as my guiding thread, I believe this book will be valuable to those who have no special interest in theories of justice and rights. For it is my belief that a proper understanding and assessment of Marx's theory of revolution, his analysis of alienation and exploitation in capitalism, and his theory of consciousness will not be possible until we have grasped the role of Marx's critique of juridical thought and practice in his social theory as a whole.

1

Hegelian Roots

I

Marx's first systematic work in social philosophy was a critique of Hegel's theory of the state. From this he progressed to a criticism of the state itself. His criticism of the state then led to a systematic investigation of the form of social organization on which the state rests. So to understand Marx's social philosophy as a whole and his position on juridical concepts in particular, we must begin with Hegel's theory of the state, as presented in the *Philosophy of Right*. The latter work, however, cannot be fully appreciated in isolation. The theory of the state it advances is embedded in Hegel's philosophy of history, and it is from the perspective of an alternative philosophy of history that Marx's most trenchant criticisms of Hegel are ultimately launched.

Even a brief summation of Hegel's philosophy of history as a whole would be out of the question here.[1] For our purposes, a basic grasp of two of Hegel's central theses and their relation to one another must suffice:

1) The goal of history is Spirit's consciousness of its own freedom through the realization (embodiment, objectification) of the fully developed concept of freedom.
2) The (modern) state is the realization of the fully developed concept of freedom; it is the synthesis of subjective and objective freedom.

To those whose view of history has been fully secularized, the first thesis will seem at worst fantastic and at best imponderable. Hegel's audience, however, was nurtured on the Judeo-Christian view of a Divine Providence whose plan unfolds in history. Thus Hegel—who often refers to Spirit as God—was able to clarify his first thesis by linking his vision of Spirit as the guiding force of world history with the Judeo-Christian conception. Indeed, Hegel believes that his concept of Spirit is the traditional concept of God in rational form. He also emphasizes two striking differences. First, according to the traditional Judeo-

1

Christian idea of Divine Providence, God's ways are for the most part mysterious to us and will always remain so. God does not publish history's itinerary, though from time to time he may permit certain select mortals (such as Moses) a glimpse at a fragment of it. In contrast, Hegel believes that the divine plan is wholly intelligible. At a certain stage of history—the stage at which the modern nation state emerges, and along with it the culmination of speculative thought in Hegel's system—Spirit's design in history is laid bare. Second, according to the traditional Judeo-Christian conception of Divine Providence, God acts self-consciously. He knows what he is doing in history and he knows it from the start. Not so for Hegel's God. The "sovereign of the world" is not conscious of its goal or its activities throughout the historical process: it only attains self-consciousness in the culmination of the process.

Though he believes that both the goal of history and the process of its attainment become fully intelligible to man (or at least to the speculative philosopher), Hegel denies that human beings can utilize this knowledge to participate purposively in the process. According to Hegel, human beings do participate in the realization of Spirit's goal, but they do so unwittingly, prompted by their private passions, in the pursuit of ends that are for the most part selfish and myopic.

The question of the *means* by which Freedom develops itself in a world, conducts us to the phenomenon of History itself. Although Freedom is, primarily an undeveloped idea, the means it uses are external and phenomenal; presenting themselves in history to our sensuous vision. The first glance at history convinces us that the actions of men proceed from their needs, their passions, their characters and talents; and impresses us with the belief that such needs, passions and interests are the sole springs of action—the efficient agents in this scene of activity.[2]

Even the speculative philosopher existing in that form of socio-political organization that is the culmination of history can only explain the way of Spirit in the world *ex post facto*. He cannot use his knowledge of history to contribute to the attainment of reason's goal, nor can he instruct others how to do so. The task of the philosopher is to explain and thereby justify the ways of Spirit to man, not to equip man for deliberate partnership in Spirit's business. Hegel leaves no doubt as to why such justification is needed.

When we look at this display of passions, and the consequences of their violence; the unreason which is associated not only with them, but even (rather we might say *especially*) with *good* designs and righteous aims; when we see the evil, the vice, the ruin that has befallen the most flourishing kingdoms which the mind of man ever created, we can scarce avoid being filled with sorrow at this universal taint of corruption. . . . Without rhetorical exaggeration, a simply truthful combination of the miseries that have overwhelmed the noblest of nations and politics, and the finest exemplars of private virtue,— forms a picture of most fearful aspect. . . .[3]

Thus Hegel's philosophy of history is theodicy—an attempt to reconcile the irrationality and destruction so evident in the world with the thesis that Reason is the creative force which rules history.

Like Hegel, Marx believed that, at a certain point in history, human beings can understand the process of history and ascertain the direction of change. Unlike Hegel, he believed this knowledge would enable human beings to cast off the role of unwitting participants and become conscious agents of historical change.

According to Hegel, the various forms of socio-political organizations preceding the modern nation state as he depicts it in the *Philosophy of Right* embody in their institutions—especially their juridical institutions—a partial, limited, or "abstract" conception of freedom, and in each there exists a correspondingly restricted consciousness of freedom.

The Orientals have not attained the knowledge that Spirit—Man *as such*—is free; and because they do not know this they are not free. They only know that *one is free*. The consciousness of Freedom first arose among the Greeks, and therefore they were free; but they, and the Romans likewise, knew only that *some* were free,—not man as such. . . . The German nations, under the influence of Christianity, were the first to attain the consciousness, that man, as man, is free: that it is the *freedom* of Spirit which constitutes its essence.[4]

In the *Philosophy of Right*, Hegel presents a detailed account of the complex array of institutions that constitute the modern state and explains how they embody the fully developed concept of freedom. The two main elements of the fully developed concept are (1) the concept of subjective freedom and (2) the concept of objective freedom.

Hegel's analysis of the concepts of subjective and objective freedom emerges most clearly in his attempt to show that only the state as he conceives it can provide an adequate response to the problems of civil society. To put it differently, Hegel's task in the *Philosophy of Right* is to show how the state can cope with the problems of civil society, yet cope in such a way that both subjective and objective freedom are given appropriate scope.

Hegel's distinction between subjective and objective freedom can best be approached indirectly through a reconstruction of two related distinctions: the distinction between *Sittlichkeit* (customary ethical life) and *Moralität* (autonomous morality), and that between objective and subjective willing.

Hegel uses the term *"Moralität"* to refer to one paradigm of how the individual is to determine what he ought morally to do or what is morally right, wrong, or permissible.[5] According to this paradigm, the individual should reflect upon the alternatives and then, relying upon his own moral judgment, follow his own conscience. Hegel emphasizes that this way of determining what one ought morally to do is *abstract* and formal in the sense that it says nothing at all that is concrete or substantive; it tells us nothing about the *content* of moral conduct.

Nothing is conveyed about *what* it is one is to do—all one is left with is a procedure by which one is to determine whatever it is one is to do. Further, the process in question is essentially individualistic—it is an act of the self-reliant individual, abstracted from his social context. Hegel identifies Kant as the philosopher of *Moralität par excellence* and criticizes him for failing to see that even the most basic moral concepts have no practical content unless they are placed in a particular institutional setting.[6]

In contrast, Hegel uses the term *"Sittlichkeit"* to refer to a paradigm according to which the moral agent is not an abstract individual, but an essentially social being who exists within the framework of institutions, practices, and laws. Further, the moral agent is conceived as a thoroughly socialized being, one who has *internalized* the various norms and standards of conduct of his society. Thus, according to the paradigm of *Sittlichkeit*, when such a person determines what he ought morally to do, that person relies on these social values. For the person of *Sittlichkeit*, determining what one is morally to do is not characteristically a matter of consciously deciding on principles or reflecting on alternative courses of action.

It is important to forestall a misinterpretation. For Hegel, neither the person of *Sittlichkeit* nor the person of *Moralität* is found in the real world—they are ideal types. Existing human beings may, however, approximate either mode of conduct to a greater or lesser extent. Hegel isolates these ideal-type concepts because he believes they each capture something essential about the moral life. Further, he does not propose a choice between *Sittlichkeit* and *Moralität*, since each is incomplete by itself. Nonetheless, it seems fair to say that he directs most of his criticisms against *Moralität*, and that his claim that the two ideals can be transformed and harmoniously united through a dialectical synthesis is far from convincing.[7]

The distinction between *Sittlichkeit* and *Moralität* can be understood as a special case of a broader contrast between objective and subjective willing.[8] Hegel uses the latter distinction to contrast two opposing paradigms of how a person is to determine what he is to do in general, rather than simply what he ought *morally* to do. In other words, the contrast between subjective and objective willing is not limited to a difference between two ways of determining one's distinctively moral conduct. We do often engage in conduct where it is assumed that no moral issues are at stake and where there is no need for moral determination.

A person's mode of determining what he ought to do (or what would be best to do) is an instance of *subjective* willing if the person's conduct is determined by his own more or less reflective consideration of what would be good or bad, etc. Subjective willing, put most simply, is a matter of making one's own decisions for one's own reasons, according to one's own independent values and priorities. As in the special case of *Moralität*, subjective willing is thus individualistic, reflective, and purely formal: to say that a person's conduct is determined through subjective willing is to say nothing of its content.

Objective willing, in contrast, is social, nonreflective, and content-ful. It is *objective* in three related senses.

a) It includes a proper *object:* When one wills objectively, what one determines to do really is the right or good thing, not just what one happens to think is so.[9]
b) One's willing is determined by principles or standards or values that are *objectified*, i.e., embodied in social institutions, which exist independently of the individual subject.
c) The "will is absorbed in its object, as, for example, the will of the child."[10]

Point (b) has already been explained, but in what sense is willing determined by objectified (i.e., institutionally embodied) principles or values like the willing of a child? Apparently Hegel means that willing determined by thoroughly internalized social rules resembles the immediate, nonreflective behavior of a child absorbed in the object of play. Or he may be referring to that stage of a person's development in which rules have already been internalized, but in which the agent has not yet separated himself from the rules so as to make critical examination of them possible. In some respects, the former analogy is especially fruitful. Just as the child at play experiences no "distance" between his action and the environment to which he responds, so the person of objective willing does not view the relevant social norm as something standing over and against his own will.

The relationship between (b), the idea that objective willing is willing determined by institutionally objectified principles or values, and (a), the claim that it is objective in the sense of having the proper object, is more complex. With considerable simplification, we can say that Hegel, like other conservatives, believes that social institutions (and the principles and values they embody) are repositories of rationality far richer than anything that can be attained by the individual's independent judgment, though he stresses that the mere existence of an institution does not establish that it is beyond rational criticism. Hegel supports this very general claim in several ways, at different levels of argument. On what might be called the level of practical empirical observation, he points out the excesses of subjective willing, arguing that socially produced principles and values are generally more objective in the sense of being impartial and judicious. At the ontological level, he advances the often repeated, but seldom understood thesis that the real is the rational and concludes that institutionally embodied principles and values are more real, more substantial, or have a higher degree of reality, than those which exist only in the ephemeral consciousness of the particular subject. At the epistemological level, Hegel advances the very general anti-Cartesian view that the community, not the individual mind, is the ultimate subject of knowledge, including practical knowledge.

Now at last we are in a position to grasp Hegel's distinction between subjective and objective *freedom* and to explain his thesis that the modern nation state as he describes it unites subjective and objective freedom. Subjective freedom is the freedom to act through subjective willing—the freedom to make one's own decisions as to what to do, for one's own reasons, without having the content of one's conduct determined by social norms or customary values. From the perspective of consequences, subjective freedom is freedom to reap the rewards of one's own practical judgment, but also to take one's own risks and to make one's own mistakes.

Objective freedom is the freedom one has when one comes to act through objective willing. But what sort of *freedom* is that? For Hegel, one whose conduct is determined through objective willing is free in several senses. Since objective willing characteristically is willing the proper object, that which is truly good or right, one is free from the harmful consequences of one's own ignorance, irrational impulses, and shortsightedness. Hence one is also free from the regret to which one would be liable had one relied upon one's own fallible judgment and failed to do what really is good or right. Finally, like the child absorbed in play, one is free from doubt, from the burdens of autonomy, from the anxieties of bearing the responsibility for one's principles of action alone.[11]

Once we understand that, for Hegel, objective willing entails freedom in each of these senses, it becomes clear that one can be free—objectively free—even if one's opportunities for exercising independent practical judgment, and in general for living the autonomous life, are severly curtailed. Indeed, Hegel's account of objective willing enables him to make perfectly good sense of Rousseau's idea that we can be forced to be free. For we can be forced to act in accordance with institutionally embodied norms, forced to forgo the burdens of autonomy, and even indoctrinated forcibly into internalizing these objectified norms.[12]

Hegel contends that the democratic theorist's obsession with subjective freedom leads to a distorted view of the state, just as the Kantian's preoccupation with *Moralität* results in a twisted conception of the moral life. If subjective freedom is not somehow kept within proper limits, Hegel argues, there can be no genuine state: a condition in which each does only what he independently judges to be right or good is anarchy. On the other hand, a state which concedes nothing or too little to subjective freedom is also intolerable.

To understand how the modern nation state is supposed to provide a synthesis of subjective and objective freedom, we must understand Hegel's conception of civil society and his analysis of the distinctive problems of that form of social life.

II

Hegel uses the phrase "civil society" *[bürgerliche Gesellshaft]* as a more or less technical term to denote the expanding, postfeudal, market society that Marx would later call bourgeois society or simply capitalism that began to emerge in Western Europe in the sixteenth and seventeenth centuries. Civil society, as Hegel conceives it, includes the following features: (a) competitive, egoistic interaction, based on the institution of private property and the market ("the war of each against all"[13]); (b) accelerating technological and organizational development in manufacturing[14]; (c) increasing urbanization, with deepening divisions between town and country life[15]; (d) class divisions, extreme wealth coexisting with extreme poverty, and the creation of a permanent, materially and culturally impoverished "rabble;"[16] and (e) rapid development of a *world* market, with the increasing interdependence of peoples and nations this brings.[17] Hegel stresses the first feature: individuals in civil society act from their own particular, limited interests, rather than from any conception of the common (or general) interest, and treat each other instrumentally, as mere means to their own private ends.

For Hegel, civil society is the sphere in which subjective freedom holds sway. Individuals rely on their own judgment, take their own risks, make their own mistakes, and reap their own rewards, unrestrained by concern for the good of others.

Hegel emphasizes two related aspects of the subjective freedom of civil society that are guaranteed by juridical institutions: the right to private property and the right to choose one's occupation. He stresses the former in his provocative but unconvincing argument that private property is necessary for the development of personality, the latter in his criticism of Plato's vision of the good society as one in which occupation is determined by heredity or by the rulers' command.[18]

In the Introduction to the *Philosophy of Right*, Hegel says that awareness of objects as mere objects is a necessary condition of our being conscious of ourselves as persons—subjects rather than mere objects.[19] Awareness of objects as mere objects leads us to appreciate that we are free, as mere things are not. Since, for Hegel, being a person requires consciousness of one's freedom, and consciousness of one's freedom comes through reflective confrontation with mere things, the conditions and modes of our access to objects become a crucial philosophical issue. As Marx will later put it: man's metabolism with nature—his interaction with the materials of life—becomes a central topic of investigation.

Later in the *Philosophy of Right*, Hegel suggests that the consciousness of our freedom through awareness of objects as mere objects is especially strong and vivid in the activity of work. The object of our labor becomes an objectification, a tangible proof of our free, creative power. In this sense, the need to labor upon objects is to be welcomed as an opportunity for the development of personality, not lamented as the curse of mankind.

The idea has been advanced that in respect of his needs man lived in freedom in the so-called "state of nature" when his needs were supposed to be confined to what are known as the simple necessities of nature, and when he required for their satisfaction only the means which the accidents of nature directly assured to him. This view takes no account of the moment of liberation intrinsic to work. . . . And apart from this, it is false, because to be confined to mere physical needs and such and their direct satisfaction would simply be the condition in which the mental is plunged in the natural and so would be one of savagery and unfreedom, while freedom itself is to be found only in the reflection of mind into itself, in mind's distinction from nature, and in the reflex of mind in nature.[20]

So far nothing has been said about the role of *private* property rights in the development of personality. But Hegel goes on to argue that mere awareness of objects and even awareness of objects we have created or transformed through work are not sufficient for an adequate consciousness of our freedom, nor hence for the full development of personality. What is required, he thinks, is that there be some objects which are exclusively *mine*—and which other persons recognize as such. Private property right is

the immediate embodiment which freedom gives itself in an immediate way . . . For a person by distinguishing himself from himself distinguishes himself from others, and it is only as owners that two people exist for each other.[21]

Hegel thinks that consciousness of oneself as a person requires awareness that others recognize one as a person, where this takes the form of their recognizing that one is the owner of certain objects. His remarks about the importance of private property reach a crescendo in the following passage:

The rationale of property is to be found not in the satisfaction of needs but the supersession [*Aufhebung*] of the pure subjectivity of personality. In property a person exists for the first time as reason. Even if my freedom is here realized first of all in an external thing, and so falsely realized, nevertheless abstract personality in its immediacy can have no other embodiment save one characterized by immediacy.[22]

As in the passage just cited, Hegel does not always explicitly say that the property right in question is a private property right. But both the context of these remarks—his analysis of civil society, which is founded on private property—and the absence of any indication that he is concerned with any communal or nonprivate form of property, make his meaning clear enough. However, even if Hegel has shown that some form of personal property is necessary for the consciousness of freedom and hence for the development of personality, this would fall short of an argument for private property *in the means of production*.

Hegel fails to show why a more restricted set of use-rights over
of production or a right to participate in control over the means
production would not suffice, when combined with a right to personal
property in things that do not qualify as means of production.[23]

The shift from an emphasis on the relationship between personality
and working on objects to the view that the individual's exclusive
control over means of production is crucial for the development of
personality is portentious. Marx will agree that consciousness of one's
freedom is essential for the development of personality and that this
consciousness is achieved through free creation of objects. But he will
contend that the institution of private property in the means of production necessarily deprives the majority of the population of opportunities for the full development of personality by excluding them from
free access to objects of labor and hence from the opportunity for free,
creative activity. Further, as we shall see in Chapter 4, Marx does not ✓
maintain that the right of private property will or should be replaced by
a new system of property *rights* in communism.

Though he values civil society precisely because it is the sphere of
subjective freedom, Hegel sees the evils of civil society as inevitable
consequences of the exercise of subjective freedom.

Particularity by itself, given free rein in every direction to satisfy its needs,
accidental caprices, and subjective desires, destroys itself and its substantive
concept in this process of gratification. At the same time, the satisfaction of
need, necessary and accidental alike, is accidental because it breeds new
desires without end, is in thoroughgoing dependence on caprice and external
accident. . . . In these contrasts and their complexity, civil society affords a
spectacle of extravagance and want as well as of the physical and ethical
degeneration common to them both.[24]

Hegel's analysis of the bitter fruits of subjective freedom is rich and
complex, anticipating many of the central elements of Marx's critique
of capitalism. The unrestricted exercise of individual freedom produces severe economic and social instability—individuals prosper fan-
tastically, then lose everything in periodic business crises which become global in scope. Markets spring up then collapse just as quickly,
ruining whole occupational groups. The juxtaposition of ostentatious
wealth with crushing poverty threatens to rend the social fabric asun-
der. Society finds itself confronted with a permanent class of losers in
the competitive struggle who lack not only the means of subsistence,
but also the rudiments of self-respect and morality.[25]

What is needed, Hegel concludes, is some means of coping with the
ills of civil society, some way of insuring that the common good, "the
universal," as he calls it, is not lost in the clash of particular interests.
There must be some power to hold "the extravagances" of civil society
"in check."[26]

At this point, Hegel confronts a crucial complication: Who can be
trusted to wield the power necessary for controlling the destructive
forces of civil society? Who can be expected to secure the universal—to

pursue effectively what really is the common
diverted by the pressures of particular interests?
ar exercise of subjective freedom from destroying
without eradicating the conditions for subjective
culty is that the active members of civil society are
because they are by definition absorbed in their own
r interests.

nced that it is unrealistic—naive—to think that one
erson can be both an active participant in the war of
each aga. ll in civil society and an agent with the objectivity,
knowledge, and dedication to ascertain and implement the common
good. In Marx's terms, the idea that the same individual can be both
bourgeois and *citoyen* is a schizophrenic fantasy. The bourgeois will
always win out over the citizen. The man who spends the greater part
of his life immersed in the competitive struggle of the market society
cannot reasonably be expected to transform himself into a farsighted,
unselfish statesman on those sporadic occasions when he participates
in the political process.

Marx's response to the difficulty is *radical* in the etymological sense
of the word—an attempt to go to the roots of the problem. He argues
that no one can control the evils of civil society: we shall be rid of them
only when we are rid of civil society itself. The problem of the incompatibility of man as bourgeois and man as citizen will likewise be
dissolved rather than solved. Despite all efforts to preserve it, civil
society will destroy itself and man as bourgeois will disappear with it.

Hegel rejects the radical solution. Instead, his response is to preserve civil society, while curbing though not eliminating its evils,
through the artifice of the division of labor. Since we cannot expect the
same persons to be both active members of civil society and guardians
of the common good, we must create a distinctive class of citizens who
are insulated from the egoistic pressures of civil society and whose
special education and training insure that they will perceive the common good as their own. Since these guardians—Hegel's bureaucratic
elite—will be drawn mainly from the middle class, rather than from the
large property owners, and since they will depend for their livelihood
on stipends provided by the state, they will be for the most part
immune to the instabilities and intrigues of market society.[27] A system
of objective examinations will insure that they have the requisite
knowledge and skills.[28] The bureaucratic elite enables us to achieve
objective freedom by protecting us from our own irrationality and
selfishness. Subjective and objective freedom are united when we
pursue our particular aims within the framework of laws and policies
laid down by the government.[29]

Hegel insists that the activities of the bureaucratic elite cannot be
limited to the police functions of the libertarian state if civil society is to
be made livable. In addition to the enforcement of contracts and
protection against theft, fraud, and physical harm, the Hegelian state,

controlled by the bureaucratic elite, is to undertake various welfare functions. Most importantly, the Hegelian state intervenes in the economy to soften the blows of periodic crises by providing a welfare safety net to catch those who lose out in the competition.

The oversight and care exercised by the public authority aims at being a middle term between an individual and the universal possibility, afforded by society, of attaining individual ends. It has to undertake street-lighting, bridge-building, the pricing of daily necessaries, and the care of public health. In this connection, two main views predominate at the present time. One asserts that the superintendence of everything properly belongs to the public authority, the other that the public authority has nothing at all to settle here because everyone will direct his conduct according to the needs of others. The individual must have a right to work for his bread as he pleases, but the public also has a right to insist that essential tasks shall be properly done. Both points of view must be satisfied, and freedom of trade should not be such as to jeopardize the general good.[30]

Hegel then goes on to say that civil society, through the operation of the government, "is responsible for feeding its members," but that bare subsistence is not enough because "it is not simply starvation which is at issue; the further end in view is to prevent the formation of a pauperized rabble."[31]

The state must not only regulate foreign trade and fix prices for certain essential commodities; it may even be necessary to exert more direct control on "the larger branches of industry" in order to "diminish the danger of upheavals."[32] Here, as elsewhere, Hegel's language makes it clear that the government's activities can at best contain the evils of civil society within tolerable limits. The state can neither eliminate economic instability nor abolish poverty. The extravagances of civil society can only be held in check.

We can now delineate three archetypal responses to the problems of civil society: (1) radical, (2) meliorist, and (3) reformist. According to the radical, the ills of civil society can neither be eliminated nor even significantly ameliorated, short of eliminating civil society itself. Further, this situation is not to be lamented, since civil society is not worth preserving anyway. The meliorist holds that the ills of civil society (or at least the most serious ones) can be significantly diminished without eliminating civil society itself, but that they cannot be abolished (without destroying civil society). Further, civil society is worth preserving. The reformer maintains that the ills of civil society—at least the more serious ones—can be eliminated (not just diminished) without destroying civil society, and that they should be eliminated.

Which of these positions a thinker adopts will depend upon his assessment of the seriousness of the defects of civil society, his appreciation of the good that is to be found in that form of social life, and perhaps most importantly, his beliefs about the possibilities for conservation on the one hand and change on the other. Hegel, as we have seen, advances a meliorist position, while Marx adopts the radical stance. Hegel not only believes that the preservation of civil society is possible, he also clearly values civil society because he believes that it alone gives sufficient scope to subjective freedom. Marx, on the other hand, not only believes the demise of civil society is inevitable, but welcomes it because he believes that the freedom of civil society is slavery.[33] As we shall see in the next chapter, when we examine his theory of alienation in capitalism and his vision of the unalienated society, Marx believed that the appropriate standard for evaluating societies rendered the distinction between subjective and objective freedom, like the contrast between bourgeois and citizen, ultimately obsolete.

Hegel's meliorism reflects a deep ambivalence about civil society. On the one hand, he recognizes the marvelous energy and efficiency of the market society proclaimed by Adam Smith and the other classical political economists, and more importantly he cherishes its scope for subjective freedom. On the other, he believes that the market cannot stand alone. It must be supported, controlled, and limited by radically different institutions: the state and the family. We have already seen how the bureaucratic elite, the heart of the Hegelian state, is constructed in conscious opposition to the organizing principle of the market: private interest. Hegel's discussion of the nature of the family completes his account of the dependence of the market upon other institutions.[34]

According to Hegel, civil society is the sphere of "abstract right," where the right to exchange one's property with another through contract is the paradigm of rights generally. In civil society itself, individuals interact only as right-holders, but they are drawn into civil society from the family, a sphere of affective interaction in which talk about rights is characteristically out of place. Thus Hegel strenuously rejects all attempts to assimilate family relations to the model of contractual rights. The family, he thinks, is an identity of interests in which persons respond spontaneously to the needs of others out of love. As such, it is to be contrasted with the sphere in which individuals' interests are not only distinct but in conflict, and in which responses to the needs of others are mediated by calculation of one's own advantage.[35]

In spite of the great differences between their responses to the problem of civil society, there are several key themes in Hegel which Marx adopted and then radicalized. Both Hegel and Marx believe that the ills of civil society are inevitable, not accidental; both reject the unrestrained right to private property; both believe that a society founded exclusively on self-interested interaction is intolerable and unworkable. We have already observed that Hegel, in criticizing Kant, stressed that moral concepts have practical import only in a particular institutional context. Similarly, we shall see in Chapter 4 that Marx's ideological critique maintains that moral concepts, including juridical concepts, can only be adequately understood by seeing how they function in supporting or challenging specific institutional arrangements. And according to both Hegel and Marx, significant gains in freedom come about through institutional change, though Hegel assigns a much larger role to changes in juridical institutions than Marx.

Further, both Marx and Hegel reject the juridical paradigm of human interaction—that conception according to which all important human relationships are understood as interactions among right-holders as right-holders. I shall show in subsequent chapters that, while Hegel is content to argue that the rational social order must contain a significant though limited juridical sphere, Marx goes much further. For him, the truly human society will find juridical concepts and juridical institutions dispensable. Marx's argument, however, must be quite different from Hegel's. Marx cannot appeal to the family as a model for the non-juridical interaction which he believes will be characteristic of communist society because for him the family as it has existed throughout the history of class-divided society is a microcosm of alienation and exploitation.[36] Thus Marx cannot argue, as other socialists have, that the harmonious family provides a preview of the affectively integrated, nonegoistic life of communist man.

It might be thought that Marx's discussions of primitive communist societies provide the needed empirical basis for his prediction that capitalism will be replaced by a non-juridical society. However, even if we assume that the tribal societies with which Marx was acquainted through the work of Morgan and others are properly described as non-juridical, it is difficult to see how one can infer anything useful about postcapitalist society from such information about preindustrial societies. For one thing, as Marx seems to acknowledge in the following passage, such primitive societies appear to achieve community at the price of individual personality and freedom, while modern communism is supposed to allow the richest development of individual personality and the most perfect freedom:

. . . . ancient social organisms of production are . . . founded either on the immature development of man individually, who has not yet severed the umbilical cord that unites him with his fellow man in a primitive tribal community, or upon direct relations of subjection.[37]

It is difficult to see how the fact that there have been non-juridical preindustrial societies in which freedom and individual personality were not allowed to flourish is supposed to make more plausible the hypothesis that capitalism will or can give way to a non-juridical industrial society which enjoys freedom and promotes the full development of individual personality. It is unpromising then, to attempt to anchor Marx's vision of communism as a non-juridical, noncoercive form of social coordination either in the example of the family or that of tribal society. Perhaps the only alternative for Marx is to try to show that all of the factors which make juridical relations necessary are peculiar to class-divided society and will disappear with it. I shall argue in subsequent chapters that Marx has not succeeded in this attempt, but that the project is nonetheless extremely illuminating.

2

Marx's Evaluative Perspective

I

The primary goal of this chapter is to articulate and assess the evaluative perspective from which Marx criticizes capitalism and judges that the transition to communism will mark not only change but progress in human history.[1] To do this, it will be necessary to present sketches of Marx's theory of alienation, his vision of communism, his unorthodox concept of human nature, and his theory of historical change. It will also be necessary to propose an answer to a perennial question of Marx scholarship: what role, if any, do the theory of alienation and the concept of human nature play in the materialist theory of history of the mature Marx?

The chief conclusions for which I shall argue are these. (1) Contrary to what many commentators have said, Marx continues to use the theory of alienation in later works, even if he seldom explicitly invokes the notion of human nature as "species being" and even if his use of terms such as *"Entfremdung"* and *"Entäusserung"* becomes less frequent. (2) In middle and late works, when Marx attacks certain versions of the concept of species being, he is criticizing those notions of human nature which are idealistic, ahistorical, and individualistic, but it is not at all clear that he is engaged in a wholesale rejection of his earlier use of the concept of species being. (3) Marx does rely upon a concept of human nature in later published works, but one which is purely descriptive and explanatory, in contrast to the partly evaluative concept of species being that dominated the *1844 Manuscripts*. (4) In later published works, the vision of communist society appears to replace the earlier concept of species being as Marx's basic evaluative perspective for criticizing capitalism and for grounding the judgment that there is progress in history. This shift from the notion of species being to the vision of communism occurs not so much because Marx rejected the earlier notion as erroneous as because it proved to be an

14

unnecessary theoretical shuffle which added nothing to the theory of history while running the risk of being confused with other conceptions of human nature which Marx had rejected. (5) If the vision of communism is to play the needed evaluative role, Marx must show not only that communism will, or at least can, replace capitalism, but also that communism would allow the fullest satisfaction of human beings' undistorted desires. (6) Marx's materialist theory of consciousness may be seen as providing the basis for a distinction between distorted and undistorted desires and for the claim that only communism can and will achieve the full satisfaction of undistorted desires. (7) Unless it includes a developed materialist theory of consciousness that grounds the distinction between distorted and undistorted desires, Marx's theory of history cannot provide an adequate basis for his radical criticisms of capitalism and his ascription of progress to history. (8) Even if the materialist theory of consciousness is sufficiently developed, it is not clear that the notion of the fullest satisfaction of undistorted desires adequately captures Marx's view of the superiority of communism. (9) The evaluative perspective supplied by the vision of communism as a society in which undistorted needs are most fully satisfied is not a juridical perspective.

<h1 style="text-align:center">II</h1>

Some commentators contend that Marx discarded the concept of species being *[Gattungswesen]* and the theory of alienation when he outgrew the intellectual straightjacket of young Hegelianism.[2] Others concede that the concept of alienation persists in Marx's middle and late works but assert that around 1846 Marx criticized and jettisoned his own youthful concept of species being. The falsity of the first claim can no longer be reasonably doubted. The *Grundrisse* (1857–1858) is replete with passages in which Marx integrates the theory of alienation with his developing economic analysis of capitalism and explicitly relies upon the concept of species being.[3] In *Capital*, while references to species being are almost wholly absent, the theory of alienation still plays a conspicuous role, most noticeably in the chapter entitled "Fetishism of Commodities," as we shall see shortly.

By the theory of alienation, I mean Marx's use of a certain family of concepts to provide a systematic account of various features of precommunist human existence which are marked by fragmentation, loss, and above all the domination of human beings by uncontrolled objects and forces which they have created but which they fail to recognize as their own creations. The key terms which Marx uses to refer to these phenomena, and which I shall sometimes lump together under the term "alienation," may be defined roughly as follows.

i) *Entäusserung:* divestiture, renunciation, loss, alienation as in alienation of one's property to another; making external to oneself, externalization.

ii) *Entfremdung:* estrangement, alienation as in alienation of affections, standing in a relationship to something such that it is alien to one, or perceived to be alien.

iii) *Vergegenständlichung:* objectification, reification.[4]

The following passage from the *1844 Manuscripts* illustrates Marx's interrelated uses of these terms:

The alienation *[Entäusserung]* of the worker from his product means not only that his labor becomes an object, an external existence, but that it becomes a power on its own confronting him. It means that the life which he has conferred on the object confronts him as something hostile and alien *[Entfremdet]*. Let us now look more closely at the objectification *[Vergegenständlichung]*, at the production of the worker, and in it at the estrangement *[Entfremdung]*, the loss of the object, his product.[5]

In this passage, Marx is clearly distinguishing objectification, which occurs whenever man creates or transforms things in the external world, and estrangement, which is a characteristic of man's relationship to the objects he makes or transforms under certain historical conditions. Further, in the work in which this passage occurs he is beginning to develop an analysis of the historical conditions of labor which shows that the process of objectification results in estrangement from the product only when that process is structured by certain social relationships—in this case the relationship of the wage-worker to the capitalist. Marx faults Hegel for failing to see that although all human production is objectification, estrangement from what is objectified is an historically limited phenomenon and will disappear with the passing of capitalism. Because Marx views the product as an objectification or embodiment of the worker's powers, he describes the worker's domination by the product as a loss or renunciation, not just of the product but of the human powers which created it. Until it is freed from estrangement, objectification will continue to be a loss, a renunciation of the worker's powers, not an affirmation or fulfillment of them.

Marx also uses the concept of objectification in a quite different way to describe certain forms of estrangement, rather than merely to characterize the making and shaping of objects regardless of the historical conditions under which production occurs. Objectification in this second sense is the process by which human qualities or human relationships come to be experienced as properties of, or relationships among, natural objects—things that are independent of human control. Capital, for example, is seen as a tangible thing with its own creative power, rather than as a social relationship among persons mediated by things (e.g., gold or paper). Commodities are experienced as things which possess value as a natural property, just as stones or stars possess properties independently of the preferences, beliefs, and social relationships of persons.[6]

Marx emphasizes that so long as we objectify human creations in this second sense we are doomed to an estranged relationship with them. We cannot overcome our subjection to them as alien forces until we realize that they are not independent things, but rather our own creations, subject to our collective control. Objectification in this second sense (what Lukács calls reification[7]) as a form which estrangement takes, then, is not to be confused with objectification in the first sense, which is present in all production of objects, whether that production involves estrangement or not.

The theory of alienation just sketched is present in Marx's early, middle, and late works. Even if the most detailed explicit uses of the terms *"Entfremdung," "Entäusserung,"* and *"Vergegenständlichung"* are found in early works such as the *1844 Manuscripts* and in the later but unpublished *Grundrisse*, the account of our estrangement from capital and commodities through objectification (in the sense of reification) comes from *Capital*. So the remaining question is whether the mature Marx employs not only the theory of alienation but also the notion of man's alienation from his *species being*.

III

To answer this question, we must first briefly outline Marx's conception of species being. In the *1844 Manuscripts*, Marx contrasts man's alienation from his species being in capitalism with the actualization of his species being in communism. According to Marx, man's species being consists of distinctively human capacities.[8] As a first approximation, we might say that man is alienated from his species being when his distinctively human capacities are not actualized or not actualized fully. We shall see later that this explication must be supplemented, but for now it is important to focus on the capacities Marx takes to be distinctively human. With one possible exception, these are all capacities for productive activity. Man alone, says Marx, is capable of (i) universal, (ii) free, (iii) conscious (or rationally controlled), (iv) social productive activity. A fifth capacity, or rather a meta-capacity, is the capacity for (v) all-around development, for exercising a wide range of skills and talents, without having to neglect some for the effective development of one or two. If we interpret "productive activity" so broadly that it includes virtually all dimensions of human development, then (v) may not be an addition, but rather perhaps an explication, of (ii) or perhaps of (i) and (ii).

Man's productive activity is *universal* both in the sense that the diversity of his products is unlimited and in the sense that he produces not just what is immediately needed by himself and his offspring, but also by beings remote from him in space and time.[9] Man is capable of *free* productive activity insofar as he can engage in productive activity for its own sake rather than as a mere means for satisfying other needs, such as survival.[10] Unlike other producing species, such as bees and ants, man is *conscious* of himself as a producer and as a member of his species in his production.[11] Finally, man has the capacity for productive activity which is *social* in the sense of being harmonious, and the degree to which his relationship with other members of his species exhibits harmonious cooperation is a measure of the extent to which his species being is actualized.

Setting aside the dubious claim that each of these capacities is in fact found only in human beings, we must clarify what it means to say that, in capitalism, man is alienated from his species being, while in communism this alienation is overcome. It will not do to say that Marx's point is simply that these capacities are not presently actualized or not fully actualized in capitalism but will be in communism. For at least some of these capacities—at least when described in a general fashion—are already actualized in capitalism, and the difference between their presence in capitalism and in communism does not seem to be simply a matter of degree of actualization. Capitalist production, for example, is already thoroughly universal in a straightforward sense. Indeed its universality marks capitalism off from earlier modes of production and makes possible the almost unlimited multiplication of needs for which Marx criticizes it. Further, Marx says that alienated labor is possible only where productive activity is conscious.

[Man] . . . is only a conscious being, that is, his own life is an object to him, precisely because he is a species being. This is the only reason for his activity being a free activity. Alienated labor reverses this relationship so that, just because he is a conscious being, man makes his vital activity and essence a mere means to his existence.[12]

This passage indicates that the difference is not that man produces unconsciously in capitalism and consciously in communism. Nor is it perspicuous to describe the contrast as merely a difference in the extent or degree to which productive activity is conscious. The difference, rather, is that in the one case the producer is conscious of his activity as merely instrumental, in the other he is conscious that non-instrumental productive activity is constitutive of himself as a being of a certain kind. Finally, Marx himself also emphasized that production in capitalism is intensely social in a straightforward sense. Capitalist production brings together large numbers of persons in cooperative activities which are in a sense harmonious, though they are not mutually advantageous for all participants.

To capture fully Marx's idea that man's alienation from his distinctively human capacities is overcome only in communism, we must recognize that his concept of species being is in part an evaluative or normative concept. The evaluative or normative element consists in the fact that it is only certain forms of the exercise of the capacities in question that are picked out as *truly human* and hence as supplying the appropriate perspective from which to criticize current and past societies. Thus not just any form of conscious production is said to be distinctively human, nor just any manifestation of universal productive capacity, nor just any form of social production.

Further, it appears that Marx's concept of species being is also partly normative or evaluative in the sense that it selects as appropriate criteria for assessing social arrangements only one subset of capacities from among those that are distinctively human. It may be, for example, that the capacity for exploitation, or for prostitution, or for the production of instruments of mass destruction, are distinctively human capacities, but Marx does not therefore propose to use these capacities as the perspective for evaluating social arrangements. Once we recognize that Marx's notion of species being rests upon normative or evaluative assumptions, we find it necessary to revise our preliminary explication as follows. To say that man's alienation from his species being is overcome only in communism is to say that certain distinctively human capacities are actualized, or actualized in their most appropriate or perfect form, only in communism. Thus capitalism is not defective because it fails to actualize *all* distinctively human capacities nor because its productive activity is not conscious or universal or social, but rather because productive activity in capitalism is not conscious, universal, and social in the appropriate senses—the senses which are fitting or fulfilling for beings such as we are. With this sketch of Marx's notion of species being in mind, we can now turn to the question of whether Marx's attitude toward the usefulness of that concept changed over the years.

Those who say that Marx explicitly rejected his earlier concept of man's alienation from his species being or from his human nature usually support their interpretation by citing two sets of passages, one in "Theses on Feuerbach," the other in *The German Ideology*.[13] They are worth quoting in full.

Feuerbach resolves religious essence into the human essence. But the human essence is not an abstraction inherent in each single individual. In its reality it is the ensemble of social relations.
Feuerbach, who does not enter upon a criticism of this real essence, is consequently compelled:
1. To abstract from the historical process and to fix the religious sentiment as something by itself and to presuppose an abstract—isolated—human individual. [Thesis VI].
Feuerbach, consequently, does not see that the 'religious sentiment' is itself a social product, and that the abstract individual whom he analyzes belongs to a particular form of society. [Thesis VII].[14] The whole process [of history] was seen [by the German ideologists] as a process of the self-alienation of "man," essentially because the average individual of the later stage was always foisted on the earlier stage and the consciousness of a later period on the individuals of an earlier. (Self-Alienation). Through this inversion, which from the beginning has been an abstraction of the actual conditions, it was possible to transform all history into an evolutionary process of consciousness. *[The German Ideology]*[15]

Contrary to what is often assumed, these passages do not decisively show that Marx rejected all conceptions of human nature or of man's species being, nor even his own conception of 1844. The passages from the "Theses" criticize Feuerbach for employing a concept of species being which is *individualistic*, as opposed to social, and *ahistorical* as opposed to historical. Nor is the passage from *The German Ideology* a wholesale rejection of the concept of man's nature nor even of the notion of his alienation from his nature or essence. Instead it is an attack upon *idealistic* conceptions of man's self-alienation. As we shall see later, *The German Ideology* offers a quite different conception of that which is common to human beings throughout history and which distinguishes humans from other species: in this sense Marx did not abandon *all* conceptions of human nature, though he did reject the notion of human essence as it has traditionally been understood.

A conception of human nature is individualistic if it presents the characteristics which are allegedly essential to man as characteristics of an individual abstracted from his social relations. Such a conception of human nature then views the overcoming of man's alienation from his nature (or the actualization of his essence) as a change in that individual, considered in isolation, rather than as a change in social relations among individuals. A conception of human nature is *ahistorical* if it mistakenly presents as essential characteristics of man certain features which are prevalent in man only at a certain point in history, within a certain form of society. A conception of human nature is *idealistic* if it presents the essential characteristics of man as features of consciousness, considered in abstraction, and understands the overcoming of his alienation from his nature (or the actualization of his essence) as exclusively or primarily a change in consciousness.

Insofar as the focus of Marx's contrast between capitalism and communism in the *1844 Manuscripts* is an account of the difference between the character of human *labor* (rather than mere consciousness) in the two forms of society, his notion of species being is emphatically *not* idealistic. In the passage from the manuscript on alienated labor considered earlier in our sketch of the theory of alienation, Marx clearly does not diagnose the problem of self-alienation as a problem of consciousness to be solved exclusively or primarily by a change in consciousness. Instead, the core of the problem is said to be the character of man's material productive activity in capitalism and his lack of control over his material products.

Further, the notion of alienation from man's species being presented there is not ahistorical in any straightforward sense. For recall that Marx takes Hegel to task for failing to distinguish objectification, which is a necessary feature of human labor throughout history, from alienation, which occurs only during historical periods prior to the advent of communism. Indeed Marx's analysis of alienated labor as the core of self-alienation in the *1844 Manuscripts* is thoroughly historical insofar as it purports to describe features of one historical form of human labor, namely, wage-labor. And because, for Marx, our species being consists of certain distinctively human *capacities*, there is nothing inconsistent in his claiming both that human beings throughout history have a common nature and that other philosophers have typically mistaken *actual* human characteristics prevalent in their own time for essential characteristics of man.

Moreover, in the *1844 Manuscripts*, both Marx's analysis of man's alienation from his species being and his vision of the actualization of man's species being in communism exhibit a *social*, not an individualistic, conception. Alienated wage-labor, as the foundation of man's self-alienation in capitalism, is not described as a characteristic of individual human beings considered in isolation. It is the productive activity of a person embedded in certain social relations, in particular, relations of effective control over the means of production. Thus Marx links the worker's lack of control over his product with the fact that someone else does control it.

If the product of labour does not belong to the worker but stands over against him as an alien power, this is only possible in that it belongs to another. Man apart from the worker.[16]

In sum, Marx's description of communism as the actualization of man's species being is an attempt to provide a *social, historical,* and *nonidealistic* conception. For Marx in the *1844 Manuscripts,* the overcoming of man's alienation from his species being or human nature is the historical development of a new set of social relations which makes possible a qualitatively different form of productive activity.

IV

If we assume that Marx's criticisms of the notion of man's alienation from his nature or species being are directed primarily toward idealistic, ahistorical, and individualistic versions of the concept rather than toward his own uses of the notion in the *1844 Manuscripts,* we are still left with a puzzle. Why does the later Marx tend to retire the notion of species being and rely more upon rather sketchy descriptions of communist society? It might be objected at this point that the question is badly put because, as I noted earlier, the notion of man's alienation from his species being is repeatedly invoked in one important later work, the *Grundrisse.* Nonetheless, the fact remains that Marx himself chose not to publish the *Grundrisse* and that in the later published works for which it was the preparation, talk about species being was almost entirely expunged. This, too, must be explained.

Brief descriptions of features of communism are scattered through Marx's middle and late works, but the most important accounts are found in a rather notorious passage in *The German Ideology* (1846) and a longer discussion in the *Critique of the Gotha Program* (1875). The passage from *The German Ideology* warrants quoting in full not only because it presents a description of communism but also because it does so by contrasting communism with previous societies in which human beings suffer from alienation.

And finally, the division of labor offers us the first example for the fact that man's own act becomes an alien power opposed to and enslaving him instead of being controlled by him—as long as man remains in natural society, as long as a split exists between the particular and the common interest and as long as the activity is not voluntary but naturally divided. For as soon as labor is distributed, each person has a particular, exclusive area of activity which is imposed on him and from which he cannot escape. He is a hunter, a fisherman, a herdsman, a critical critic, and he must remain so if he does not want to lose his means of livelihood. In communist society, however, where nobody has an exclusive area of activity and each can train himself in any branch he wishes, society regulates the general production, making it possible for me to do one thing today and another tomorrow, to hunt in the morning, fish in the afternoon, breed cattle in the evening, criticize after dinner, just as I like, without ever becoming a hunter, a fisherman, a herdsman, or a critic.[17]

In this and other passages in middle and late works, Marx incorporates in his vision of communism many of the same elements subsumed in the *1844 Manuscripts* under the notion of the actualization of man's species being. In particular, communism is described as a form of society in which productive activity will be engaged in for its own sake, rather than as a mere means toward survival, and in which harmonious social relations will foster the all-around development of persons, the fullest development of individual personality.

In *Critique of the Gotha Program*, Marx presents an account of the development of communism out of capitalism. The first stage (referred to by later Marxists as socialism) is

. . . communist society, not as it has developed on its own foundation, but on the contrary, just as it emerges from capitalist society, which is thus in every respect, economically, morally, and intellectually, still stamped with the birthmarks of the old society from whose womb it emerges.[18]

The principle of distribution of this first stage, according to Marx, is "to each according to his product," where this means that each ". . . individual producer receives back from society—after the deductions have been made—exactly what he gives to it."[19] The deductions are for replacement of instruments of production, insurance, subsidization of those unable to work, and various public services, including education.[20] So, although the producer does not get back a share of the social product equivalent to what he contributes, his share is proportional to his contribution.

Marx then goes on to predict "a higher phase of communist society." Since its interpretation will occupy us now and in a later chapter, I shall quote the passage in full.

. . . [A]fter the enslaving subordination of the division of labor, and therewith also the antithesis between mental and physical labor, has vanished; after labor has become not only a means of life but life's prime want; after the productive forces have also increased with the all-around development of the individual, and all the springs of cooperative wealth flow more abundantly— only then can the narrow horizon of bourgeois right be crossed and society inscribe on its banners: "From each according to his ability, to each according to his needs."[21]

Later in the same work Marx also predicts that "Between capitalist and communist society" there is "a political transition period in which the state can be nothing but the revolutionary dictatorship of the proletariat."[22] This is the *last* form of the state, for in communism the state finally disappears. It is not altogether clear where the dictatorship of the proletariat fits into the two-stage sequence described above. If "communist society" in the passage predicting the dictatorship of the proletariat refers to stage one, then we get a three-stage sequence:

1) dictatorship of the proletariat
2) first stage of communism
3) higher stage of communism,

where *both* stages of communism are stateless.

On the other hand, if "communist society" in the passage predicting the dictatorship of the proletariat refers to the higher stage of communism then we get a two-stage sequence:

1) first stage of communism, including dictatorship of the proletariat,
2) higher stage of communism.

Both interpretations are consistent with Marx's statement that the dictatorship of the proletariat is a transitional phase between capitalism and communism and both are consistent with his prediction that the developed communist society (the higher stage) is stateless.

For our purposes, the important thing to notice is that in *Critique of the Gotha Program* Marx picks out at least two stages in the development of communism and says that each stage will satisfy a distinctive principle of distribution. In the lower stage, the principle is "to each according to (i.e., in proportion to) his product;" in the higher stage, the principle is "to each according to his needs." Further, Marx refers to the former, but not the latter, as a principle of *right*, or as we might say, a principle of distributive justice. I shall argue in Chapter 4 that these two principles are to be understood quite differently, and that, for Marx, the great increase in harmony and productivity that makes possible the satisfaction of the second principle marks the obsolescence of principles of justice.

Principles of distributive justice are characteristically thought of as prescriptive principles which play a certain role in social life in circumstances of scarcity: they serve as a basis upon which individuals can press their claims to scarce goods. They are the ultimate normative principles for adjudicating conflicting claims, and they are regarded by members of the society as playing this role. If this is so, then not every society in which a particular principle of distribution is satisfied will be a society in which that principle functions in social life as a principle of justice. A society might satisfy a distributive principle without the principle functioning as a prescriptive principle to establish rights to shares of scarce goods for the simple reason that the satisfaction of that principle may be incompatible with the existence of conditions of conflict over scarce goods which make prescriptive principles necessary. I shall argue later that the principle Marx believes will be satisfied in the higher stage of communism is just such a principle because "needs" as it occurs in that principle is to be interpreted broadly to cover the whole range of desires that persons in that society will have, not just "needs" in the sense of "basic desires" or "minimal desires." Understood in this way, the principle of distribution according to needs is a principle *describing* a state of greatly increased harmony and abundance, not a principle *prescribing* the appropriate way to cope with competing claims to scarce goods, and as such its satisfaction marks the end of the circumstances in which principles of distributive justice are needed. But for now I wish to point out only that neither in *Critique of the Gotha Program* nor in other works in which Marx describes developed communist society does he describe it as a *just* society or a society which upholds *rights* of any kind, whether coercively backed or not.

Marx's description of the stages of communism in *Critique of the Gotha Program*—which he believes to be grounded in his scientific work in *Capital*—is remarkable in two respects. First, it differs importantly from his earlier account of the stages of communism in the *1844 Manuscripts*,[23] though Marx nowhere explains what theoretical advances in the intervening years led him to change his mind. Second, neither in *Critique of the Gotha Program* nor elsewhere does Marx even attempt to show how these particular stages, having these specific characteristics, can be predicted on the basis of definite features of his analysis of the "laws of motion of capitalism" in *Capital*.

The negative function of these sketchy descriptions of communist society is to make vivid the defects of capitalism and earlier class-societies by contrast. Their positive function is to serve as a perspective from which human progress may be gauged. Communism is said to be the culmination of man's prehistory and the beginning of truly human history.

V

Those who wish to see Marx as a purely scientific theorist will no doubt object here that Marx himself eschewed attempts to offer blueprints for the future and insisted that he was not to be confused with utopian socialists who exhort us to realize their ideals by an act of will. Moreover, the objection continues, to ask why communism as Marx describes it, rather than some other conception of the good society, is to serve as the yardstick of human progress and the basis for criticizing capitalism is to misunderstand Marx's conception of communism. For, according to Marx, communism is not one possibility among others. It is the unique successor to capitalism and hence there is no need to explain its superiority to other social ideals. Communism is not an ideal among competing ideals; it is *the* social form which *will* replace capitalism.

I shall probe Marx's account of the role that social ideals play in the motivation for social change in Chapter 5. But at present I shall only note that there are two reasons for examining the vision of communism in order to understand the basic evaluative perspective in Marx's theory in spite of Marx's cautionary remarks about how we are to take his descriptions of communism.

First, even though Marx denies that the motivating power of ideals is the fulcrum of social change, his work is clearly not limited to description and explanation. He condemns capitalism and class-societies generally and presents communism as a form of life in which none of the defects he criticizes in previous social forms is present. Communism for Marx is not simply that society which will in fact follow capitalism. Though communism is not the final stage of human development, it is the beginning of truly human history because it is the necessary condition or framework for man's fulfillment. To fail to determine precisely in what the superiority of communism consists is to leave Marx's theory incomplete.

Second, regardless of the importance or lack of it which Marx himself attached to articulating the vision of communist society as an evaluative perspective, the task is inescapable for us because we know, as Marx did not, that communism as he described it is not the unique successor to capitalism. Marx gravely underestimated the possibility that exclusive control over the means of production by a minority of persons exercising control *as individuals* (capitalism) would give way to exclusive control over the means of production by a minority exercising control *as a collectivity* (totalitarian state socialism). But once the theoretical gap between Marx's scientific analysis of the dissolution of capitalism and his account of the stages of communism is appreciated, and once the empirical falsity of his prediction of communism as the unique successor of capitalism is seen, the question of developing an adequate evaluative perspective for guiding social change is reopened. If there is no scientifically predictable, unique successor to the current system, but at most a limited range of practical alternatives; if the successor will in part be determined by political action we now undertake; and if coherent political action must be informed by an articulated and rationally defensible evaluative perspective, then some way of choosing among evaluative perspectives is needed. Nor will it do to say that the distinctive values of autonomy and community which Marx espouses are uncontroversial and not in need of theoretical backing. They are only uncontroversial when stated at a level of abstractness which renders them inadequate as guides for social change, as Marx himself emphasized. Moreover, once they are given determinate content, these ideals may become vulnerable to Marx's own ideological critique. Even if they should turn out to be widely accepted ideals, they can no more be taken as unproblematic than can the bourgeois ideals of individual freedom and equality. For it can be argued that unless the distinctive ideals of communist society are grounded in a theory of practical rationality or of human nature or in some other way, Marx is liable to the charge that these values are themselves ahistorical abstractions, parochial products of distorted consciousness. I shall suggest later that if this objection can be met, the reply must rely upon the same element of Marx's social theory that gives rise to the objection in the first place: the historical materialist theory of consciousness.

Allen Wood and others have suggested, however, that Marx's most important criticisms of capitalism rest not upon controversial normative ideals such as Marx's distinctive conceptions of community or autonomy, but rather upon quite unexceptional values which require no theoretical explication or support.[24] For example, Marx condemns capitalism for causing avoidable death, waste, hunger, mental and physical exhaustion, monotony, and loneliness. Thus even if communist society provides *one* standard by which Marx criticizes capitalism, it is an exaggeration to claim that it is Marx's *basic* or *ultimate* evaluative perspective.

The word "avoidable" here is extremely important. If Marx had merely shown that capitalism causes the evils in question he would not be the revolutionary radical social critic he is. In addition, he asserts that these evils can be eliminated (or greatly reduced) only by a radical transformation of the social order. So long as capitalism exists, these evils are necessary and unavoidable. Hence, it is only by comparison with the new social order he calls communism that Marx can support his judgment that capitalism causes *unnecessary* and *avoidable* death, hunger, etc. In other words, because Marx is neither a reformist nor a meliorist, but a radical, his indictments of capitalism are implicitly *comparative* and the standard of comparison is external to capitalism: the hunger, death, exhaustion, and loneliness of capitalism are seen to be avoidable—and hence irrational—only by reference to communism. It is in this sense that the vision of communist society provides Marx's basic or ultimate evaluative perspective: without reference to life in communism, Marx's criticisms lose their radical character. For this reason, it is implausible to claim that Marx's main interest was in criticizing capitalism *rather* than in providing an account of communism. Nor is it helpful to reply that the comparative nature of Marx's indictment of capitalism implies only a reference to socialism, not communism. This later Marxist terminology simply obscures Marx's insistence that what he calls the early stages of communism are themselves defective and incomplete and that they too must be understood in relation to developed communism.

Further, unless we take Marx at his word when he says that the emergence of a society having these characteristics can be *predicted* on the basis of his analysis of capitalism, we ignore his insistence that he is a scientific rather than a utopian radical. Nonetheless, the thesis that Marx's basic or ultimate evaluative perspective is communist society (because his radical criticisms are implicitly comparative) does *not* depend upon the assumption that Marx's descriptions of communism are to be taken as scientific *predictions*. Whether a society that avoids the evils of capitalism can be scientifically predicted or merely shown to be practically possible, the charge that those evils are unnecessary and hence irrational can be sustained as a radical, rather than a reformist, criticism only by reference to a description of communism. I conclude, then, that it would be very misleading to say that for Marx the vision of communist society provides only one evaluative perspective among others.

Granted that an account of communism must provide the basic evaluative perspective from which Marx's radical criticisms of capitalism are launched, in what does the superiority of communism consist?

It will not suffice to say that the superiority of communism lies in the fact that it is the only form of society which is truly human, if this means that it alone accords with human nature. To make this move is to regress to the evaluative concept of human nature of the *1844 Manuscripts* when what is needed is an explanation of its apparent replacement in later works by the vision of communism. What we require is an interpretation which links the shift from the early evaluative concept of species being or human nature to the account of communism with the development of Marx's theory of history.[25]

The concept of species being which Marx evoked in the *1844 Manuscripts* was, so to speak, suspended in midair. Though the early Marx did locate the core of man's alienation from his species being in the social labor process rather than in pure consciousness and though he did acknowledge that the overcoming of this alienation was a historical process, the concept of species being was not itself anchored in Marx's materialist theory of history because that theory was not yet developed. Marx's first systematic attempt to lay out the elements of the materialist theory came in *The German Ideology* in 1846, and it is in this book that we find Marx retiring the evaluative concept of man's nature as a species being and employing instead a descriptive-explanatory concept which I shall call the Protean core concept of human nature. At the beginning of *The German Ideology* Marx (and Engels) introduce this concept in a passage which deserves to be cited at length.

. . . [W]e must begin by stating the first premise of all human existence and hence of all history, namely, that men must be able to live "to make history". . . . But life involves above all eating and drinking, shelter, clothing, and many other things. *The first historical act is thus the production of means to satisfy these needs, the production of material life itself.* This is a historical act, a fundamental condition of all history which must be fulfilled in order to sustain human life every day and every hour, today as well as thousands of years ago. . . . The first principle therefore in any theory of history is to observe this fundamental fact in its entire significance and all its implications and to attribute to this fact its due importance. . . . The second point is that *once a need is satisfied, which requires the action of satisfying and the acquisition of the instrument for this new purpose, new needs arise.* . . . we now find that *man also possesses "consciousness."* Men have history because they must produce their life . . . in a certain way [and] . . . *their consciousness is determined in this same way.* [emphasis added][26]

According to this passage—and basically the same theme is expressed later in the famous Preface to *A Contribution to the Critique of*

Political Economy—a scientific theory of history must begin with what is distinctive of human beings, namely, that *they change themselves, their needs, their social relations, their consciousness, by changing the means for satisfying their basic material needs.* Human nature, then, is simply whatever it is about human beings that enables them to change themselves in this way.[27] This Protean capacity (or set of capacities) is the core of being human—it is constant through history and universal to the species.

It is from the vantage point of this lean but fertile concept of human nature that Marx criticizes thinkers as disparate as Proudhon and Bentham. He accuses both of mistaking the latest transient historical expression of the Protean capacity for human nature itself. Marx puts the point paradoxically when he charges that "M. Proudhon does not know that all history is nothing but a continuous transformation of human nature."[28] The idea is that, while the Protean core capacity remains constant throughout history and is in that sense not itself transformed, its exercise gives rise in various epochs to successive configurations of psychological attributes which for a time enjoy sufficient generality and persistence that superficial thinkers such as Proudhon mistake them for universal features of human beings as such. Virtually the same accusation is levelled at Bentham in volume I of *Capital*.

To know what is useful for a dog, one must study dog-nature. This nature itself is not to be deduced from the principle of utility. Applying this to man, he that would critique all human acts, movements, relations, etc., by the principle of utility, must first deal with *human nature in general*, and then with *human nature* as modified *in each historical epoch*. Bentham makes short work of it. With the driest naiveté he takes the modern shopkeeper, especially the English shopkeeper, as the normal man . . . this yard-measure, then, he applies to past, present, and future.[29]

It is vital to note that the Protean core concept itself is purely descriptive or explanatory, in contrast to the notion of species being, which was evaluative insofar as it selected a subset of distinctively human capacities as truly human—as constituting the perfection or fulfillment of man. The Protean concept speaks only of one distinctively human capacity (or set of capacities). Yet this capacity is so broad that both the free communal production picked out by the concept of species being and the capacity for the competitive, exploitative production said to be incompatible with the actualization of species being are subsumable under it. How, then, can what appears to be an all-embracing, purely descriptive or explanatory concept of human nature serve as a perspective from which to criticize capitalism, exhibit the superiority of communism, and ground the judgment that there is progress in human history?

One initially plausible answer is that the Protean concept focuses on the idea that human history is basically the activity of *satisfying needs* and that Marx's sole criterion of evaluation is simply the extent to which this activity is successful. On this interpretation, capitalism is condemned not because it is unjust or immoral, or because it does not accord with human nature, but because it fails at the constitutive task of all human societies: it fails to satisfy needs. Communism, then, is not superior because it better measures up to principles of justice or other moral ideals, or because it actualizes human nature, but simply because it better satisfies needs. And progress in history in general is to be gauged by the same simple criterion of satisfaction.

One immediate difficulty with this understanding of Marx is that a great deal must be done to clarify the notion of needs if it is to be at all illuminating. The first point to note is that "needs" should not be interpreted narrowly as in "subsistence needs," for Marx makes it clear that while communism will do a better job of discharging the first task of human society its superiority is not limited to this. The full satisfaction of basic needs is for Marx only the prerequisite for the pursuit and satisfaction of the need for creative production and for the all-around development of the autonomous, socially integrated individual. Indeed once the extent to which the latter exceed needs in the minimal sense it might be more appropriate to say that, on this interpretation, success in the satisfaction of basic and nonbasic needs, or of needs and desires, is Marx's ultimate evaluative yard-stick.

Another problem is that Marx emphasizes that needs and desires are not constant throughout history. The character of one's consciousness, and hence one's needs and desires, so far as these are informed and structured by consciousness, depend, according to Marx, upon the nature of the processes by which one's society produces the materials of life and, more specifically, upon one's relationship to the means of production employed in those processes. Hence once we look beyond the most basic survival needs, there is no single set of actual needs or desires which is common to all of the epochs Marx describes, the satisfaction of which could serve as a standard of evaluation.

One response to this difficulty is to relativize the notion of satisfaction: we evaluate a given form of society according to the extent to which it succeeds in satisfying the desires which *it* engenders. We judge that there is progress in history if (in general) later social forms do a better job of satifying the desires they engender than earlier forms did in satisfying the desires they engendered. On this reading, Marx criticizes capitalism only for its failure to satisfy, or to satisfy fully, the desires characteristic of capitalist man, while he praises communism for its ability to satisfy fully the distinctive desires of communist man.

This interpretation, however, cannot be right, for it overlooks Marx's emphasis on the qualitative differences between the desires of capitalist man and those said to be distinctive of communist man. The former Marx portrays as slavish, destructive, in conflict with one another, and grounded in a consciousness that is distorted by the alienated social relations of class-divided society. To take only two important types of examples, consider the cases of fetishism discussed earlier and what might be called the possessive obsession of capitalist man. In the fetishism of commodities, men are driven to produce and to strive to purchase ever more commodities because they suffer from the illusion that these things possess value independently of social relations. I come to desire a certain expensive piece of furniture not because I recognize its use-value as something sturdy and comfortable to sit upon, but because I perceive it as having great monetary value, as if this were a natural property of the thing, where my perception of this value is determined largely by the fetishistic behavior of others toward the object.[30] In the phenomenon of the fetishism of capital, I pursue an insatiable desire for more capital in part because of my illusory belief that capital is a thing—ultimately the only thing—with creative power, the power to move mountains and to change men's hearts.

The possessive obsession of capitalist man, according to Marx, is a certain motivational "set" informed by the false belief that the sole mode of appropriation and enjoyment of objects is exclusive individual *possession*. Opportunities for enjoyment through appropriative *activities*, especially activities of joint appropriation, are eclipsed by the virtually limitless compulsion to *have* things, to "enjoy" them through passive, private, exclusive possession.[31]

Marx's theory of ideology supplies additional examples of the relationship between distorted consciousness and desires. Such consciousness includes, for example, the belief that human beings are greedy by nature and can only be motivated to work by incentives for private gain, or that happiness requires dominance over others. Marx's ideological critique is designed, in part, to explain the existence and persistence of such beliefs by articulating the role they play in motivating people to perpetuate the very social relationships which engender and reinforce those beliefs. Since such distorted beliefs have motivational force, we may, by extension, speak of the corresponding desires as distorted.

A promising way of capturing Marx's emphasis on the qualitative differences between communist and capitalist desires might be, then, to understand it as corresponding to a distinction between *distorted* and *undistorted* desires. Marx describes communism as a form of society in which relations among persons are no longer distorted, but rather transparent and thoroughly intelligible. In communism the gap between the surface appearances of social life and the underlying reality— the chasm Marx strives to bridge in *Capital*—will no longer exist.[32] Utilizing this distinction, we might then say that for Marx the superiority of communism is not simply that it makes possible the fullest satisfaction of the desires it engenders, but that

C: Communism, and only communism, makes possible the fullest satisfaction of those desires which persons at this stage of history would have or would develop, were their consciousness, and hence their desires, not distorted by the positions they occupy in class-society.

According to this view, one important role of the materialist theory of consciousness is to explain both the distortions of consciousness in pre-communist society and the evolution of undistorted consciousness in the transition from capitalism to communism. By the materialist theory of consciousness I mean, roughly, the application of Marx's general doctrine of historical materialism to the explanation of the evolution of forms of consciousness in history. There is, of course, tremendous controversy concerning the proper formulation of Marx's doctrine of historical materialism.[33] But for our purposes much of the dispute need not be resolved. It will suffice to say that in its simplest, most general form historical materialism is the thesis that

HM: Social phenomena existing within a society at any given time, transitions from one form of society to another, and differences and similarities between different forms of society existing at the same or different times, are all explained primarily by the level of the productive forces of the societies in question and the nature of the economic structure within which those productive forces are employed.

"Social phenomena" here includes political, cultural, and economic institutions, roles, patterns of behavior, and forms of consciousness. By restricting the thesis of historical materialism, HM, to the phenomena of consciousness, we get the main thesis of the materialist theory of consciousness

MC: The nature of the forms of consciousness predominant in a given society, changes in consciousness in the transition from one form of society to another, and the differences and similarities between the forms of consciousness in different societies at the same or different times, are all explained primarily by the level of the productive forces of the societies in question and the nature of the economic structures within which those forces are employed.

Our efforts to ascertain the basic evaluative perspective of Marx's enterprise have led us to the conclusion that the materialist theory of consciousness plays a more fundamental role than might have at first been suspected. The explication of the distinction between distorted and undistorted needs, the truth or falsity of thesis C, and hence the plausibility or implausibility of using the vision of communism as the basic standard for radically criticizing capitalism and as the basis for the judgment that there is progress in history—all of this depends upon the materialist theory of consciousness.

VI

The notion that the appropriate evaluative perspective is or includes the preference-structure one would have were one's desires undistorted or adequately informed is not uniquely Marxian. Variants of it are found in John Stuart Mill's so-called "choice criterion of value" and in John Rawls' notion of "deliberative rationality." According to a plausible interpretation of Mill, what is truly valuable (as distinct from what is in fact valued by someone or other) is that which would be preferred or commended by those who are fully or adequately informed as to the qualities and consequences of the thing in question, where becoming informed is largely a matter of practical acquaintance, both with the thing in question and with competing objects of choice, either through one's own experiences or through testimony of the experience of others. Put most simply, the good is that which would attract and sustain the interest of a fully, or at least adequately, informed evaluator.

Rawls employs the notion of deliberative rationality as one element in the definition of a rational life plan. A person's life plan is said to be rational only if it "would be chosen by him with full deliberative rationality, that is, with full awareness of the relevant facts and after careful consideration of the consequences."[34] Rawls makes it clear that the attainment of full deliberative rationality excludes preferences based on illusions or false beliefs, and this presumably rules out at least some of the desires grounded in Marxian false consciousness.[35]

Despite these similarities, however, there is a great difference between the Marxian evaluative perspective employed above in C and the notions proposed by Mill and Rawls. For Marx the attainment of an undistorted or adequately informed preference-structure is possible only for persons living within a certain nexus of social relations and the latter can only exist once a long path of historical development has been traversed. Thus Marx would reject Mill's choice criterion of value and Rawls' conception of deliberative rationality as ahistorical and individualistic abstractions. For Marx, adequately informed or undistorted preferences are a social achievement, attainable only at a certain stage of man's historical development as a being who evaluates through experience and whose experience is social. And this achievement can only be won, according to Marx, through the abolition of private ownership of the means of production.

Granted the materialist theory of consciousness, the idea that the appropriate evaluative perspective is the preference-structure that persons would have were their preferences not affected by distorted consciousness is *not* a purely formal notion. If the interpretation I am suggesting is correct, Marx is committed to the view that the materialist theory of consciousness can both *explain* the gradual replacement of distorted preferences by undistorted ones and *predict* in important respects the results of the continuation of that process. Therefore, if the materialist theory of consciousness could be developed as Marx thought it could, we would not be left with a contentless conception of undistorted preferences as simply whatever preferences would emerge if certain ideal conditions for evaluation were met. Instead, we would have a theory which enables us to predict with increasing completeness both the occurrence of the conditions under which undistorted preferences will be formed and the content of those preferences. A crucial job of the materialist theory of consciousness, then, would be to provide solid justification for Marx's predictions that certain sorts of desires—in particular desires for creative, cooperative productive activity and autonomous living—will be constitutive of human psychology in communism.

If Marx did hold the view I have been exploring, or would have advanced it had he addressed the questions I have posed, then his theory appears to be extremely rationalistic. For Marx characterizes communism as a condition of harmony in which the full satisfaction of one person's desires does not thwart the full satisfaction of another's. It appears, then, that Marx may have held the very strong thesis that all serious interpersonal conflicts are artifacts of defective modes of production or of the distorted consciousness which defective modes of production engender. This is much stronger than the thesis that the various preferences which any given individual would form if his beliefs were undistorted would harmonize with each other. For as Mill, Rawls, and others recognize, different individuals, each of whom has achieved harmony in his own system of desires, may find themselves in serious conflict with one another.

Those who recognize this possibility and who are not so rationalistic as to reduce all serious interpersonal conflict to problems of ignorance, false consciousness, ultimately remediable defects of the mode of production, or weakness of the will, have typically offered principles of justice or principles of rational social choice, designed to achieve congruence among potentially colliding systems of desires. As I shall argue in detail in Chapter 4, however, Marx does not envisage a role for principles of justice in communism because he denies that conflicts in communism will be significant enough to require such principles. Further, Marx flatly rejects the best-developed example of a theory of social coordination which purports to harmonize conflicting desires— the market theory of the classical economists. Yet he nowhere articulates an alternative—a competing *theory* of social coordination of comparable explanatory and predictive power.

The problem may be put differently. Others who utilize the idea of adequately informed or undistorted preferences view it as only the first component of a theory of practical rationality because they recognize the problem of harmonizing informed or undistorted preference-structures as a major task of that theory. For these theorists, the notion of adequately informed or undistorted preferences, even when combined with the notion of rationality as adoption of the most efficient means for achieving given ends, does not suffice. They believe that principles of justice or other principles of social choice for coordinating the pursuits of different individuals are also needed and that no adequate conception of the good society is complete without them. Marx, in contrast, at least gives the appearance of having collapsed rationality into only two components: the elimination of false or distorted beliefs and preferences and the adoption of the most efficient means for achieving given ends. While it would be uncharitable to say that Marx is committed to such a simplistic view, it seems fair to say that he does not provide a richer theory. In sum, Marx offers neither a theory of social coordination for communism, nor an adequate basis in his analysis of capitalism for the prediction that an adequate theory will emerge in the revolutionary process. As we shall see later, Marx's belief that scarcity will be greatly reduced in communism and his faith in the idea of democracy may in part account for the absence of a richer theory of practical rationality.

Assuming again that Marx did hold the view under consideration or would advance it in reply to queries I have raised, the precise nature of his basic evaluative perspective is still not clear. Nothing said so far provides a conclusive anwer to this question: is the basic Marxian criterion of evaluation that underlies his radical criticisms simply the maximization of satisfaction, where the importance of the prediction that communism will allow the full satisfaction of undistorted preferences is simply that satisfaction is maximized only in a society whose members have undistorted preferences? Or does the Marxian view attach some importance to undistorted preferences independently of whether satisfying these preferences maximizes satisfaction? Marx himself apparently never posed, much less answered, this question because he discounted the possibility that maximization of satisfaction, the satisfaction of undistorted preferences, and the satisfaction of the particular desires (for autonomy, etc.) that he attributes to communist man, might diverge. Moreover, unlike utilitarian theorists, Marx does not propose any method for measuring satisfaction which may be applied to all desires regardless of their qualitative character and irrespective of whether they are grounded in distorted or undistorted consciousness.

It would be extremely difficult to defend adequately either the thesis that the satisfaction of undistorted desires maximizes satisfaction or the thesis that undistorted desires will turn out to be just those desires—for autonomy, cooperative productive activity, and all-around development—which Marx confidently attributes to communist man. It is not at all obvious that desires which are not grounded in false belief yield greater satisfaction than distorted desires. Nor is it clear that the failure to cherish autonomy, community, or the other distinctive values Marx attributes to communist man must rest, even in part, on false beliefs or distorted consciousness.

A richer theory of practical rationality, such as Kant's, or a normative theory of human nature, such as Aristotle's, might be powerful enough to show that an adequately informed and rational agent would exhibit just the desires Marx assigns to human beings in communism. But as I have noted earlier, Marx nowhere offers such a theory of practical rationality, and even if he had rehabilitated his early normative concept of human nature, that concept is not adequate to the task. It seems, then, that those who recognize the need for developing a defensible Marxian radical evaluative perspective are faced with these alternatives. Either the superiority of communism and the radical defects of capitalism are to be gauged by the standard of the satisfaction of undistorted desires or by reference to a set of ideals, including autonomy and community, which are not reducible to the standard of satisfaction. The former strategy is unsatisfactory because it either commits us to the yet unsupported view that undistorted desires will turn out to be the very desires Marx attributes to the members of communist society or to the uninspiring claim that communism is superior simply because it maximizes satisfaction, where the qualitative character of the desires of communist man is itself of no significance. The second strategy, though more promising, is also not without difficulties: it leaves us with a set of distinctive normative ideals which can be and have been challenged. To say that these ideals are not adequately supported by Marx is not, of course, to say they are unsupportable. My aim, rather, is to state more clearly the requirements for a more adequate Marxian theory and to indicate that Marxians cannot neglect some of the basic problems of traditional moral philosophy.

If the interpretation I have been exploring best accords with what is most distinctive in Marx's radical thought and has the additional virtue of explaining Marx's shift from the early evaluative concept of species being to the later vision of communist society grounded in the theory of history, then critical attention should focus squarely upon the materialist theory of consciousness.[36] Assuming that the proposed interpretation is correct, Marx's radical criticisms of capitalism, his judgment that there is progress in history, and his predictions of the nature of communist man, all hinge upon whether a materialist theory of the evolution of undistorted consciousness, and hence of undistorted desires, can be developed and defended. Marx himself, as is well known, did not achieve this. His most detailed discussions of the relationship between productive forces and economic structures, on the one hand, and forms of consciousness, on the other, are found in *The German Ideology*. But after 1846, Marx postponed the task of developing the materialist theory of consciousness in order to investigate the productive processes in relation to which consciousness was to be understood. *Capital*, which was to have been only the first stage of a larger project that would include the development of the theory of consciousness, ballooned into a life's work.

3

Exploitation and Alienation

I

There is an important element of Marx's criticism of capitalism that has until now been purposely kept in the background of our discussion of his evaluative perspective: the concept of exploitation. No one denies that the concept of exploitation plays a key role in Marx's attack on capitalism. Yet there is much confusion as to just what Marx's concept of exploitation is.

Recent discussions tend to fall into two groups. In the first are those that offer extensive analyses of Marx's concept of alienation, but seldom mention exploitation. When writers in this first group do mention exploitation they mistakenly assume that the concept is transparent and unproblematic.[1]

The second group has little to say about alienation, but does attempt an account of exploitation. These writers mistakenly confine Marx's concept of exploitation to the labor process itself.[2] Both approaches fail to articulate important connections between alienation and exploitation.

In this chapter, I shall present a more comprehensive account of Marx's concept of exploitation. First, I shall argue that Marx's work includes three distinct but related conceptions of exploitation: (a) a conception of exploitation in the labor process in capitalism; (b) a trans-historical conception of exploitation that applies not only to the labor process in capitalism but to the labor processes of all class-divided societies;[3] and (c) a general conception of exploitation that is not limited to phenomena within the labor process itself. Second, on the basis of this more comprehensive account I will do three things: (i) I will articulate connections between exploitation and alienation by arguing that the theory of alienation provides content for the concept of exploitation; (ii) I will rebut certain prevalent objections against Marx's views on exploitation by showing that these objections are

36

based on misunderstandings about what Marx's concept of exploitation is; (iii) I will examine the relationship between Marx's concept of exploitation and the radical evaluative perspective articulated in the preceding chapter.

II

I begin with the most specialized of Marx's three conceptions of exploitation: the conception of exploitation in the labor process of capitalism.[4] The labor process that defines capitalism as a distinctive mode of production is the wage-labor process of commodity production.[5] The key to this special conception of exploitation is the distinction between necessary and surplus wage-labor. According to Marx, the wage-laborer's work can be divided into two parts: the work by which he produces commodities whose value is equivalent to the value of those goods required for his own subsistence, and the work by which he produces commodities whose value exceeds the value of these subsistence goods. The former Marx calls "necessary wage-labor," the latter "surplus wage-labor."[6] Marx invites us to conceive of the wage-laborer's working day as divided into two parts. During the first part, the worker works for himself in the sense that he produces commodities whose value is equivalent to the wages he receives. During the remainder of the working day, the wage-laborer works for the capitalist in the sense that what he produces is appropriated by the capitalist and not returned to the worker in the form of wages. Since the product of *surplus* wage-labor is not returned to the worker, Marx calls surplus labor "*unpaid* labor."

Marx also holds that wage-labor is *forced* labor. Because the capitalist controls the means of production, the wage-laborer is compelled by threat of unemployment and, ultimately, starvation, to enter the wage contract. Finally, though the worker receives wages in return for a portion of the commodities he produces, all the commodities he produces are *controlled* by the capitalist.

Granted this skeletal analysis of wage-labor, it is not difficult to see why Marx would brand it as exploitation. As Nancy Holmstrom succinctly puts it: "It is the fact that the [capitalist's] income is derived through *forced, unpaid, surplus* [wage] labor, *the product of which the workers do not control*, which makes [wage labor] exploitive."[7] Exactly why the term "exploitation" is so appropriate here will become clearer once we see how Marx's conception of exploitation in the labor process in capitalism is related to the second and third conceptions of exploitation.

According to Marx, each of the class-divided social formations preceding capitalism had its distinctive labor process and each of these distinctive labor processes constituted a distinct form of exploitation. In the *Grundrisse*, he distinguishes three social formations prior to capitalism: oriental despotism, ancient slave-holding society, and feudalism. The method by which a surplus is extracted from the workers differs in each case, as does the form which the worker's product takes. In the feudal labor-process, for example, the worker is not a wage-laborer who produces goods in the form of commodities on pain of unemployment. He is a serf who receives the use of a small plot of land instead of wages and who produces goods for the personal consumption of the lord on pain of physical coercion. Yet in each case, four elements are present: (1) the labor is *forced;* (2) a portion of it is *uncompensated* labor; (3) the worker produces a *surplus;* and (4) the *workers do not themselves control their product.* The conception of exploitation in the capitalist labor process simply specifies each of these four elements which constitute the trans-historical conception of exploitation in the labor process. Marx's conception of exploitation in the wage-labor process, then, is simply a specialized version of his trans-historical conception of exploitation in the labor processes of all class-divided societies.[8]

To grasp Marx's most general conception of exploitation, one must begin with one of his earlier works, *The German Ideology,* written in 1846. In the following passage from this work Marx first introduces the term "exploitation," explicates its meaning, and notes the French phrase from which he borrowed the term—all in the course of a discussion of the bourgeois view of interpersonal relations as relations of utilization *(Brauchbarkeit).*

In Hollbach, all . . . activity of individuals in their mutual intercourse e.g., speech, love, etc., is depicted as a relation of utility and utilization. . . . In this case the utility relation has a quite different meaning, namely that I derive benefit for myself by doing harm to someone else *(exploitation de l'homme par l'homme).* . . . All this actually is the case with the bourgeois. For him only one relation is valid on its own account—the relation of exploitation; all other relations have validity for him only insofar as he can include them under this one relation, and even where he encounters relations which cannot be directly subordinated to the relation of exploitation, he does at least subordinate them to it in his imagination. The material expression of this use is money, the representation of the value of all things, people and social relations.[9]

This passage is crucial because it clearly articulates Marx's general conception of exploitation. This general conception includes three elements: first, to exploit someone is to *utilize* him or her as one would a tool or natural resource; second, this utilization is *harmful* to the person so utilized; and third, *the end* of such utilization *is one's own benefit.*[10]

What is most striking is the extreme generality of this characterization: exploitation is not limited to the labor process itself. It is not simply that the bourgeois exploits the worker *in the wage-labor relationship.* Nor is it simply a matter of the bourgeois exploiting the *worker.* The point, rather, is that, for the bourgeois, human relations *in general* are exploitative, and this includes not only his relations with the worker, but with his fellow bourgeois as well.

In the *Excerpt-Notes of 1844,* Marx describes mutually exploitative exchange-relations among individuals in the mythical simple commodity-exchange society portrayed by John Locke and other bourgeois theorists. These Lockean individuals produce and exchange their own surplus products with other individuals of the same description. Since they only exchange goods, no wage-relation exists. Hence the special conception of exploitation in the capitalist labor process—the wage-labor process—does not apply. Further, since neither party has a monopoly on the means of production that forces the other to perform uncompensated labor for him, the more general trans-historical conception of exploitation in the labor process is inapplicable as well. Yet as the following passage shows, Marx condemned these exchanges as mutually exploitative—as relationships in which one individual utilizes another as a mere means to his own benefit, to the disadvantage of the other, and *vice versa*.

As soon as exchange occurs, there is an overproduction beyond the immediate boundary of ownership. But this overproduction does not exceed selfish need. Rather it is only an indirect way of satisfying a need which finds its objectification in the production of another person. . . . I have produced for myself and not for you, just as you have produced for yourself and not for me. . . . No one is gratified by the product of another. Our mutual production means nothing for us as human beings. . . . Human nature is not the bond of our production for each other. . . . Each of us sees in his product only his own objectified self-interest and in the product of another person, another self-interest which is independent, alien, and objectified. As a human being, however, you do have a human relation to my product; you want my product. It is the object of your desire and your will. But your want, desire, and will for my product are impotent (as such). My social relationship with you and my labor for your want is just plain deception. . . . Mutual pillaging is at its base.[11]

The fact that Marx views relations between Lockean producer-exchangers as mutually exploitative according to the general conception of exploitation is extremely important. Like the passage in *The German Ideology* in which Marx describes all bourgeois relations as relations of harmful utilization for gain, it shows that Marx did not restrict the term "exploitation" to relationships between classes, much less to the wage-relationship between capitalist and worker.

More importantly, Marx's general conception of exploitation is broad enough to apply to relationships between persons who are not producers. For it applies with equal force to more sophisticated exchange-relationships between members of the bourgeoisie in fully developed capitalist society. Even though two merchants or two bankers, for example, are members of the same class, even though both have property in means of production and stand in no wage-relation to one another, they nonetheless exploit one another in their transactions. Each harmfully utilizes the other as a mere means to his own advantage. Each views the *needs* and *desires* of the other not as needs and desires, but rather as levers to be manipulated, as weaknesses to be preyed upon. In the Essay *On the Jewish Question*[12] and the

Excerpt-Notes of 1844, Marx presents a detailed account of the ways in which money serves as the medium of exploitation in the wage-relation between workers and capitalist and in relations among members of the bourgeoisie. And this, of course, is just what we should expect, granted the general conception of exploitation Marx introduced in *The German Ideology.*

Money facilitates the exploitation of every human capacity because it enables us to attach a price to every human capacity and to purchase control over its exercise. As Marx puts it in *The German Ideology,* money is the "material expression" of our purely instrumental relations with human beings because money is "the representative of the value of all things, people, and social relations."[13]

Marx's comments on proletariat prostitution provide further evidence for the claim that his general conception of exploitation extends beyond the labor process itself and applies to *intra*-class as well as inter-class relations. In 1844, Marx notes that workers regularly prostitute their wives and daughters to supplement their wages.

You must make everything that is yours saleable, i.e., useful. If I ask the political economist: Do I obey economic laws if I extract money by offering my body for sale, by surrendering it to another's lust? (The factory workers in France call the prostitution of their wives and daughters the Xth working hours, which is literally correct.) . . . . Then the political economist replies to me: you do not transgress my laws. . . .[14]

Marx's point here is that the exploitation of the worker by the capitalist in the labor process encourages exploitative relations among the workers, even within the worker's family itself. In the labor process, the worker sells the use of his capacities, the control over his mind and body to the capitalist. Thus the labor process accustoms the worker to think of human capacities as saleable. Further, the use of money makes it possible to price and purchase all human capacities—sexual capacities as well as capacities for industrial operations in the labor process. Finally, both the meagerness of his wage and the bourgeois ethic of "self-improvement" encourage the worker to exploit his wife and children in the way in which the capitalist exploits him.[15]

Marx's recurrent remarks on the exploitative character of the modern state furnish still more evidence that his analysis of exploitation in capitalism is not limited to exploitation in the labor process. It has often been noted that Marx has two distinct views of the state.[16] The first is that the coercive apparatus of the state is a weapon wielded by the bourgeoisie to enforce the conditions of its exploitation of the proletariat. This first view of the state is most clearly expressed in the *Communist Manifesto:*

The executive of the modern representative state is but a committee for managing the common affairs of the bourgeoisie.[17]

Marx's other view of the state is more complex. On this second view, the state achieves a degree of autonomy from the interests of the bourgeoisie as a class. The state bureaucracy approaches the status of a distinct class, pursuing its own interests, above the class-division between bourgeoisie and proletariat. Marx's most penetrating criticisms of the semiautonomous exploitative state bureaucracy are found in his early work *Critique of Hegel's Philosophy of Right*,[18] but this second view of the state is also found in middle and late works. In the *Eighteenth Brumaire* (1852), Marx describes the state bureaucracy as "an appalling parasitic body, which enmeshes French society like a net and chokes all its pores . . . ."[19] He proceeds to describe the process by which the parasite grew by increasing its control over the wealth produced by the citizens and by then using this control to extract ever more wealth and control.

Every common interest was straightway severed from society, counterposed to it as a higher general interest, snatched from the activity of society's members themselves and made an object of government activity, from a bridge, a schoolhouse and the communal property of a village community to the railways, the national wealth. . . .[20]

The simpler conception of the state as the instrument of the bourgeoisie and the more complex conception of the semiautonomous bureaucratic state are mutually consistent. In fact, it would be more accurate to say that the more complex conception assimilates the simpler. The richness and originality of the complex view is that it enables us to understand how the state can be most effective as an instrument for the bourgeoisie's exploitation of the proletariat when it attains a degree of autonomy from the bourgeoisie. Because effective control over the proletariat includes political as well as economic domination, the bourgeoisie finds it necessary to delegate power to the leadership of the state bureaucracy; yet this power endows the state with a dangerous degree of independence, a life which is partly its own. The theory of alienation aptly captures the ambivalent and ambiguous relationship between the bourgeoisie and the state that is its creation but which is no longer fully within its control.

In the *Civil War in France*, Marx reiterated this conception of the state bureaucracy as a semiautonomous power standing partly above class-divided society and exploiting *all* its members, proletarian and bourgeois alike. The glory of the Paris Commune uprising of 1871 was that it was the first attempt to smash the exploitative state, to restore "to the social body all the forces hitherto absorbed by the State parasite feeding upon them and clogging the free movement of society."[21]

The parasite simile, which vividly captures the exploitative character of the state bureaucracy, is also Marx's favorite figure for the exploitation of the worker by the capitalist. In *Capital*, Marx frequently describes the capitalist as a vampire feeding on the life-blood of the worker.[22] Since, on this second view, the victims of state exploitation are capitalists as well as workers, no conception of exploitation in the labor process is broad enough to cover the relation between the state and citizenry in capitalism.[23]

I conclude, then, that Marx's concept of exploitation is broader and more complex than previous accounts have assumed. Exploitation, for Marx, is not confined to relations within the labor process, nor even to relations between classes. Accounts that overlook these points impoverish Marx's condemnation of capitalism as an exploitative social formation. Marx's criticism is not just that the capitalist labor process is exploitative—his criticism is that capitalist society is exploitative through and through. The exploitation of the worker by the capitalist is the foundation of the exploitative society, but it is not the whole edifice. Any account which restricts Marx's concept of exploitation to the labor process ignores Marx's fundamental thesis that the labor process of a society exerts a pervasive influence on all human relations within that society.

III

I now want to suggest that the relation between Marx's concept of exploitation and his theory of alienation is more intimate than has generally been thought.[24] My suggestion is that *the theory of alienation supplies content for the concept of exploitation by providing a systematic classification of the ways in which human beings are utilized and the forms of harm that this utilization inflicts on them.* There are two important reasons why Marx's theory of alienation is well suited to this task. First, the theory of alienation provides an account of the basic conditions under which exploitation in capitalism occurs. Second, the theory of alienation is rich enough to encompass the pervasiveness of exploitation in capitalism—including the more subtle forms of exploitation lying outside the wage-labor process.

According to Marx, the chief conditions for the existence of the exploitative labor process of capitalism are (a) capital in the form of money, (b) a pool of "free" workers, and (c) a minority with a monopoly on the means of production.[25] Marx employs the concept of alienation to characterize elements which these three conditions have in common.

In the essay *On the Jewish Question,* he uses the concept of alienation to describe capital in the form of money as the medium by means of which the capitalist exploits the worker.

Selling is the practice of externalization. . . . [Man] thereby converts his nature into an *alien,* illusory being, so under the domination of egoistic need he can only act practically, only practically produce objects, by subordinating both his products and his activity to the dominion of an alien being [the capitalist], bestowing upon them the significance of an alien entity—money.[26]

In the *Grundrisse,* Marx describes the process by which the feudal serf was "freed" from his ties to land and lord as a process by which the worker is *alienated* from the means of production.[27]

The bifurcation of society into the class of propertyless producers and the class of propertied nonproducers Marx describes as the *aliena-tion* of one group within the human community from another.[28]

The theory of alienation is rich enough to provide a comprehensive account of the ways human beings are utilized in capitalism and the ways this utilization harms them. In the wage-labor process, Marx distinguishes between the worker's alienation from his *product* and his alienation in the work *activity* itself.[29] Marx describes the worker's *product* as an alien being to stress the worker's lack of control over what he produces and the destructive results of this lack of control.

The harm the product inflicts on the worker is of two sorts. First, the product harms the worker by contributing to periodic overproduction crises which in turn force capitalists to lay off workers: the product becomes an alien force which cuts the worker off from his means of livelihood. Second, in producing commodities for the capitalist, the worker is helping to reproduce the whole capitalist system—the sys-tem that methodically degrades and impoverishes him.

According to Marx, what is most harmful about the *activity* of wage labor itself is that it alienates the worker from creative, self-conscious productive activity by robbing him of control over his actions, exhaust-ing his body, and stunting his mind. In this activity, the capitalist utilizes the worker as a mere means, as an *alien* being, not as a fellow human being with human capacities which must be nurtured if they are to develop.

The theory of alienation is also rich enough to encompass the various forms of harmful utilization outside the labor process and Marx does employ it for this purpose. We have already seen how Marx uses the language of alienation to characterize the function of money as a medium of exploitation in all human relations. He also employs the concept of alienation to describe the exploitative relationship between the semiautonomous bureaucratic state and its citizens. The state is alienated social power, an alien thing standing over and against the society it is supposed to serve and exploiting it. Like the commodity the worker produces, the bureaucratic state is the creation of capitalist society—but a creation over which the creator has lost control and which has become an alien, menacing force.[30]

IV

The preceding account of Marx's concept of exploitation and its con-nections with his views on alienation can now serve as a basis for evaluating three objections frequently raised against Marx's attack on capitalist exploitation.

The first objection is that exploitation is no longer widespread, at least in the United States, because workers' real wages have risen significantly since Marx's time. Marx's paradigm of the wage-laborer who works for a subsistence wage is a vanishing species. This objec-tion is based on two misconceptions. First, it rests on an erroneous conception of Marx's views on exploitation in the wage-labor process. According to Marx, exploitation is not simply a matter of meager wages and will not be eradicated if wages rise. Marx's conception of exploitation in the wage-labor process, it will be recalled, included four elements. What makes wage-labor exploitative is that it is *forced, unpaid* labor *which produces a surplus*, where *the product is not under the worker's control*.

Attention to the general conception of exploitation makes the inadequacy of this first objection even clearer. If exploitation occurs wherever persons are harmfully utilized as mere instruments for private gain, and if the money system encourages such utilization in all spheres of human activity, then merely paying workers more money cannot be expected to end exploitation.

A second, more serious objection to Marx's views on exploitation was recently raised by Robert Nozick.

The charm and simplicity of [Marx's] theory's *definition* of exploitation is lost when it is realized that according to the definition there will be exploitation in any society in which investment takes place for a greater future product . . . and in any society in which those unable to work . . . are *subsidized* by the labor of others.[31]

Nozick's argument here can be reconstructed as a *reductio ad absurdum* of Marx's alleged definition of "exploitation."

   i) According to Marx, "exploitation" is defined in such a way that exploitation exists if (and only if) the workers do not themselves receive their total product.
   ii) In any society in which there is investment and in any society in which those unable to work are subsidized, workers will not receive their total product.
   iii) But in some circumstances, at least, neither investment nor subsidization of those unable to work involve exploitation; and any society will require some investment and some subsidization.

Therefore,

   iv) Marx's definition of "exploitation" is absurd or at least severely flawed.

Nozick is not alone in subscribing to premise (i). Both Marc Blaug in *Economic Theory in Retrospect* and Paul Samuelson in his immensely influential textbook *Economics* also assume that Marx defines "exploitation" as appropriation of the worker's surplus product.[32]

One obvious difficulty with premise (i) is that it erroneously restricts Marx's concept of exploitation to the wage-labor process. But even if we view premise (i) as referring only to exploitation in the wage-labor process, there are at least three good reasons for rejecting it. The first is that, by focusing only on the appropriation of the worker's product, the definition in (i) neglects Marx's claim that the labor is *forced* and his view that in the labor process itself the worker is *harmfully utilized* in the various ways described in the theory of alienation. The second is that

Marx himself explicitly rejects any such definition in the *Critique of the Gotha Program*. The third reason for rejecting premise (i) is that any such definition would be guilty of an error that Marx repeatedly attacked throughout his career—the error of viewing the ills of capitalism as primarily distributive problems. Granted the preceding account of the connection between alienation and exploitation, the first reason for rejecting premise (i) should be clear enough. Let us consider the second and third reasons in turn.

Marx was quite aware of both the need for investment and the need for subsidization of those unable to work.[33] In the *Critique of the Gotha Program*, he stated that even in communist society it will be necessary to rake off a portion of the social product to be used for these purposes. Indeed, Marx criticized the authors of the *Gotha Program* of the German Workers for committing the very error which Nozick and Blaug attribute to him. The authors of the *Program* confused the reasonable demand for an end to exploitation with the unreasonable demand that the workers receive the "undiminished proceeds" of their labor. For Marx, the mere fact that the worker does not receive the full product of his labor is not sufficient for exploitation. Whether there is exploitation depends upon *how* the product is produced and *what happens to* the surplus product.

Third, and finally, to define "exploitation" as appropriation of the worker's surplus product would be to treat it as a purely distributive matter. And to treat exploitation as a purely distributive matter is to be well on one's way toward what Marx viewed as a major error of non-Marxist socialist theories. If one views it essentially as a matter of distribution, one may be tempted to assume that exploitation is simply a violation of some appropriate standard of distributive justice. One will be tempted to equate the demand for an end to exploitation with the demand for a "just" or "fair" wage. To yield to this temptation is doubly disastrous according to Marx. First, to focus on distribution is to overlook the fact that distribution is a function of production and that attempts at distributive reform without fundamental changes in the mode of production are doomed to failure. Second, focusing on exploitation as primarily a problem of distribution directs attention toward confused abstract ideals of justice and away from concrete revolutionary goals.[34] Marx derides preoccupation with ideals of justice or fairness in the following passage, also from the *Critique of the Gotha Program*.

What is "a fair [just, *gerechte*] distribution"? Do not the bourgeois assert that the present-day distribution is "fair"? . . . Have not the socialist sectarians the most varied notions about "fair" distribution?[35]

In sum, Marx's views on the connection between alienation and exploitation, his remarks on subsidization and investment in communist society, and his refusal to view the ills of capitalism as primarily distributive defects all provide strong reasons for rejecting the claim that Marx simply (and absurdly) identified the exploitation of the wage-laborer with appropriation of the laborer's surplus product.

The third objection to Marx's theory of exploitation is that it is fatally dependent upon the defective labor theory of value.[36] As Nozick puts it: "With the crumbling of the labor theory of value, the underpinning of [Marx's] theory of exploitation dissolves."[37]

Granted the preceding account of Marx's three conceptions of exploitation, the claim that his views on exploitation cannot survive the demise of the labor theory of value is indefensible. It is true, of course, that Marx held a version of the labor theory of value—the theory that the value of a commodity is determined solely by the labor-time required to produce it. It may even be true that Marx himself was convinced that the adequacy of his analysis of exploitation in the labor process depended upon the truth of this theory. But neither of these claims entails that Marx's views on exploitation are in fact fatally dependent on the labor theory of value.

To recognize that the labor process in capitalism is exploitative according to the general conception of exploitation one certainly need not subscribe to the labor theory of value. For the general conception of the harmful utilization of a person as a mere means to one's advantage is not tied to anything so specific as that theory. Further, even the special conception of exploitation in the labor process in capitalism can be captured without reliance on the labor theory of value. All that is needed for the special conception is a distinction between necessary labor-time and surplus labor-time, not the claim that labor is the sole source of the value of the product.

Nozick might reply, however, that without the labor theory of value, the special conception fails to capture a crucial feature of Marx's views on exploitation in the capitalist labor process: the claim that *the degree of exploitation* can be expressed mathematically as the ratio of total value produced to value expended in wages.[38] Nozick might argue that Marx must use the labor theory of value to arrive at this ratio and that without this ratio there can be no measure of the extent to which the worker is exploited.

This reply, however, will not do. To express the degree of exploitation quantitatively, a Marxist need not maintain that the total value of the product is determined solely by the labor-time expended. He need only argue that, granted Marx's analysis of the myriad ways in which capital is used against persons in exploitative relationships, *the rate of capital accumulation* provides an adequate indicator of the degree of exploitation. And to calculate the rate of capital accumulation one certainly need not rely upon the labor theory of value.

Those who have limited Marx's concept of exploitation to the labor process and equated exploitation with the workers not getting the full product of their labor may have been misled by Marx's discussion of the degree of exploitation in *Capital*, vol. I (p. 218), where we are told that "The rate of surplus value is an exact expression for the degree of

exploitation of labor-power by capital or of the labourer by the capitalist." It is tempting—but erroneous according to my interpretation—to
infer from this passage that, for Marx, exploitation just *is* the appropriation of surplus value and that consequently exploitation exists wherever workers do not receive the full product of their labor. On my
interpretation, we must distinguish between Marx's proposal for measuring exploitation in wage-labor and his conception of what exploitation is, both inside and outside the wage-labor process.

It appears, then, that Marx's attack on exploitation in capitalism is
not vitiated by the three objections just considered. Exploitation has
not been eliminated by increases in the real wage; Marx's definition of
exploitation is not absurd; nor are his views on exploitation fatally
dependent on the labor theory of value.

V

With the main lines of Marx's analysis of exploitation before us, we
must now explore a perplexing but central question: what is the connection between Marx's notion of exploitation and the radical Marxian
evaluative perspective articulated in Chapter 2? We have seen that
there is a tendency in middle and later published works to retire the
normative concept of human nature and to replace it with a vision of
communism as the evaluative perspective from which Marx's radical
criticisms are to be understood. I have also argued that this radical
evaluative perspective is more epistemological than moral in any traditional sense. Claims about what sort of life is fitting or proper or natural
for human beings tend to give way to statements about what sorts of
social arrangements engender and satisfy undistorted desires—preferences grounded in an accurate perception of social and natural relations, rather than in the estranged and illusory consciousness that
class-divided societies produce.

We saw that, insofar as Marx's criticisms of capitalism are radical
rather than reformist or meliorist, they are comparative, where the
standard of comparison is communism. Marx's critique is radical because he stresses that the main defects of capitalism are necessary so
long as that system endures, but unnecessary in the sense that they can
be eliminated by the transition to a different type of social order,
namely, communism.

Charges of exploitation may also be radical or otherwise. It is true
that one can criticize capitalism for its exploitation without even implicitly invoking a comparison with nonexploitative relations in communism. But Marx castigated those reformists who believed that a nonexploitative form of wage-labor is possible as vehemently as he rejected
the cynical assertion that exploitation is an inevitable feature of human
labor and one whose evils could at best be somewhat ameliorated. It
seems clear that Marx cannot support his claim that exploitation, while
necessary so long as capitalism endures, is unnecessary and hence

irrational in a deeper sense without appealing implicitly to his characterization of an alternative form of society which is nonexploitative. And if these radical criticisms are to avoid the charge of utopianism, the implied standard of comparison must at least be shown to be practically possible on the basis of his scientific analysis of capitalism. Consequently, if we are to understand Marx's criticisms of capitalist exploitation as he intended them—as radical and nonutopian criticisms—it seems that we must attempt to integrate his theory of exploitation with the evaluative perspective of communist society.

In *Capital* and *Theories of Surplus Value*, Marx concentrates on defining the rate (or "degree") of exploitation in wage-labor and on examining relationships between the rate of exploitation and the ways in which the capitalist strives to maximize his extraction of surplus value. In these later works, we find no attempt to clarify and develop the basic but vague notion of what it is to treat a person as a mere instrument, nor of the exact nature of the evil perpetrated when a person is treated in this way. There is, in particular, no sustained endeavor to provide an explication of the contrasting notion of utilizing a person's skills in production without treating him or her as a mere instrument. There are, however, indications of how such an account might be developed. Most obviously, utilizing a person's skills in production would not involve treating him as a mere instrument for Marx only if his activity is not "forced"—i.e., if he is not compelled either by physical coercion or by the threat of economic deprivation. But even this much is far from unproblematic, as it stands, because of the lack of an explicit analysis of the notion of compulsion. One might argue, for example, that even in the higher stage of communism as Marx describes it, persons will be compelled to work in order to avoid deprivation for themselves and others. Marx would reply, presumably, that they would not be compelled in the sense of "compulsion" relevant to the notion of treating a person as a mere instrument. Collectively they would freely choose to produce the bounty of communist society and individually they would freely choose which particular productive activity to engage in. More importantly, when human skills are utilized for production in communism, Marx would say, the utilization is not for any individual's or group's private gain and the process is not harmful to the producer in the various ways set out in the theory of alienation.

The closest Marx comes to developing an explanation of how human skills can be utilized for the production of social goods without treating persons as mere instruments is in his scattered descriptions of free, mutually beneficial productive activity in communism. However, as we have seen, his most detailed descriptions occur in the *1844 Manuscripts* and employ a normative concept of human nature that he seems to have abandoned in his middle and later published works. Nonetheless, what I referred to earlier as Marx's epistemological shift does perhaps provide a framework for developing a Marxian account of when the social utilization of human skills does not involve treating persons as mere instruments. The idea, roughly, is that productive activity will be free, rather than compulsory, and mutually beneficial, rather than harmful, when and only when individuals choose to engage in particular activities on the basis of undistorted preferences and when the collective result of these choices is a social order in which all persons' undistorted preferences can be fully satisfied. This suggestion of how we are to understand the notion that exploitation involves the harmful, merely instrumental use of human beings has the virtue of not relying upon the early, unsupported normative concept of human nature. It does not assimilate treating a person as a mere means to treating him in a way that fails to accord with his nature or impedes the actualization of his essence as a species being.

Nevertheless, this strategy has problems of its own. As we saw in the preceding chapter, Marx's prediction that the disintegration of capitalism will usher in a form of social life that engenders and fully satisfies undistorted preferences depends upon two of the weakest elements of his social theory. First, though Marx recognizes that labor can be neither free nor mutually beneficial so long as a minority has exclusive control over the means of production, he never adequately examined his belief that exclusive control by a minority of individuals acting as individuals will not be replaced by exclusive control by a minority acting as a collectivity. Second, he did not develop a materialist theory of consciousness capable of yielding a substantive account of the transition from distorted to undistorted preferences. So long as these two fundamental problems are not successfully addressed, the foundations of the Marxian theory of exploitation will be incomplete. Once again I wish to emphasize that in articulating these problems I do not claim to have demonstrated their insolubility; my aim, rather, is to indicate clearly the gaps in what I take to be the most defensible reconstruction of Marx's theory that remains true to what is distinctive in his thought.

Aside from these difficulties, which cannot be pursued further here, an important question remains: is exploitation, according to Marx, a form of injustice? Answering this question will require a systematic reconstruction of Marx's puzzling and provocative discussions concerning justice and rights. To this task the next chapter is devoted.[39]

4

The Marxian Critique of Justice and Rights

I

Before Marx's critique of justice and rights can be assessed, it must be articulated in all its complexity. But efforts so far have been incomplete and sometimes confused. Accounts of Marx's views on *distributive* justice—and on rights of distribution—have passed as accounts of his views on justice and rights in general. Marx's complex and penetrating critique of the justice of nondistributive rights, in particular, civil rights and rights of political participation, has been neglected. Finally, even within the unduly restricted sphere of distributive justice, certain fundamental dimensions of Marx's critique have been overlooked. I aim to build on the contributions of recent literature while remedying these defects.

My plan is as follows. First, I shall present a more comprehensive account of Marx's views on distributive justice, arguing that they are both more complex and much more radical than previous analyses indicate. Second, I shall reconstruct Marx's critique of the justice of civil and political rights. Third, I shall articulate Marx's criticism of what may be called the generic notion of justice—the notion that covers both distributive and nondistributive rights and can be extended to a critique of criminal justice. Fourth, I shall examine Marx's position on the question of what role, if any, conceptions of right or justice play in revolutionary motivation. I shall explore certain striking implications of Marx's multidimensional critique of rights and justice—implications which have hitherto been wholly neglected or not fully appreciated. The most important of these may be listed briefly as follows.

1) One of the most serious indictments of capitalism—and of all class-divided societies—is not that they are unjust or that they violate persons' rights, but

that they are based on defective modes of production which make reliance upon conceptions of justice and right necessary.

2) The demands of justice cannot be satisfied in the circumstances which make conceptions of justice necessary; thus efforts to achieve justice inevitably fail.

3) Conceptions of rights or justice will not play a major motivational role in the revolutionary struggle to replace capitalism with communism.

4) Communism will be a society in which juridical concepts—including the juridical concept of respect—have no significant role in structuring social relations.

5) The concept of a person as essentially a being with a sense of justice and who is a bearer of rights is a radically defective concept that could only arise in a radically defective form of human society.

II

I noted at the outset of this book that there are two basic roles which juridical concepts—concepts of justice and rights—can play in a social philosophy: a *critical* role and an *explanatory* role. A social philosophy assigns a basic *critical* role to juridical concepts when it frames its most fundamental assessments of a society in terms of justice or injustice or the preservation or violation of rights. Such a theory appeals to our sense of justice or our commitment to rights in an attempt to motivate us to act—either in support of some existing social structure or to reform it or to replace it with one which more adequately respects rights or achieves justice. Perhaps the most explicit contemporary example of this critical or action-guiding use of juridical concepts is John Rawls' thesis that "Justice is the first virtue of social institutions. . . ."[1]

A social philosophy assigns a fundamental *explanatory* role to juridical concepts if it adheres to what one author aptly calls the juridical model of society.[2] According to the juridical model, the key to understanding a given society and to grasping how it differs from or resembles other societies is to analyze its concepts of justice and rights, both as theoretical concepts and in their actual embodiments in practices and institutions. With some qualifications, Hegel can serve as a good example of a philosopher who assigns a basic explanatory role to juridical concepts. For Hegel, the key to understanding a society is to articulate its distinctive conception of freedom, as it is embodied in the civil and political rights of that society.

In both Hegel and Rawls, juridical concepts play a crucial role in explaining the *consciousness* of individuals in a society. For Hegel, as we have seen, being recognized by others as a being with rights—in particular, property rights—is a necessary condition of the development of personality. According to Rawls, it is characteristic of members of a well-ordered society that they conceive of themselves and others as *beings with rights, who possess a sense of justice.* Further, Rawls argues that respect for oneself and others as citizens with equal rights is a great stabilizing force in society.[3]

Juridical concepts may, however, play a quite different role in an account of self-consciousness and consciousness of others. A social philosophy may offer a theory of *social change* in which juridical concepts play a crucial explanatory role. For example, revolutionary motivation may be explained as arising from the recognition that one's society fails to satisfy the demands of justice or that it violates rights. The same social philosophy may use juridical concepts both to motivate persons to effect social change and in an explanation of how change comes about.

Keeping in mind these two different roles, we can begin with what is least controversial about Marx's views on justice and rights: his general rejection of the idea that juridical conceptions are the most fundamental conceptions for *explaining* social phenomena. This rejection of the juridical model is, of course, an inference from Marx's materialist views on the relation between the base and the superstructure of a given society. Achieving an accurate and informative formulation of Marx's materialism is no easy task,[4] but for our purposes all that is necessary is the recognition that for Marx an analysis of the basic productive forces and productive processes of a society, rather than its conceptions of justice and rights and the juridical institutions that embody them, provides the key to understanding that society as a whole. Because he believes that these basic productive forces and processes are "the real foundation on which rises a legal and political superstructure" and which determine (or condition) "the general character of the social, political, and intellectual life-process" of a society, Marx concludes that conceptions of justice and rights cannot serve as the most fundamental explanatory concepts.[5]

Recent analyses have focused primarily on Marx's critique of the *critical* role of juridical conceptions—the use of such conceptions to make fundamental assessments of a given society. Robert Tucker[6] and Allen Wood have both argued that Marx does *not* condemn capitalism as being unjust, and their view has become prevalent.[7] As we shall see later, one problem with these writers' discussions is that they both fail to distinguish Marx's critique of distributive justice from his critique of civil and political justice. Both Tucker and Wood slip from texts concerning distributive justice to general conclusions about Marx's critique of justice, without examining his distinctive criticisms of the justice of civil and political rights.[8] But for now let us set this complication aside and examine the Tucker-Wood thesis as the claim that Marx does not condemn capitalism as a system which violates some standard of distributive justice.

Since Wood's argument in support of this claim is more developed than Tucker's, I shall concentrate on it, noting divergences from Tucker only when necessary. Wood's argument can be outlined as follows:[9]

1) According to Marx, a standard of justice can only be meaningfully applied to that mode of production from which it arises and to which it corresponds (and each mode of production has its distinctive standard of justice).
2) According to Marx, the wage-relation between worker and capitalist is just according to the only standard of justice which applies to it, namely, the standard which requires that equivalents be exchanged for equivalents.

On the basis of premises (1) and (2), Wood concludes that for Marx the exploitation of the worker by the capitalist, though evil because it is a form of servitude, is not unjust. Similarly, he says that, on Marx's view, slavery in ancient Greece was evil but not unjust, since the juridical relation of master to slave corresponded to the mode of production in ancient Greece, just as the juridical relation between wage-laborer and capitalist corresponds to the capitalist mode of production.[10]

It is important to note that on Wood's interpretation, Marx is committed not only to (1) above, but also to the much stronger thesis that a given mode of production *always satisfies* that standard of justice to which it gives rise and which is the only standard of justice applicable to it. For Wood's point is not that Marx deems capitalism and slavery just, while acknowledging that they *might* have failed to satisfy their respective standards of justice. His claim, rather, is that for Marx there is, as it were, a preestablished harmony between a mode of production and its standard of justice.[11] Wood cites the following passage from *Capital*[12] in support of premise (2).

The sphere within whose boundaries the sale and purchase of labour-power goes on, is in fact a very Eden of the innate rights of man. There alone rule Freedom, Equality, and Bentham. Freedom, because both buyer and seller of a commodity, say of labour-power, are constrained only by their own free will. They contract as free agents, and the agreement they come to, is but the form in which they give legal expression to their common will. Equality, because each enters into relation with the other, as with a simple owner of commodities, and they exchange equivalent for equivalent.

As further evidence for premise (2), Wood also cites another passage from *Capital* in which Marx says that, since the transaction by which the capitalist extracts surplus value from the worker satisfies the requirement that equivalents are exchanged for equivalents, "this circumstance is, without doubt a piece of good luck for the buyer, but by no means an injustice [*Unrecht*] to the seller."[13]

Wood explains that the transaction between worker and capitalist is an exchange of equivalents because the worker does receive a wage which is equivalent to the exchange-value of his labor-power; and it is, after all, his labor-power which the capitalist buys. According to Marx, the capitalist is nonetheless able to extract surplus value from the worker because the use-value of labor-power (i.e., the value produced through the exercise of that power) is greater than the exchange-value of the labor-power itself. Wood concludes that, for Marx, though wage-labor is exploitative, and the exploitation is a form of servitude, it is not unjust.

There are several important objections to Wood's interpretation. First, as Nancy Holmstrom[14] has noted, Wood's argument is far from conclusive because it "views the exchange between the capitalist and worker too narrowly, abstracted from its background."[15] Holmstrom says that Marx's point is that even if the transaction is an exchange of equivalents it is not a *free* exchange: the worker is *forced* to sell his labor-power to the capitalist because it is the latter who controls the means of production. She concludes that once we understand Marx's account of the coercive background of the transaction "we now see that calling it a just exchange could only be done tongue-in-cheek, or to mean: 'This is [erroneously] taken to be just.' "[16]

Holmstrom's point is a sound one and well worth elaborating. The most plausible reading of the passages just cited is that they express what I shall call *internal* criticisms of certain notions of justice endemic to capitalism—in particular the notions of freedom and equality. Roughly, I take Marx's point to be this. The notion of justice—and more specifically of distributive justice—that prevails in capitalist ideology places great emphasis on freedom and equality. By restricting their vision to the wage-labor transaction itself, those enthralled by capitalist ideology are able to enlist the ideals of freedom and equality to justify the wage-labor relation and ultimately the whole set of social relations built upon it. But this feat of tunnel vision is a rather fragile accomplishment. Once we look beyond the transaction itself, we see that the exchange is not free because of the profound inequalities in the respective positions of the worker and the capitalist. Marx emphasizes that the freedom and equality of the wage-labor transactions is an illusion:

> The "free" laborer—*agrees*, i.e., is compelled by social conditions to sell the whole of his active life . . . no matter how much it may appear to be the result of a free contractual agreement.[17]

So long as the principle that exchanges are just if and only if they are free agreements among equals is applied myopically—to what Marx calls the mere surface of capitalist society—the wage-relation appears to be just. But once we take seriously and apply consistently the ideals of freedom and equality and refuse to narrow their application arbitrarily, capitalism's own standard of justice provides material for a critique of capitalism itself. For this reason I refer to the preceeding passages as examples of Marx's internal criticism of justice in capitalism.[18]

There are further, perhaps even more conclusive, objections to the Wood-Tucker interpretation of Marx's critique of distributive justice. First, even if it were true that, for Marx, the wage-relation is just according to the only standard that can be applied to it, Marx's theory of ideology offers a broad range of other internal objections. But the

Tucker-Wood preestablished harmony view rules out the possibility of any internal criticisms.

The conceptions of justice, indeed even the narrower conception of distributive justice that Marx finds in capitalism is much more complex than Wood or Tucker recognize. It is certainly not restricted to a standard for the exchange of commodities. Marx's theory of ideological thinking—what Engels calls false consciousness—makes this quite clear. One goal of Marx's theory of ideology is to expose those false empirical beliefs that play a crucial role in attempts to show that capitalism is just. Capitalist conceptions of justice, like other juridical conceptions, presuppose certain factual generalizations that are usually taken for granted.

We have already seen that, for Marx, the view that the wage-relation is just rests either on false factual beliefs about the symmetry of the worker's and capitalist's respective situations or at least upon a failure to take into account certain facts about its asymmetry. Perhaps Marx's most brilliant attack on the Lockean notion of distributive justice is his assault on the myth of primitive accumulation, or original acquisition, as it is also called.

This primitive accumulation plays in Political Economy about the same part as original sin in theology. Adam bit the apple, and thereupon sin fell on the human race. Its origin is supposed to be explained when it is told as an anecdote of the past. In times long gone by there were two sorts of people; one, the diligent, intelligent, and, above all, frugal elite; the other, lazy rascals, spending their substance, and more, in riotous living. The legend of theological original sin tells us certainly how man came to be condemned to eat his bread in the sweat of his brow; but the history of economic original sin reveals to us that there are people to whom this is by no means essential. Never mind! Thus, it came to pass that the former accumulated wealth, and the latter sort had at last nothing to sell except their own skins. And from this original sin dates the poverty of the great majority that, despite all its labour, has up to now nothing to sell but itself, and the wealth of the few that increases constantly although they have long ceased to work. Such insipid childishness is every day preached to us in the defense of property. In actual history it is notorious that conquest, enslavement, robbery, murder, briefly force, play the great part. In the tender annals of Political Economy, the idyllic reigns from time immemorial. Right and "labour" were from all time the sole means of enrichment, the present year of course always excepted. As a matter of fact, the methods of primitive accumulation are anything but idyllic.[19]

The distinction between internal and external juridical criticisms also shows that Wood is in error when he says that, for Marx, it would make no sense to criticize slavery as being unjust. The ideology by which a slaveholder in ancient Greece or in the American South would justify slavery included certain false empirical generalizations about the differences between slaves and free men. Slaves were thought to be *naturally* inferior, morally and intellectually. The slaveholder's view was that the slave lacked those characteristics of rationality and moral agency that are distinctive of a human being, or a fully human being. In juridical language, the slaveholder believed that he may treat the slave in ways in which it would be unjust to treat a free man because the slave does not possess those natural characteristics which bestow rights.

To criticize the slaveholder by attacking his false beliefs about the natural differences between slaves and free men is to employ what I have called an internal critique. For such a critique does not depend upon any juridical conceptions other than those already dominant in slaveholding society. The abolitionist need not appeal to a new concept of justice. He or she need only point out that the old concept of justice is being grossly misapplied as a result of socially reinforced false empirical beliefs about the range of individuals to which the concept of a human being, or of a full-fledged juridical person, applies. This internal criticism is only one obvious application of one of Marx's most distinctive and fruitful contributions to social theory: the insight that distorted beliefs about what belongs to the nature of various individuals play an important role in the ideological justification of repressive social institutions.

Those who, like Wood and Tucker, have concluded that Marx did not primarily criticize capitalism for its distributive injustices were correct in their conclusion, but for the wrong reasons. As attention to Marx's internal criticisms shows, he did not think that capitalism was just according to its own standard of justice, even if he did think that was the only standard of justice appropriate to it. In the next section I shall explain why, in spite of his frequent use of internal criticisms, Marx refrained from calling capitalism unjust.

III

What I have called internal criticisms of the distributive justice of capitalism are to be contrasted with *external* criticisms. External criticisms are of two sorts. In both cases, the perspective from which the criticism is advanced is external to the conception of justice under criticism. The external perspective, however, may be either an alternative conception of justice or some non-juridical evaluative conception.

Holmstrom and others have suggested that at least some of Marx's external criticisms of capitalism are launched from the perspective of a communist conception of justice—a conception of justice based on the communist mode of production and one whose demands will be satisfied in communism.[20] I have argued elsewhere[21] that, at least in the case of distributive justice, this is false. Moreover, to fail to see why it is false is to fail to see how radical Marx's critique of distributive justice is.

As William McBride[22] has emphasized, Marx not only ridicules those critics of capitalism who speak of socialist justice, he seems deliberately to avoid the use of the language of justice and rights himself. There are at least two excellent reasons why Marx should do this. First, he continually emphasizes that distribution in any society is a derivative phenomenon: its general features are determined by the character of the society's basic productive processes.[23] As I noted earlier, Marx seems to infer that, since the key to understanding a society as a whole is an analysis of its basic productive processes, the most fundamental way of criticizing a society is to lay bare the defects of those processes. This Marx attempts to do in *Capital*. Now just as the root defects of capitalism lie in its basic productive processes, so, one might conclude, the fundamental superiority of communism will be found in its distinctive productive processes rather than in its distributive arrangements. For this reason it would be strange if Marx launched his most profound criticisms of capitalism from the perspective of a communist conception of distributive justice.

There is, however, a second, much stronger, reason to reject this claim that Marx criticizes capitalism from an external perspective of communist distributive justice. The claim that Marx relies upon a standard of communist distributive justice cannot be squared with his charge that talk about "just distribution" and "equal right" is "obsolete verbal rubbish" and that socialists should cease their preoccupation with such "ideological nonsense."[24] Marx believed that communism will be a society in which what Hume and Rawls call the circumstances of (distributive) justice either no longer exist or have so diminished that they no longer play a significant role in social life. The circumstances of distributive justice, roughly, are those conditions of scarcity—and of conflict based on competition for scarce goods—that make the use of principles of distributive justice necessary. Marx holds that the new communist mode of production will so reduce the problems of scarcity and conflict that principles of distributive justice will no longer be needed.

This prediction, I shall argue in Chapter 7, rests in part upon Marx's belief that communism will be a *democratic form of social coordination* and that democratic control over social and natural resources will be both much more efficient (i.e., productive) and much more harmonious than anything hitherto known. For now, I wish only to observe that this prediction that democratic social coordination will eliminate the circumstances of distributive justice does *not* commit Marx to the extremely implausible thesis that scarcity and conflict will wholly disappear in communism. The idea, rather, is that democratic social coordination will be sufficiently harmonious and bountiful that whatever conflicts remain will not require reliance upon juridical principles prescribing rights to distributive shares. The basic principles of social organization will not include principles of distributive justice.

According to this interpretation, Marx factors what others call the circumstances of distributive justice into *objective* and *subjective* elements. In capitalism, the objective element consists in what Engels calls anarchy in production, the inefficient and wantonly wasteful use of human and natural resources. The subjective element includes egoism, competition, and the ever-increasing and ultimately self-frustrating needs that the system engenders in the individual. According to Marx, the communist mode of production will unfetter the tremendous productivity latent in capitalism. At the same time, it will transform the individual into a cooperative, communal being, who finds work itself intrinsically satisfying and whose need for human association will dwarf his need for things. Marx's most extended discussion of the transformation of the human subject is found in the *Economic and Philosophic Manuscripts*, especially in the sections on "Private Property and Communism" and "Alienated Labor."[25] As we saw in Chapter 2, it is in these early manuscripts and in scattered remarks in later works that we find the basis of Marx's most radical criticisms of capitalism and its juridical concepts: his evaluative (though non-juridical) conception of fully developed, socially integrated communist man, the free and creative producer who participates in democratic rational control of the social and natural environment.

In one of the scattered, all-too-brief passages in which Marx predicts the transcendence of the circumstances of distributive justice, he echoes a familiar socialist slogan which might be taken to be a standard of distributive justice for communism.

In a higher phase of communist society, after the enslaving subordination of the individual to the division of labour, and therewith also the antithesis between mental and physical labour, has vanished; after labour has become not only a means of life but life's prime want; after the productive forces have also increased with the all-round development of the individual, and all the springs of co-operative wealth flow more abundantly—only then can the narrow horizon of bourgeois right be crossed in its entirety and society inscribe upon its banners: from each according to his ability, to each according to his needs![26]

How are we to reconcile Marx's use of this slogan with his charge that talk about justice and rights is obsolete verbal rubbish and ideological nonsense and his view that scarcity and conflict will be greatly reduced in communism? The answer, as I suggested earlier, is that Marx is not offering the slogan as a communist principle of distributive justice, but rather as a description of the way things will in fact be in communism.[27]

Once the circumstances of distributive justice have been left behind, there will be no place for any such principle as a *prescriptive principle* that lays down demands for society to satisfy and specifies rights for it to protect. One of the virtues of this interpretation is that it allows us to explain some of Marx's most important remarks about justice— remarks which would otherwise seem incoherent or utterly baffling.

We can now see why Marx would refrain from calling the capitalist's exploitation of the worker unjust, even though he himself thought it was unjust according to the standard of distributive justice distinctive of capitalism, once that standard was applied consistently and not

arbitrarily restricted to the surface of the wage relation. For had he
reviled exploitation as a form of injustice, Marx would have encouraged the conclusion that communist society will be a just society and
that its superiority will consist in this. This conclusion would obscure
the radical character of Marx's condemnation of capitalism and his
vision of communism. For once we understand the depth of Marx's
analysis, we realize that, for him, perhaps one of the most damning
indictments of capitalism—and of all class-divided societies—is that
their modes of production have defects so serious that they make
principles of distributive justice necessary. For Marx, the very need for
principles of distributive justice is conclusive evidence of defects in the
productive processes that form a society's core. And from the point of
view of a discussion of justice, the superiority of communism is not
that it finally solves the problem of distributive justice by at last hitting
upon and effectively implementing the correct principle of distributive
justice. The superiority of communism, rather, is that it makes the
whole issue of distributive justice otiose. The virtue of this interpretation is that it assimilates Holmstrom's judicious criticism of Tucker and
Wood, while accounting for three data which Holmstrom's interpretation cannot explain: (i) Marx's refusal to refer to communism as a just
society; (ii) his view that communism will abolish the circumstances of
distributive justice (and the implication that principles of justice will
not be needed in communism); and (iii) his charge that talk about
justice and rights is "obsolete verbal rubbish" and "ideological nonsense".[28]

At this point, it might be objected that Marx's point is only that
principles of *distributive* justice are too restricted and that in communism they will be replaced by what might be called principles of
productive-distributive justice.[29] On this interpretation, Marx's external critique of distributive justice is launched from a perspective of a
more fundamental notion of justice, but a notion of justice nonetheless. Communist principles of productive-distributive justice would
avoid the superficiality of conceptions of distributive justice. They
would be based on a clear understanding of the derivative character of
distributive arrangements and upon a commitment to eliminating
those inequalities in control over production that are the root of all
other social inequalities. Such communist principles of productive-
distributive justice would specify rights to distributive shares, but
much more importantly, they would determine each individual's right
to share in directing society's productive processes.

For those who are persuaded by Marx's criticisms of the inadequacy
of the preoccupation with distributive justice, but who are skeptical
about his prediction that a new mode of production will greatly reduce
problems of scarcity and competition, the idea of productive-distributive justice is attractive. Nonetheless, it appears that Marx's external
criticisms of capitalism are not based on any such conception. His point
is not that a broader notion of communist productive-distributive

justice is needed to solve traditional problems of distribution. His much more radical claim is that, once the new productive arrangements appear, there will be no need for principles of justice for production or distribution.

The superiority of this new mode of production will not lie in institutions by which society recognizes and protects each individual's claim to a share of control over production and, derivatively, to a share of the goods produced. Its superiority will consist, instead, in the fact that it is a form of social organization in which no one will find it necessary to press such claims, nor to rely upon an institutional apparatus to recognize and enforce them.

In a few scattered passages, Marx does speak very vaguely about the organization of productive processes under communism,[30] but he never so much as suggests that production will be regulated by principles of justice. Nor does he say or even imply that communist productive processes will be structured by conceptions which recognize the individual's *right* to participate in the direction of those processes. His view, rather, seems to be accurately captured by Engels' famous remark that in communism "the government of persons is replaced by the administration of things."[31] The idea seems to be that democratic decisions about production will consist mainly of collective scientific judgments concerning the most efficient means for satisfying needs, not political or juridical judgments. And there is no suggestion that these democratic decisions will take place within a juridical framework that specifies roles and positions of authority or even the opportunity to participate in the process of decision-making itself, in terms of rights.

IV

So far my analysis, like the others cited above, has focused on Marx's critique of *distributive* justice. Now we must broaden our field of vision to examine Marx's criticisms of the justice of civil and political rights. The single most important source for these criticisms is Marx's essay, *On the Jewish Question*. Only when this essay is combined with Marx's writings on the justice of distributive rights can we appreciate the comprehensiveness of Marx's critique of rights. Unfortunately, Tucker, Wood, Holmstrom, McBride, and others have neglected this rich and provocative early manuscript.

In *On the Jewish Question*, Marx distinguishes between (1) human rights, (2) the rights of man, and (3) the rights of the citizen. "Human rights" is the most general category—it includes the other two as subcategories. The rights of the citizen are rights of political participation, especially the right to vote.[32] The rights of man include:

a. The right to freedom of expression, thought, and belief (especially religious belief);

b. the right to equality before the law (the rights of due process);
c. the right to private property;
d. the right to security (the right to freedom of the person—protection of life and limb); and
e. the right to liberty.[33]

Marx introduces these categories of rights in the course of a multidimensional criticism of the limitations of what he calls political emancipation. The rights of man and of the citizen are those rights by which individuals become politically emancipated. Political emancipation is that emancipation which is granted to individuals by the modern liberal state. The main thrust of *On the Jewish Question* is that political emancipation falls short of genuine human emancipation—the comprehensive freedom that Marx believes can only be achieved in communism, once the state has disappeared.

Granted the context of a criticism of political emancipation and granted his references[34] to rights specified in actual political constitutions, it is clear that when Marx refers to the rights of man or of the citizen, he means, in the first instance at least, *legal* rights—rights specified in a coercively backed system of rules. For example, the (legal) right to private property is the coercively backed freedom to use or sell or give one's goods to another. Stated negatively, it is the coercively guaranteed freedom *from* being interfered with by others when one uses, sells, or gives one's goods.

Now as Mill emphasized,[35] rights may be either coercively backed or backed by less formal sanctions such as peer pressure or public opinion. Later I shall consider the question of whether Marx's criticisms of the rights of man and the citizen are applicable to these rights regardless of whether they are coercively backed or not. At present, we will restrict ourselves to coercively backed rights.

The heart of Marx's most radical criticism of the justice of nondistributive rights is the following claim:

E ". . . the so-called rights of man as different from the rights of the citizen are nothing but the rights of the member of civil society, i.e., egoistic man, separated from other men and from the community."[36]

By "civil society," Marx means what he later refers to simply as capitalism—roughly, that form of social organization characterized by private ownership of the means of production, a market for commodities, including labor power as a commodity, and increasing industrialization. But what does it mean to say that these rights are *only*, or *nothing but*, the rights of the man of civil society? If these rights are understood as their proponents viewed them, as valuable social guarantees of freedoms, then E may be more clearly stated as follows:

E[1]. The rights of man as different from the rights of the citizen are valuable (as social guarantees of freedom) only for the member of civil society, i.e., the egoistic man, separated from man and from the community.

Let us waive the issue of whether, as Marx implies, all members of civil society are egoists. Instead, for simplicity, let us concentrate on the following reformulation of E^1.

E^2. The rights of man are valuable only for egoistic, isolated man.

Notice that E^2 is much stronger than the following historical-epistemological claim which Marx frequently advances.

H-E. The conception of the rights of man only arises (and becomes a dominant political conception) at a certain stage of historical development, namely, with the rise of civil society and the egoistic man of civil society.

H-E may be called an historical-epistemological claim because it states that the conception of the rights of man is not available to human beings throughout history. It only arises and becomes known (or widely known) after certain historical developments have occurred. More specifically, H-E implies that the conception of the rights of man is not self-evident or discoverable on reflection by every rational person, regardless of his location in history and regardless of the development of his society.

It is important to note that H-E does *not* imply anything as strong as E^2. Even granted that civil society is egoistic and that political conceptions arise only when they have value to someone, H-E would at best imply the weaker claim:

E^w. The rights of man are valuable for the egoistic, isolated man of civil society.

E^2, the claim Marx apparently advances, is much stronger than E^w because it says that these rights are *only* valuable for egoistic, isolated man. E^w leaves open the possibility that some or all of these rights will be valuable for the nonegoistic, socially integrated members of the new society which Marx believes will supercede civil society. E^2, on the other hand, excludes this possibility: the rights in question are "nothing but" those sorts of social guarantees which are valuable for the sorts of individuals that civil society produces.

What are we to make of E^2? Consider the right of man to which Marx devotes the most attention: the right to private property. By "the right to private property" Marx means a person's "right to enjoy his possessions and dispose of the same arbitrarily, without regard for other men, independently from society, the right of selfishness."[37] Marx also states that "the practical application of the rights of man to freedom [liberty] is the right . . . to private property," and that this right to liberty is "the right to do and to perform what does not harm others." He then notes that

The limits within which each person can move without harming others are defined by the law, just as the boundary between two fields is defined by the fence. The freedom in question is that of a man treated as an isolated monad and withdrawn unto himself.[38]

We can now formulate the application of E^2 to the special case of one of the rights of man, the right to private property:

E^{2p}. The right to private property—the right to dispose of one's goods as one wishes—is valuable only for egoistic, isolated persons.

It seems simply false to say that the right to private property is valuable only for egoists. After all, the right to use one's goods as one sees fit can be valuable regardless of whether one's ends are egoistic or not, i.e., regardless of whether they are exclusively self-interested ends.

The key to Marx's claim here lies in the notion of "an isolated monad" who is "separated from other men and from the community." His point seems to be that the existence of the right to private property—the very need for such a right—both marks and perpetuates a situation in which there are basic conflicts of interest between individuals. In such a situation, secure possession of his goods is a person's only guarantee that he will be able to satisfy his basic interests, including his survival interests. In these circumstances, other individuals are perceived either as mere means for increasing one's own possessions, and hence for increasing one's prospects for achieving one's interests, or as intruders who wish to gain control over one's goods and who thereby threaten one's basic interests.

If the existence of private property does lead persons to view each other at best as mere means and at worst as lethal threats, and if private property rights are needed to secure oneself against intrusions by others, then it makes sense to describe the right to private property as a right which is valuable for man in so far as man is an isolated, egoistic monad. And *if* individuals would not so view each other but for the existence of private property, then it is plausible to say that the right to private property is valuable *only* for egoistic, monadic man. Further, the right to private property could then be said to separate a person from the community in the sense that it protects him from interference by others and absolves him of any responsibility for the welfare of others.

Notice that even if one condemns the right to private property as a boundary line conception that guarantees noninterference while absolving the individual of all responsibility for others, one might nonetheless advocate a quite different kind of property right. Such a right would be a guarantee of a share of the fruits of community cooperation. Or, one might wish to replace the boundary line right to private property with a right to property that guarantees not only a share of the social product but also a share of control over the means of production.

As I argued earlier, however, Marx does not himself advocate the replacement of a defective capitalist right to property with a superior communist right to property. He nowhere formulates such a communist right to property, nor even says that in communism there will be a right to property. Instead, he calls talk about rights and justice obsolete rubbish and ideological nonsense. For as I noted earlier, his criticism goes much deeper than the idea that one property right should be replaced by another. He believes that in communism the sources of conflict will be so diminished that there will be no need for a system of rights to *guarantee* the individual's freedom to enjoy his share of the social product or to *guarantee* him a share of control over the means of production.

So far I have concentrated only on the application of Marx's criticism of the rights of man to the right of private property. The charge that the *other* rights of man are valuable only or even chiefly for the isolated, egoistic individual of civil society is much less plausible. The right to equality before the law and the right to free speech, for example, do not seem to be criticizable as boundary line rights for isolated persons who view each other only as means or as dangerous competitors. It is true that the right to free speech established boundaries to prohibit certain sorts of interferences, but in what sense is this a *criticism* of the right?

The answer lies, I believe, in the very simple but very general assumption Marx makes about the sources of these interpersonal conflicts which make rights necessary. He assumes that any society in which the potential for interpersonal conflict is serious enough to warrant the establishment of rights to serve as limits on conflict is a deeply defective society. Only this assumption is powerful enough to explain Marx's scorn for rights in general, his attack on *all* the rights of man, and what McBride correctly calls his deliberate refusal to characterize communism as a society in which an appropriate conception of rights is effectively implemented.

The extent to which Marx's criticism of the rights of man carries over to the rights of the citizen now becomes clear. Early in *On the Jewish Question*, Marx has already pointed out two basic limitations on the rights of the citizen, i.e., rights of political participation. First, by relegating differences in religion, wealth, education, and other factors to "private life," i.e., by officially excluding their influence from the political and legal systems, the rights of the citizen in fact give these factors free rein in "private life." Second, even where the influence of wealth, education, etc., is officially excluded from the legal and political systems, pervasive and profound unofficial influences flourish. These influences may be either legal or illegal. Illegal influences include bribery of government officials and corruption in the electoral process and the courts. Marx's major emphasis, however, is on the prefectly legal ways in which differences in wealth and status produce inequalities in the effectiveness with which different individuals can exercise their equal citizenship rights. The role of wealth in election campaigns and in securing effective legal representation[39] provide all too familiar contemporary examples. The celebrants of the rights of the citizen help perpetuate the illusion that the state is above the clash of class interests in civil society.

In the section of *On the Jewish Question* in which Marx examines the connection between the rights of man and the rights of the citizen, it is perhaps not altogether clear whether he intends his criticism of the rights of man as purely egoistic rights to extend to the rights of the citizen. The following passage, however, suggests that he does.

Political emancipation is the reduction of man, on the one hand, to a member of civil society, an egoistic and independent individual, on the other hand to a citizen, a moral person. The actual individual man must take the abstract citizen back into himself and, as an individual man to his empirical life, in his individual work and individual relationships become a species-being; man must recognize his own forces as social forces, organize them, and thus no longer separate social forces from himself in the form of political forces. Only when this has been achieved will human emancipation be completed. [40]

Consider a similar passage from Marx's *"Critique of Hegel's Philosophy of Right"*:

In actually establishing its political existence as its true existence civil society has simultaneously established its civil existence, in distinction from its political existence, as inessential. And with the one separated, the other, its opposite falls. [41]

In the first passage, Marx is apparently saying that the rights of man and the rights of the citizen are *correlatives* which mark a division between man's existence as an independent egoist in civil society and his idealized life as a citizen, a moral agent concerned with the common good rather than his own narrow self-interest. The implication is that in communism, where the concept of the egoistic, isolated individual is no longer applicable, the correlative concept of man as citizen, along with the notion of rights of the citizen, will also no longer apply. In the second passage, Marx seems to be saying that civil society, the sphere of egoistic, instrumental interaction, and the political sphere, the sphere in which individuals exercise the (legal) rights of the citizen, are correlative—and that when the one is abolished the other falls with it.

If this interpretation is correct, then Marx holds that, just as the state can exist only in opposition to civil society, so the rights of the citizen can exist only in opposition to, or as distinguished from, the rights of man. Just as the state is needed only so long as civil society exists, so political participation *rights* are needed—and hence are valuable—only where the rights of man are needed. But the rights of man, Marx believes, are valuable only for egoistic, isolated individuals—persons who are not integrated into a genuine community. Hence, he must conclude, both the rights of man and the rights of the citizen will have no value and hence no place in communism, even though he might acknowledge that some political participation rights for members of the proletariat may be valuable during the transition from capitalism to communism, while some elements of civil society remain. Indeed, so far as the state included the legal system of rights of man and of the citizen, Marx's view that the state will disappear with the last vestiges of capitalism implies that these rights—as coercively backed guarantees—will disappear, too. If this interpretation is correct, then Marx is committed to

E^3. The rights of man and of the citizen are valuable only for the egoistic, isolated man of civil society, and will not be needed in communism.

E^3 is a very radical claim, but it is important not to mistake it for a more radical claim which Marx is not committed to.

E^4. The *freedoms* guaranteed by the various rights of man and of the citizen will disappear with the disappearance of capitalism.

Marx does not believe that persons in communist society will not enjoy free speech or that they will not be free from assaults on their lives and limbs. E^3 only implies that in communism there will be no need for (legal) *guarantees* of these freedoms.

It might be argued that Marx's attitude toward one of the civil rights, the right to vote, underwent a significant shift after he wrote *On the Jewish Question*. A well-known passage in *The Communist Manifesto* tells us that a first step in the revolution is to win the right to vote for all proletarians, and in an article on the Chartist movement published in *The New York Tribune* (August 25, 1852) Marx predicts that the result of universal suffrage will be "the political supremacy of the working class."

However, even if Marx did change his estimate of the value of political participation rights, this in no way implies that he believed that the form of society which will eventually emerge when the struggle is completed will have need for a system of political participation rights. All the later passages indicate is that, at a certain point, the right to vote becomes an effective weapon in the class war; and in the absence of any suggestion here or elsewhere that Marx assigns a different role for this right to play when the war has been won, we have no reason to reject the hypothesis that Marx viewed this civil right, like the others, as headed for obsolescence.

The key to understanding why Marx would wish to advance E^2 or E^3 is to consider the circumstances in which rights—as legal guarantees of freedoms—are needed and hence valuable. Most simply, a legal guarantee for a particular freedom is needed only where there is at least a significant potential for serious infringements of that freedom. Keeping this in mind, we can reconstruct Marx's argument for E^2 (or E^3).

i)   Rights, as (legal) guarantees for freedoms specified under the rights of man (and the citizen), are needed only where there is a potential for serious infringements of the freedoms.
ii) Serious infringements of the freedoms specified under the rights of man

(and the citizen) can arise only from clashes of class interests and the egoism to which class conflict gives rise.

iii) In communist society there will be no classes, hence no clashes of class interest, and no egoism arising from class interests.

Therefore

iv) In communism there will be no need for the rights of man (or of the citizen, if these are correlatives of the rights of man) as legal guarantees.

The importance of this sketch of an argument in support of E^2 (or E^3) is that it enables us to focus on the crucial premise (ii)—a very strong, extremely general thesis about those sources of interpersonal conflict that are serious enough to make legal rights valuable. It asserts that interpersonal conflicts serious enough to require a system of coercively backed rights principles are based on class conflict and the destructively competitive, egoistic interaction to which class conflict gives rise. This hypothesis on the sources of conflict is, of course, quite questionable. Indeed, I will argue in Chapter 7 that it signals a failure to understand the diversity of problems in response to which rights may be invoked.

The distinction between internal and external criticisms applies to Marx's critique of civil and political rights as well as to his attack on distributive rights. In each case, some of Marx's criticisms are launched from a perspective within the conception of rights he is attacking, while others are advanced from a vantage point which is external. In *On the Jewish Question*, Marx's main internal criticisms of civil and political rights are found in his discussion of the inadequacy of political emancipation from the influence of inequalities in wealth and educational and occupational status. The alleged goal of political emancipation is to free the legal and political systems from the influence of those factors by means of constitutional measures to accord every individual equal rights of political participation and equality before the law, regardless of his social position—all are to be equal citizens. Yet political emancipation, according to Marx, inevitably fails to achieve its own goal. Inequalities in social position continue to exert a pernicious influence through both legal and illegal channels. So long as wealth can corrupt legal and political processes and so long as differences in social position create inequalities in the effectiveness with which different individuals can exercise their equal rights, political emancipation fails to live up to its own ideal of equal citizenship.

As in the case of distributive rights, Marx's external critique of the rights of man and the citizen is more radical than his internal critique. The external critique is advanced from a perspective external to the conception of civil and political rights it attacks. And as in the case of Marx's external critique of distributive rights, it is the perspective of a society that is beyond the circumstances of rights.

It might be objected that the text of *On the Jewish Question* does not conclusively support my conclusion that Marx is attacking the very concepts of the rights of man and of civil and political rights, rather than simply the peculiar historical version of those concepts exemplified in bourgeois society. It may be true that Marx's criticisms in that essay taken in isolation do not conclusively rule out the possibility that, for Marx, there could be "non-bourgeois" or communist versions of some or all of these rights which are not rights for the egoistic, isolated man of civil society. On this less radical interpretation, Marx would be seen as only rejecting certain specific *bourgeois* rights along with the strongest version of the doctrine of natural rights, the thesis that there is a unique, "eternal" set of rights appropriate for all human beings regardless of their place in history and the type of society they live in.

It is true, of course, that Marx rejects the doctrine of natural rights understood in this way. There are several reasons, however, for taking seriously my conclusion that he also condemns the very notion of a (legal) right as being an artifact of defective modes of production and believes that such a notion will become obsolete when a superior mode of production comes into being. First, only the more radical interpretation can convincingly explain the fact that Marx nowhere even suggests that defective bourgeois rights will be replaced by communist rights—for example, communist rights of free speech or of political participation. It is one thing to say that Marx's epistemological views prohibit him from predicting the precise nature of various rights that will be established in communism; it is quite another to explain why he would refrain even from claiming that communism will include rights of some sort or other. Moreover, in criticizing the rights of man and of the citizen, Marx nowhere says that he is criticizing only the bourgeois version of these rights. Indeed, it seems that he never even distinguishes between, e.g., a general concept of the right to political participation and the specific form such a right takes in bourgeois society.

Second, as we have already seen, Marx charges that talk about equal rights—not just talk about *bourgeois* equal right—is ideological nonsense and outdated verbal rubbish. If he were condemning only certain historical versions of the concept of a right, then we would expect him to qualify carefully this as well as his other scornful remarks about rights. He does not, however, provide such qualification.

Third, in the *Critique of the Gotha Program* Marx argues explicitly that *the very concept of a right* implies the application of an equal standard, but that whenever an equal standard is applied to different individuals, those individuals will be treated in an unsatisfactory way. This claim occurs in the context of Marx's criticism of the principle that producers have a right to a share of the social product proportional to the labor they supply, but he makes it clear that it is a criticism of *rights as such*.

> The right of the producers is proportional to the labour they supply; the equality consists in the fact that measurement is made with an equal standard, labour.

But one man is superior to another physically or mentally and so supplies more labour in the same time, or can labour for a longer time; and labour, to serve as a measure, must be defined by its duration or intensity, otherwise it ceases to be a standard of measurement. This equal right is an unequal right for unequal labour. It recognizes no class differences, because everyone is only a worker like everyone else; but it tacitly recognizes unequal individual endowment and thus productive capacity as natural privileges. It is, therefore, a right of inequality, in its content, like every right. Right by its very nature can consist only in the application of an equal standard in so far as they are brought under an equal point of view, are taken from one definite side only, for instance, in the present case, are regarded only as workers and nothing more is seen in them, everything else being ignored. Further, one worker is married, another not; one has more children than another, and so on and so forth. Thus, with an equal performance of labour, and hence an equal share in the social consumption fund, one will in fact receive more than another, one will be richer than another, and so on. To avoid all these defects, right instead of being equal would have to be unequal.[42]

If Marx were limiting his criticism to certain historical conceptions of rights, this passage would be very difficult, if not impossible to explain.

V

There is still a very general element of Marx's internal critique of justice and rights which has not been explored. Briefly, it is the thesis that the quest for justice is futile because the circumstances of justice are just those conditions in which the demands of justice can never be met. Robert Tucker comes close to articulating this thesis in the following passage, though his discussion is marred by a conflation of justice with distributive justice.

The ground of Marx's aversion to justice is now not far to seek. The idea of justice connotes a rightful balance in a situation where two or more parties or principles are in conflict. It typically involves an adjustment or settlement based on a delimitation of mutual claims. Now for socialists to raise the cry of justice with reference to economic relations in capitalist society was to imply that a rightful balance might be struck, or an adjustment reached, in the conflict between capital and labor. It was to suggest the possibility of a negotiated peace or, at any rate, armistice, in the warfare between capital and labor. This was anathema to Marx. As he saw it, there was no possibility of settling this conflict, no way of achieving a delimitation of claims between these two antagonists.[43]

Though this passage occurs as the conclusion of Tucker's attempt to show that Marx's condemnation of capitalism was not rooted in a concern for distributive justice, Tucker can be seen as making an important point about what might be called the generic concept of justice. Rawls articulates this generic concept when he says that, above the conflict of competing conceptions of justice, there stands the core notion that principles of justice are needed for "assigning basic rights and duties and for determining . . . the proper distribution of the benefits and burdens of social cooperation." Rawls then goes on to note that those who hold different conceptions of justice can agree that "institutions are just when no arbitrary distinctions are made between persons in the assigning of basic rights and duties and when the rules determine a proper balance between competing claims. . . ."[44]

This generic concept of justice is broad enough to encompass the conceptions of distributive justice and of civil and political justice against which Marx directs his critical fire. Marx's theory of class conflict, when taken together with his theory of the state, implies that the generic concept of justice makes demands that cannot be met in those circumstances which give rise to that concept and to which it applies. As Tucker rightly points out, Marx's view is that class conflict can only be ended by the abolition of classes—no proper or impartial balance of competing claims is possible. Further, as we have seen, Marx believes that the state—including the whole system of rights and duties it enforces—is the creature of class conflict and will disappear with it.

Now as we saw earlier,[45] Marx's writings contain two distinct conceptions of the state. The first, which is found most explicitly in *The Communist Manifesto*,[46] is that the state is a weapon in the class war wielded by the dominant economic class.

Marx's second conception of the state is found primarily in *The Civil War in France* and in *The Eighteenth Brumaire*, where he emphasizes that under certain conditions the bureaucratic state can achieve a degree of independence from the struggle between capitalists and proletarians. Under these conditions, state officials are able to rule in their own interest by playing off the warring classes against each other.[47]

It is crucial to see that according to both of Marx's conceptions of the state, the state does not fulfill the only function which, according to traditional political theory, would give it a legitimate title to authority. For in neither case is the state an institution which satisfies the demands of the generic concept of justice by achieving a "rightful" or "proper" or "fair" or "impartial" balance among competing claims. On Marx's view, the state inevitably either serves to enhance the oppression of one class by another or exploits the public in general for its own aggrandizement or does both.[48] In neither case does it act as an impartial arbiter of conflict or secure the common interest. This is true even of the transitory socialist state and for this reason Marx calls it the *dictatorship* of the proletariat, emphasizing that here too the state is a weapon wielded by one class against the other, not an impartial arbiter seeking to strike a rightful balance of claims or to promote a common interest. Indeed, for Marx there can be no genuine common interest in class-divided society.

When the idea that the demands of justice cannot be satisfied in the circumstances that generate them is applied to our earlier discussion of distributive justice in the exchange between worker and capitalist, its attribution to Marx becomes even more plausible. I argued earlier that one of Marx's internal criticisms of capitalism is that, in the wage-relation, it violates its own principle that exchanges are to be *free* exchanges between *equals*. But we have not yet captured the radical character of Marx's criticism until we add the charge that this principle of free and equal exchange between the buyer and seller of labor power is not only unsatisfied but *unsatisfiable*.

For Marx no genuinely free and equal exchange is possible between those who own the means of production and those who do not, and it is in terms of ownership or nonownership of the means of production that "capitalist" and "worker" are defined. Thus it is impossible for the capitalist and the worker, so long as they remain capitalist and worker, to engage in a free and equal exchange. It follows that the only change profound enough to overcome the objection that the exchange is only apparently free and equal is the abolition of private ownership of the means of production. But since the capitalist, the worker, and the exchange relation between them only exist where there is private ownership of the means of production, this change cannot count as one which satisfies a principle or just exchange between worker and capitalist. If Marx had stopped short of this more devastating internal critique, he would not have succeeded in distinguishing himself from those reformists who admit that the principle of free and equal exchange is not satisfied but who propose to satisfy it by increasing the worker's wages or by supplementing wages with welfare benefits, as in Bismark's Germany.

There is a related, but even deeper, internal juridical criticism which Jeffrie Murphy develops by expanding on the following comments made by Marx on the topic of crime and punishment.[49]

Punishment in general has been defended as a means either of ameliorating or of intimidating. Now what right have you to punish me for the amelioration or intimidation of others? And besides there is history—there is such a thing as statistics—which prove with the most complete evidence that since Cain the world has been neither intimidated nor ameliorated by punishment. Quite the contrary. From the point of view of abstract right, there is only one theory of punishment which recognizes human dignity in the abstract, and that is the theory of Kant, especially in the more rigid formula given to it by Hegel. Hegel says: "Punishment is the *right* of the criminal. It is an act of his own will. The violation of right has been proclaimed by the criminal as his own right. His crime is the negation of right. Punishment is the negation of this negation, and consequently an affirmation of right, solicited and forced upon the criminal by himself."

There is no doubt that something is specious in this formula, inasmuch as Hegel, instead of looking upon the criminal as the mere object, the slave of justice, elevates him to the position of a free and self-determined being. Looking, however, more closely into the matter, we discover that German idealism here, as in most other instances, has but given a transcendental sanction to the rules of existing society. Is it not a delusion to substitute for the

individual with his real motives, with multifarious social circumstances pressing upon him, the abstraction of "free will"—one among the many qualities of
man for man himself? . . . Is there not a necessity for deeply reflecting upon an
alteration of the system that breeds these crimes, instead of glorifying the
hangman who executes a lot of criminals to make room only for the supply of
new ones? (Karl Marx, "Capital Punishment," *New York Daily Tribune*, 18
February 1853).

Murphy plausibly concludes from this passage that Marx recognized
the moral attraction of a retributivist theory of punishment over utilitarian theories, but denied the "applicability" of retributivism. Utilitarian theories commit us to the morally repugnant view that the criminal
may be *used* as a means toward benefiting society, especially by way of
deterring others from breaking the law. Retributivism, at least in its
more plausible versions, justifies punishment as a mechanism by
which a proper balance of burdens and benefits among the members of
society is restored: the criminal must be made to suffer a deprivation
because he has freely chosen to take unfair advantage of the restraints
on conduct that others have observed, where these restraints are
imposed on all for the benefit of all.

According to Murphy, Marx's remarks about the predictability of
crime, when taken together with his views on class conflict, suggest
that in the conditions of capitalism that make a justification of punishment necessary, even the most plausible justification—retributivism—
fails. Murphy points out that the plausibility of retributivism's
justification of punishment depends upon certain empirical assumptions about the character of the society in which the institution of
punishment exists. Salient among these is the assumption that social
relations are, in the main, mutually beneficial and that consequently
the burden of restraint imposed on individuals by the law is shared
roughly equally by all.

In "Persons and Punishment," Herbert Morris emphasizes that the
retributivist justification of punishment sketched above also rests on
another assumption, namely, that " . . . individuals [are] capable of
[freely] choosing and capable of choosing on the basis of consideration
with respect to rules."[50] If this assumption is not satisfied, then punishment cannot be justified as the correcting of a situation of unfairness
created by the criminal's having freely chosen to take advantage of
others' compliance with the constraints necessary for mutually
beneficial social cooperation.

Marx would presumably argue that the burdens of constraint imposed by the law are not only unequally distributed among members
of different social classes. He would also charge that, in some cases,
they are so onerous for the dominated class that it will be false to say
that a member of the dominated class freely chose to break the law,
where this implies that he could have freely chosen not to break it.
Thus, in the passage cited above, Marx stresses the reliable predictability of crime in a system that "breeds" crime and suggests that retri-

butivism substitutes "for the individual with his real motives, with multifarious social circumstances pressing upon him, the abstraction of a 'free will' . . . ." This line of argument may be most plausible in the case of property law. The claim is that the same system that produces laws demanding that the propertyless worker restrain himself from taking the property of another precludes him from any other means of satisfying his needs or at least makes any other means extremely difficult.

Both of the Marxian criticims sketched above are *internal* criticisms of what many, including apparently Marx, take to be the most plausible justification for punishment, since both argue that a necessary assumption for the applicability of the retributivist view is not satisfied. In the one case, the assumption is that society is (in general) a mutually beneficial arrangment; in the other, that all individuals can freely choose to obey the law, to bear the burden of restraint it imposes. In neither case does the criticism rely upon an alternative theory of punishment.

In their most radical form, these objections would assert that the assumptions in question not only are not satisfied but are *not satisfiable* in the conditions that make the institution of punishment, and hence a justification for the institution of punishment, necessary. In other words, the conditions of class conflict that engender the behavior to which the institution of punishment is a response are just those conditions in which the assumptions of mutually beneficial social relations and of the freedom of all to obey (or disobey) the law are not satisfied. It would perhaps be difficult to attribute either of these internal critiques of criminal justice, especially in their most radical form, to Marx on the basis of his brief, scattered remarks on crime and punishment. Nonetheless, they do seem at least to be strongly suggested when we place those remarks in the context of his broader theory of class domination, and they do exhibit the same general structure as Marx's internal critiques of civil, political, and distributive justice.

VI

At the outset, I distinguished between two different roles which a conception of justice or of rights can play in a social theory: (i) a critical or action-guiding role and (ii) an explanatory role. It was noted earlier that Marx's materialism precludes any major explanatory role for juridical concepts. Once we have a grasp of his position on the critical use of juridical concepts, certain surprising facts about Marx's explanation of social change come to light.

One of the most striking features of Marx's theory of revolutionary motivation is its refusal to rely upon the individual's sense of justice or his commitment to rights.[51] Setting aside for a moment the important tactical and educational role Marx assigns to leadership groups such as the Communist League, Marx's scenario for revolutionary action includes the following elements.[52] As capitalism develops, what Marx calls its "contradictions" become so extreme that they become evident to the proletarian. An ever-diminishing minority of propertied non-workers (the capitalists) confronts an ever-increasing majority of propertyless workers (the proletarians). The property-owners—those who control the means of production—become wealthier, while those who own only their own labor power become poorer. Society is confronted by the paradox of poverty produced by overabundance: because the worker produces more than he and his fellows can afford to purchase, overproduction crises occur and workers are laid off. Once the proletarian recognizes these basic facts of the class war, he comes to realize that his own interest and the interest of his class as a whole require the overthrow of capitalism.

This conception of proletarian revolutionary action renders otiose any significant motivational role for principles of justice or for moral principles of any kind. All that is required, according to Marx, is the motivation of self- or class-interest—no appeal to the sense of justice or to any moral standard is necessary. In fact, Marx has only scorn for those moralizing socialists, like Proudhon, who would exhort the masses to social revolution by appealing to their sense of justice. In *The Communist Manifesto*, Marx stresses that communists "preach no morality" and makes it clear that the proper role for communists is to educate the masses so that they perceive their own interests more clearly and to channel the resulting revolutionary efforts into the most efficient course of action.[53] The communist is not one who formulates principles of justice or uses skills of persuasion to stimulate the proletarian's sense of justice.

According to Marx, self-interest or class-interest has always been the chief motivation in revolutionary struggles. In eighteenth-century France, the emerging bourgeoisie found it necessary to destroy the Monarchy in order to achieve its own good, just as the proletariat's interest lies in the destruction of the bourgeoisie. But there is an important difference between the way in which the bourgeois revolutionaries presented their cause and the way in which the proletariat presents its attack on capitalism. In every previous revolution, including the French, the revolutionary class, being a minority, found it necessary to portray its own special interests as universal rights, its special advantage as the common good, in order to gain the support of other classes. But once the proletariat becomes the vast majority in opposition to a tiny minority, all subterfuge about rights and justice can be cast aside. Nor is Marx's appeal to the proletarians to achieve universal suffrage directed to their sense of justice. It is an appeal to their sense of strategy, their growing awareness that they must achieve political domination if they are to crush their class enemies. In *Critique of the Gotha Program*, Marx suggests another reason to eschew appeals to justice: they are not only unnecessary, but also divisive and confusing, since each of the various socialist sects has its own notion of justice and rights.[54]

We can now at last understand why Marx thought talk about justice
and rights was obsolete verbal rubbish. First, his materialist analysis
led him to deny any fundamental explanatory role to juridical notions
in general. Second, in his criticisms of capitalism, conceptions of justice and rights play no major role. He does sometimes turn bourgeois
conceptions of justice and rights against themselves in what I have
called his internal criticisms, but his most radical attacks on capitalism
are offered from a perspective external to the concepts of justice and
rights. Third, for Marx conceptions of communist justice and rights are
simply not needed either to evoke or explain revolutionary motivation
or as basic normative principles for the new society toward which that
struggle is directed. Thus, for Marx, talk about rights and justice is
obsolete in all these senses.

Now that we have before us the main dimensions of his positions,
we can understand how Marx's internal and external criticisms are
related. His internal criticisms play only a secondary, destructive role.
They are designed to demolish the arguments by which bourgeois
ideologists attempt to show that capitalism is just. While Marx's thesis
that rights will not be needed in communism does not preclude the
possibility that they will be useful in some stages of the transitional
period prior to communism, his rather sketchy and cautious descriptions of the transitional period do not rely explicitly on juridical concepts. Further, Marx assigns no positive, constructive role to conceptions of justice or rights in his account of how the proletariat becomes
motivated to effect the revolutionary transformation of society. His
attacks on the confused exhortations of the moralizing socialists have
only the destructive aim of clearing the way for an appeal to proletarian
self-interest.[55]

VII

Let us set aside for now Marx's dubious assumptions about the sources
of interpersonal conflict and his optimistic prediction that the circumstances of rights and justice will be transcended in communism. We
must now concentrate instead on the implications of Marx's views for
the *form of consciousness* which persons in communism—as Marx conceives it—will manifest. The idea is that persons in communism will
not conceive of themselves or others as bearers of rights.

To understand the implications of this feature of communist consciousness, we must make somewhat more explicit the intuitive notion
of a right upon which we have relied in our discussion thus far. The
analysis of the concept of right is, of course, a complex and controversial task, but this much is relatively simple and uncontroversial. If a
person conceives of himself as a bearer of rights, he conceives of
himself as having a valid or legitimate claim or entitlement to something—either to be treated in certain ways or not to be treated in certain
ways. He thinks of himself as being able to demand what he has a right
to as his due, rather than as something he may merely request as being

desirable. Writers such as Ronald Dworkin and John Rawls offer an even stronger characterization of what it is to conceive of a person as a bearer of rights: it is to conceive of that person as having a claim that cannot be overridden by considerations of utility.[56]

In an article entitled "The Nature and Value of Rights," Joel Feinberg adds flesh to this skeletal concept of a right-bearer.

Having rights, of course, makes claiming possible; but it is claiming that gives rights their special moral significance. This feature of rights is connected with the customary rhetoric about what it is to be a human being. Having rights enables us to "stand up like men," to look others in the eye and feel in some fundamental way the equal of anyone. To think of oneself as the holder of rights is not to be unduly but properly proud, to have the minimal self-respect that is necessary to be worthy of the love and esteem of others. Indeed respect for others (this is an intriguing idea) may simply be respect for their rights, so that there cannot be the one without the other; and what is called "human dignity" may simply be the recognizable capacity to assert claims. To respect a person, then *is* to think of him as a potential maker of claims.[57]

There are two important points here. First, there is the idea that to conceive of oneself as a bearer of rights is to think of oneself as having claims on the basis of which one may demand something from others, as having something firm "to stand on." The notion of advancing claims against others and the metaphor of "standing up like men" are quite revealing. They indicate a crucial fact about what it is to conceive of oneself as having rights, namely, that it is to view oneself as a potential party to interpersonal conflicts in which it is *necessary* to assert claims and to "stand up" for what one claims as one's due. Were interpersonal relations sufficiently harmonious or were conflict resolution spontaneous, there would be no occasion for claims or demands and hence no place for a conception of rights. Similarly, were there no potential divergence between individual interests and social utility, there would be no need for the strong concept of a right advanced by Dworkin and Rawls.

Second, Feinberg suggests what many other theorists of rights have often only implied—that to respect a person, whether oneself or another, is to respect him as a being who is a bearer of rights.

Suppose that conceiving of a being as worthy of respect does entail thinking of him as a bearer of rights. If this is the case, and if members of communist society will not conceive of themselves as right-bearers, then it follows that they will not conceive of themselves as worthy of respect. This is not to say, of course, that they will think of themselves as being unworthy of respect, but rather that they will have no use for either the concept of rights or of respect. For them, the world will be peopled by lovers, or friends, or comrades, but not by right-bearers who are worthy of respect.

Nor is it to say, however, that in communism, as Marx envisages it, persons will not *have* rights or *be* worthy of respect. Whether or not Marx could consistently maintain it, there seems to be nothing logically inconsistent in the idea of a society in which nobody ever finds it necessary to demand what he or she is in fact entitled to or to respect another's claims. This idea is coherent—at least if one assumes that there are certain rights human beings have simply by virtue of being human. To say that, in communist society, persons will have rights, but will employ no conception of rights, would then be to say two things: that those persons spontaneously treat each other in certain ways, and that if this spontaneity failed each would be justified in demanding such treatment. Though an external observer of communist society might, in the course of his investigations, assert that persons in communism have rights, the concept of rights would have no place in communist life.

If, as Marx seems to believe, the concept of a right plays a significant role in social organization only in societies that have failed to control and minimize competition, scarcity, interpersonal conflict, and the separation of man from man, and if having the concept of respect entails having the concept of persons as right-bearers, then it follows that any society which needs the concept of respect is fundamentally defective. If this is indeed Marx's position, then it follows that, for Marx, what is wrong with capitalist society is not that it fails to live up to the standards imposed by its conceptions of rights and respect, but that it is so ill-organized that it needs such conceptions.

Though it has been uncritically assumed in much recent literature, the thesis that respect for persons as such essentially involves proper recognition of their status as right-bearers is quite problematic. In order to argue plausibly that there is a coherent and useful concept of respect for persons as such which is *not* a juridical concept, one would have to do two things. First, one must articulate some basic criteria that such a concept must satisfy if it is to count as a concept of respect for persons as such. Second, one must exhibit a concept that satisfies the criteria but which does not rely upon the concept of rights (or justice).

Though I cannot argue for them here, I submit that the relevant criteria will include the following:[58]

a) The concept of respect for persons as such must include the idea that *all* persons—simply by virtue of being persons—are objects of *equal* respect, regardless of differences in characteristics such as intelligence, attractiveness, etc.

b) The concept of respect for persons as such must apply *only* to persons and must apply to them in virtue of their possessing certain agency-characteristics which distinguish them from nonpersons.

c) The concept of respect for persons as such must include the idea that respecting persons as such consists in manifesting a proper recognition—in thought and action—of the fact that the being in question is a person (as distinct from a nonperson or "mere thing").

It seems clear enough that juridical concepts of respect for persons as such are typically presented as satisfying all three criteria. There may be, of course, deep disagreement about how the notion of "proper recognition" is to be filled out, and competing sets of rights-principles may be invoked to provide it with content.

Interestingly enough, Kant provides us with a concept of respect for persons as such which satisfies all three criteria, but which is not itself explicitly juridical. According to this concept, respecting persons as such involves a proper recognition of the fact that they are not mere things, but ends in themselves, and proper recognition of this fact requires that we never treat persons as mere means. Kant also suggests that this notion of respect for persons as such includes the notion that persons are not suitable objects of commensurate evaluation in the way in which mere things are: persons, he says, have a dignity that is beyond all price.[59]

Kant himself, in the *Metaphysics of Ethics*, goes on to provide more determinate content for this notion of respect for persons by arguing that it requires the observance of various substantive moral principles which specify our rights and duties *vis-à-vis* persons. Nonetheless, the fact that moral philosophers can engage in reasonable disputes over what sorts of rights and duties are required by respect for persons at least suggests that the connection between respect for persons and the notion of rights is neither obvious nor unproblematic.

We have seen that some of Marx's most trenchant criticisms of alienation in capitalism focus on the ways in which social interaction in capitalism fails to recognize, or even subverts, the distinction between persons and mere things. He condemns capitalism as a system in which persons are treated and treat themselves as mere means in the service of things: the worker is a mere appendage of the machine, and worker and capitalist alike are slaves of capital. Further, Marx emphasizes that the money system in capitalism transforms persons and their qualities into commodities—items of commensurate value, things with a price.

Communism, in contrast, is said to be a form of social interaction in which human beings are not treated as commodities, in which mere things are in the service of human enrichment, and in which human beings do not function as instruments in the service of things. It seems plausible to describe such a society as one in which individuals and institutions express a proper recognition of the distinction between persons and things, and where this recognition extends equally to all persons simply by virtue of their characteristics as agents. If this description is accurate, then communism, as Marx understands it, is a society in which there is an operative concept that satisfies all three of the criteria listed earlier. And if this is so, there seems to be no reason to deny that a concept of respect for persons as such will play a role in communism. Granted, as I have argued, that Marx believes that communism will be a society in which concepts of rights will play no significant role, we must assume that whatever the content of the communist concept of respect for persons turns out to be, it will not consist of a specification of persons' rights. The more difficult question is this: If reliance upon the concepts of rights is excluded, could such a concept be provided with sufficient content so that it could fulfill the basic role of structuring human relationships which theorists typically assign to juridical concepts of respect?

VIII

Whether or not Marx's vision of the unalienated society includes a non-juridical conception of respect for persons, his theory of alienation does contain a brilliant critique of the juridical conception of respect for persons found in capitalist society. Since Marx himself provides no explicit analysis of respect, it might be more accurate to say that his theory of alienation provides the materials for such a critique. Consequently, what follows might best be regarded more as an attempt to develop conclusions from Marx's work rather than as a reconstruction of it.

Marx argues that the money and credit systems subvert that distinction between persons and mere things that is made so much of by rights theorists as diverse as Kant and Hegel. Human beings and all their qualities—including their moral qualities—become commodities, things among things, objects of commensurate value. In a market society in which not only one's labor power, but also one's sexual capacities and artistic talents are viewed primarily as items with an exchange value, the moral exhortation to treat persons as beings who have an "inner worth," not a price, becomes an impotent verbal ritual.

In the credit system, even moral virtues—which are supposed to be valued for their own sake, not as means to private gain—are valued primarily as collateral useful for obtaining capital.

What is the nature of *credit?* By a good man the trusting man here understands, like Shylock, the man who can pay. . . . Take the case where a wealthy man gives credit to a poor man whom he considers diligent and reliable. . . . Even if this exception and this romantic possibility are assumed, the life, talent, and activity of the poor man *guarantee* for the rich man the repayment for the money loaned. All social virtues of the poor man, then, the substance of his living and his very existence, represent for the rich man the reimbursement of his capital with the usual interest. The death of the poor man is the worst possibility for the creditor. It is the death of his capital and interest as well. Consider the ignominy in the *evaluation* of a man in terms of money as it takes place in the credit system. . . . Credit is the economic judgement of man's morality. . . . *Human individuality* and human *morality* have become an article of trade and the *material* in which money exists.[60]

Bourgeois ideology attempts to conceal this subversion of the distinction between persons and mere things by celebrating its own distinctive, juridical conception of respect for persons. This conception ruthlessly abstracts from the inequality, exploitation, and subversion of values which occur when market relations invade the whole of human life. It reduces recognition of persons as persons to two forms of juridical recognition, corresponding to the two basic categories of rights in bourgeois society. Respect for persons as such is identified with recognition of their status as property right-holders and as holders of equal rights of political participation. Impoverished worker and opulent *rentier* capitalist, prostitute and customer, high government official and politically impotent "citizen," all have an equal right to make contracts in the market and the equal right to vote in elections.

It is interesting to note that even the most sophisticated advocates of the market society typically assume without serious argument that recognition of the individual as a being with an equal right to make exchanges is an adequate expression of respect for persons as such. In the following passage, Robert Nozick opts for a grievously impoverished conception of what is required by the principle that we are to treat persons as ends, not as mere means, without seriously addressing the objection that a society based on private exchange violates that principle in obvious ways.

It is sufficient that the other party stands to gain enough from the exchange so that he is willing to go through with it, even though he objects to one or more uses to which you shall put the good which you receive from him in the exchange. Under such conditions the other party is not being used solely as a means, in that respect.[61]

As usual, this picture of the equal right to freedom of contract ignores the background of severe inequality in initial assets from which actual exchanges emerge, while denying any moral relevance to the fact that the "good" which one party receives may be used to help reproduce institutions which systematically disadvantage the majority by distorting the legal and political processes and limiting their opportunities for meaningful work and autonomous activity. Nozick's conception of exploitation appears to be correspondingly anemic: there is no exploitation, so long as the exchange did not result from physical coercion or fraud!

We have already seen the power of Marx's criticism of the superficial equality of those who have nothing to exchange but their labor power and those who control the means of production. And we have also examined in some detail his forceful critique of the defects of political emancipation, which stops at equal citizenship rights, while ignoring vast inequalities in the effectiveness with which members of different social classes can exercise those rights. In both cases, Marx regards the recognition of right-holder status as not only failing to establish the distinction between persons and mere things, but as playing a major role in its obliteration. Mere recognition of an individual as a being with the right to engage in exchange and the right to participate in the political process is an abstract and superficial conception of respect for persons, but it plays a very concrete and foundational role in a system which treats persons as mere things.

Though Marx predicts and endorses a new form of society in which persons are treated as persons, we have seen that he does not characterize it as a juridical society. Therefore we cannot regard his critique of capitalism's juridical conception of respect as an effort to prepare the way for a more adequate *juridical* conception of respect, based on a more adequate conception of rights. Instead, we must conclude either that communism as Marx conceives it is a society in which respect for persons is not recognition of right-holder status or that it is a form of social life so radically different from ours that it has no use for the concept of respect for persons as such.

IX

At this point, a significant objection might be raised against my interpretation. Like Tucker, Wood, Holmstrom, McBride, Murphy, and other recent writers on the Marxian critique of rights, I have tended to neglect the important distinction between the concept of coercively backed rights and the concept of rights as being backed by noncoercive means, such as peer pressure or public opinion. Marx's most radical critique of rights (this objection would continue) is only directed toward the former, the concept of coercively backed rights. Thus Marx is committed only to the thesis that communism will have no need for the concept of a coercively backed right, not that it will have little or no need for any concept of a right. Marx's claim that the state, as a mechanism for enforcing rights, will disappear in communism and his thesis that all coercion is "inhuman"[62] and will have no place in the truly human communistic society only imply that the notion of a *coercively backed* right will become obsolete. Nor, assuming a connection between the concept of rights and the concept of respect, does his radical critique of rights commit Marx to the prediction that in communism there will be no place for the concept of respect for self or others.

In a more extreme form, this objection would assert that Marx is not even committed to the disappearance of coercively backed rights, but only to the disappearance of the enforcement of rights *by the state* as a separate, alienated, apparatus for coercion. This extreme form is very implausible. It ignores the fact that Marx criticizes the *content* and *function* of the rights of man, not merely their enforcement by the state. Further, in none of the passages cited above in which Marx criticizes rights does he indicate any such strong connection between defects in the content and function of juridical concepts and the fact that they are enforced by a separate coercive apparatus. The extreme form of the objection is able to explain neither Marx's consistently derisive remarks about rights and justice (not just about their enforcement by the state), nor the fact that he portrays communism as a noncoercive form of social organization, not merely as a stateless one.

I shall concentrate, therefore, on the more moderate form of the objection, which acknowledges that Marx is committed to the obsolescence of coercively backed rights (not just the disappearance of the state as an apparatus for enforcing rights), but which denies that he is committed to the obsolescence of rights that are not coercively backed. There are at least three good reasons to reject the more moderate form of this objection as well. First, to my knowledge, Marx himself never distinguishes between rights and coercively backed rights. Second, though it is true that by itself his charge that coercion is inhuman and his description of communism as a noncoercive form of social organization commit him only to the obsolescence of coercively backed rights, Marx's claim is that talk about rights and justice is obsolete ideological nonsense—not simply that talk about enforcement is. Third, as I argued earlier, it would be very implausible to attempt to restrict Marx's criticisms of the rights of man and of the citizen to the concept of coercively backed rights. Marx's thesis is apparently that, by virtue of their content and function, rights are valuable only for precommunist man—the isolated individual who views his fellows suspiciously from behind the boundary lines laid down by principles of right. It would be *ad hoc*, I believe, to interpret Marx as saying that the socially integrated individual of communism will need and value rights, but not coercively backed rights. Nonetheless, my evaluation of Marx's views will not depend on the assumption that he was committed to the more radical prediction of the obsolescence of rights, not just coercively backed rights. Instead, in Chapter 7, I will evaluate both the claim that communism will have no use for coercively backed rights and the thesis that in communism there will be no significant or major role for rights that are backed by other sanctions such as public disapproval.

There is, however, a possible Marxist reply that suggests an important qualification of my reading of Marx's views on rights, both on the more and the less radical interpretation. A Marxian might object that at most only a plausible case has been made for the thesis that Marx predicts only that what some recent writers call *general* rights will not play any significant role in communist social organization—nothing has been said which shows that Marx also predicted the obsolescence of *special* rights. General rights, roughly, are rights that are ascribed to persons independently of their having engaged in some particular voluntary acts, such as the making of contracts, and independently of their standing in certain special relationships, for example, of child to parent. The rights of man are the most general of general rights. Special rights are said to include rights created through certain voluntary actions which individuals perform, such as promising, or which accrue to certain special relationships.

In the absence of an explicit extension of his critique to such special rights, it might be both implausible and uncharitable to saddle Marx with the thesis that social life in communism will not rely in important ways upon the institution of promising or other voluntary acts which are said to generate special rights. Consequently, I will restrict my conclusions about Marx's critique of rights to the category of general rights, which include rights of distributive justice and civil and political rights.

However, I will only note in passing that an interpretation which holds that Marx predicted the obsolescence of general rights, while acknowledging the persistence of special rights, may in fact place a greater burden upon the defender of Marx. For it might be argued that any society which possessed the concept of a special right would have the conceptual resources for formulating general rights-principles and would also appreciate their usefulness for coping with a wide range of problems of social coordination and conflict resolution, including those which are not rooted in egoism or class conflict. In other words, once it is admitted that people in communism would rely in important ways upon special rights, it may become even more difficult to support the prediction that communism will achieve harmony and greatly increased productivity without employing general juridical principles as important elements of social organization. In Chapter 7, I shall explore in some detail the various roles which juridical principles may play even in a society in which egoism and class conflict are either minimal or nonexistent and where problems of scarcity have been significantly ameliorated.

Another, more profound qualification of our findings concerning Marx's views on justice will be required if the concept of justice is sufficiently broadened. We have proceeded on the assumption that principles of justice are prescriptive principles whose distinctive role is to provide the ultimate basis for ordering competing claims of individuals or groups. And we have noted that the circumstances of justice so understood are those conditions in which there is at least a serious potential for recurrent conflict of the sort which makes such principles necessary. According to this view, justice is in a broad sense an *adjudicative* and *adversarial* concept.

It might be argued, however, that we should either construe the concept of justice more broadly or acknowledge that there is another, quite different, concept according to which justice is more a matter of harmonious, spontaneous order than of the ordering and mutual delimitation of conflicting forces. Indeed, it might be argued that Plato's vision of the just polis in the *Republic* is a premier example of the latter concept of justice. On a plausible interpretation, Plato's point is that a properly designed society would be one in which the proper assignment of roles and functions would minimize or at least greatly reduce the sources of conflict which make necessary a reliance upon adjudicative principles, and in particular upon the extremely adversarial notion of rights. Though an institutional artifice is needed to achieve this harmony, once the appropriate institutional arrangements are in place, the harmony is spontaneous in the sense that adversarial relations and the need for adjudication are largely avoided.

Even if we take the step of acknowledging that there are two distinct concepts of justice, we need not assume that they have nothing in common. There may be some extremely abstract maxims of justice that can be accommodated by both—for example, the principle that equals are to be treated equally, or perhaps that justice is giving each his due. In an adjudicative theory of justice, however, the latter maxim would mean something quite different than in a theory of justice as spontaneous harmony. In a society such as Plato's, individuals or groups will not find it necessary to appeal to principles which provide a basis for balancing or delimiting their competing claims on social resources or political authority. Instead, where each is given his due in Plato's sense, each will perform his assigned function spontaneously and the various functions will mesh in a harmonious order.

If we recognize this basic distinction between concepts of justice, we should qualify our interpretation with the cautionary statement that Marx offers a systematic critique of adjudicative or adversarial conceptions of justice. We might be tempted to go further, however, and assert that Marx not only rejects adjudicative or adversarial conceptions, but also endorses a particular conception of justice as spontaneous harmonious order. Further, we might then attribute to Marx the view that the key to achieving and maintaining a spontaneous order of the appropriate sort is that each person is to participate as an equal in shaping and controlling the natural and social environment, and that when this condition is satisfied it will be possible to say that equals are treated equally, and that each has his due. These last two assertions, however, would be extremely misleading. For it is important to remember that Marx himself neither distinguishes between the two concepts of justice, nor explicitly limits his criticisms to the former, nor ever applies the language of justice to that vision of spontaneous harmonious order which he calls communism. This is not to say, of course, that we are barred from concluding that he should have or could have presented his critique of capitalism and his vision of communism as applications of an alternative concept of justice. But it is to set aside his determined efforts to expunge all talk about justice from the basic vocabulary of radical social criticism.

X

The main results of our investigation can now be briefly summarized. Recent explorations of the Marxian critique of rights and justice have not captured the complexity of Marx's position. First, attempts to reconstruct Marx's position have sometimes not clearly distinguished between the explanatory and critical roles which a social philosophy may assign to juridical conceptions. Second, they have also been hampered by a failure to distinguish between Marx's attacks on rights of distributive justice and his criticisms of rights of nondistributive justice on the one hand and his internal and external critiques on the other. Third, writers have not distinguished between two quite different sorts of external critiques—those from an alternative conception of justice and those from a new perspective beyond considerations of justice altogether. Finally, previous analyses have not explored the radical implications of Marx's critique for the ways in which human beings will conceive of themselves in communism.

I have argued that Marx's critique of rights and justice extends to the explanatory and critical functions of these concepts; that it includes both internal and external criticisms; and that it applies both to rights of distributive justice and to civil and political rights, and may also be applied to the theory of criminal justice. Further, I have argued that, granted a certain strong connection between respect and rights, Marx is committed to the prediction that communism will not only be a society beyond rights, but also beyond respect. Finally, I have cast some doubt on the existence of such a strong connection between respect and rights and consequently upon the claim that Marx is committed to such a prediction.

The value of Marx's critique is that it constitutes perhaps the most radical challenge imaginable to contemporary moral and political theory. Marx offers nothing less than a systematic attack on two doctrines which we may be tempted to view as self-evident: the principle that justice is the first virtue of social institutions and the principle that respect for persons as right-bearers is the first virtue of individuals.

5

Revolutionary Motivation and Rationality

I

We have seen that recent literature concentrates on the question of whether Marx's analysis of capitalism uses moral concepts, especially a concept of justice, or whether it is a nonmoral, strictly scientific analysis. Less attention has been paid, however, to what role, if any, Marx assigns to juridical principles in his account of revolutionary motivation.

Marx repeatedly asserts the superiority of his views to those of moralizing socialists, who appeal to moral principles, including principles of justice, to spur the masses to revolt.[1] Thus the claim that Marx offers a nonmoral, or at least a non-juridical, analysis of capitalism would seem to be in harmony with his account of revolutionary motivation. I shall argue, however, that Marx's account of revolutionary motivation is deficient as it stands and that remedying its defects may require significant revisions in his social theory.

II

We can begin by reviewing some of the main features of Marx's account of the revolutionary motivation of the proletariat discussed in the preceding chapter. At a certain stage in the development of capitalism, what Marx calls the "contradictions" of the system become so extreme that they become plain to any but the most abject bourgeois hypocrite.[2] A contracting minority of propertied nonworkers stands in undisguised opposition to an expanding majority of propertyless workers. Caught in the toils of worsening business cycles, workers are laid off because they have been too productive. Wealth accumulates in the hands of the minority, while accelerating impoverishment and mental and physical degradation are the lot of the majority. Once the proletarian—aided by the work of the revolutionary leadership—recognizes these basic facts of the class struggle (which Marx articulates and systematizes in his materialist conception of history and his analysis of capitalism), he will realize that his own interest, as well as that of every other proletarian, requires the overthrow of the system.[3]

It is something of an understatement to say that for Marx the proletarian's revolutionary motivation is self-interest or class interest. For, at times, Marx goes so far as to identify the interest as the most basic one of all—the interest in survival. For Marx the phrase "class war" is no hyperbole. In the *Communist Manifesto,* he declares that the existence of society itself is no longer compatible with the rule of the bourgeoisie.[4]

As I noted in the preceding chapter, what is striking about Marx's conception of proletarian revolutionary motivation is that it purports to make any motivational role for moral principles, including juridical principles, otiose. Where self-interest—indeed the interest in survival—is adequate, there is no need to appeal to a sense of justice or to any moral standard. Marx believes this is all to the good, since every unscientific socialist sect has its own conception of justice or fairness. There is no need for a careful analysis of these moral conceptions, since effective revolutionary motivation in no way depends upon them. Marx concludes that talk about justice is "obsolete verbal rubbish"[5] and that communists need "preach no morality." This striking tendency to treat juridical principles in particular and moral principles in general as dispensable is surely one of the most distinctive features of Marx's theory of revolution.

According to Marx, the motivation of previous revolutionary classes has also been self-interest. The rising bourgeoisie in France, for instance, found it necessary to destroy the *ancien regime* to achieve its own good. There is, however, a crucial difference between the way in which the bourgeois revolutionaries presented their struggle and the way in which the proletariat presents its attack on the social order. In every revolution in the past, including the French, the revolutionary class, not being a majority, found it necessary to present its own special interests as universal rights in order to enlist the support of other classes.[6] Granted Marx's assumption that the intermediate classes become "proletarianized," so that the proletariat becomes the vast majority, with only one tiny class confronting it as its implacable foe, such ideological window-dressing is no longer necessary. The proletariat, like previous revolutionary classes, is motivated by its own interests; but unlike its predecessors, it can boldly acknowledge this fact. And granted the confusion and divisiveness Marx associates with appeals to moral principles, there is something to be gained by insisting upon the self-interested character of the proletarian struggle.

III

Criticisms of Marx's account of revolutionary motivation have often focused on its apparent inapplicability to nonproletarians who strive for socialist revolution. The most notorious instances of this puzzling phenomenon are Marx and Engels themselves—the one a petty bourgeois, the other a big bourgeois, both dedicated to the cause of the proletariat. Though such cases pose problems for Marx's account of revolutionary motivation, they are not the most interesting ones. The most interesting challenge for Marx's theory is to see if it can respond to the much more radical charge that it is unsatisfactory even as an account of the *proletarian's* revolutionary motivation.

This more radical type of criticism may impugn either the *descriptive* accuracy of Marx's account or its *normative* adequacy. Descriptive criticisms purport to show that Marx's theory is inaccurate as an explanation of how proletarian revolutionaries are in fact motivated. Normative criticisms contend that Marx has not shown that a proletarian has adequate reason to become a revolutionary, whether in fact he becomes one or not.

Some have argued that Marx's theory is normatively adequate but descriptively inaccurate. The overthrow of capitalism is in the interest of the proletariat, and if its members believed this and acted rationally on this belief, they would undertake revolutionary action. But, in fact, many workers, still in the thrall of bourgeois ideology, fail to perceive what is in their own best interests. Their motivational failure has a cognitive root.

Another standard objection is that the theory fails both normatively and descriptively. Marx underestimated the resilience of capitalism and its potential for reform. Many workers have not become revolutionaries for the simple reason that their lot has improved significantly since Marx's day. The crushing contradictions of capitalism have given way to the tolerable tensions of the welfare state. The normative inadequacy of Marx's view seems to follow as a matter of course: granted the proletariat's improved condition, it is no longer obvious that revolutionary activity is rational.

IV

There is, however, a much more radical objection that has received little scrutiny.[7] The purpose of this chapter is to articulate this objection, to elicit its implications for Marx's social theory as a whole, and to evaluate its force. Stated in the baldest and boldest form, it is the charge that even if revolution is in the best interest of the proletariat, and even if every member of the proletariat realizes that this is so, so far as its members act rationally, this class will *not* achieve concerted revolutionary action.[8] This shocking conclusion rests on the premise that concerted revolutionary action is for the proletariat a public good in the technical sense. By a public good is meant any object or state of affairs such that if it is available to anyone in a group it is available to every other member of the group, including those who have not shared in the costs of producing it.

There are five features of public goods which together result in a basic problem of social coordination. (i) Action by some but not all members of the group is sufficient to provide each member with the good. (ii) If the good is produced, it will be available to all, even to those who did not contribute to its production. (iii) There is no practical way, or no way not involving excessive costs, to prevent those who did not contribute from enjoying the good.[9] (iv) The individual's contribution is a cost to that individual. (v) The value of what each individual would gain from the good outweighs his share of the costs of producing it.[10]

Granted these five features, provision of the public good in question is threatened by the free-rider problem. Each member of the group, if rational, will reason as follows: "Regardless of whether I contribute or not, either enough others will contribute to provide good G or they will not. If the former, then the good will be available to me free of charge and my contribution would be wasted. If the latter, then my contribution would again be a loss to me. So rational self-interest requires that I not contribute and go for a 'free ride' on the efforts of others."

The free-rider problem arises for such public goods as clean air, energy conservation, population control, and preventing inflation. The situation can be illustrated by matrix M.

OTHERS

	Contribute	Don't Contribute
Contribute	Benefits of G 2 Costs of Contribution	No Benefits of G 4 Costs of Contribution
Don't Contribute	Benefits of G 1 No Costs of Contribution	No Benefits of G 3 No Costs of Contribution

INDIVIDUAL

The numbers in the four cells of M represent the individual's preferences among the outcomes: the lower left cell is most preferred, the upper right is least preferred.

It is often assumed that the public goods problem arises only for rational egoists—individuals who seek to maximize their own utility. This is not the case, however, as matrix M shows. Assume that the individual contemplating contribution or noncontribution is not a maximizer of his own utility but a maximizer of overall utility for the group. Matrix M still captures this situation accurately and reveals the same free-rider problem. Each maximizer of group utility would reason as follows: "Regardless of whether I contribute or not, either enough others will contribute or they won't. If the former, then my costs of contribution would do no good, while constituting a subtraction from the utility the group gains from G. If the latter, then my costs of contribution are again a subtraction from the group's utility. So maximizing group utility requires that I be a free rider." And again, since every other maximizer of group utility reasons in the same way, the good G will not be secured. Matrix M, then, represents the problem for the maximizer of group utility as well as for the maximizer of individual utility, since the result is the same whether "costs" and "benefits" are calculated solely for the individual or for the group as a whole.[11]

Application to the case of the proletarian is straightforward. Concerted revolutionary action is a public good for the proletariat as a group. Yet each proletarian, whether he seeks to maximize his own interests or those of his class, will refrain from revolutionary action. The radical character of this objection must not be underestimated. The point is not that inaction is *compatible* with rationality. Rationality *requires* inaction. Further, the problem does not depend upon an assumption that the costs of contribution for the individual are very high, much less sacrificial. The phenomenon of revolutionary self-sacrifice presents interesting problems for the moral psychologists, but they are not the problems I shall deal with here.

The public goods objection to Marx's account of proletarian revolutionary motivation can be understood either descriptively or normatively. As a normative objection, it is the claim that the proletarian, far from having conclusive reasons to join the revolutionary struggle, has conclusive reasons to withhold his support from it. Granted the assumption that the proletarian is in fact either a maximizer of his own utility or of his group's, the descriptivist objection follows.

V

The seriousness of the public goods objection to Marx's theory of revolutionary motivation is intensified once it is related to Marx's views on the role of capitalist competition in the downfall of capitalism. According to Marx, the capitalists, by producing an impoverished, exploited proletariat whose only salvation lies in the overthrow of the system, produce "their own gravediggers."[12] The mechanics of the capitalists' self-destruction is an integral part of Marx's economic theory and the details are quite complex. For our purposes, however, a simple sketch will suffice.

Each capitalist must either compete successfully or eventually lose his capital. To compete successfully, he must extract more and more surplus value from his workers; he must increase what Marx calls the degree of exploitation.[13] But this increasing pressure on the proletariat eventually makes its condition unbearable: the victims become revolutionaries. It is compellingly rational for each capitalist to squeeze more and more surplus from his workers, since to moderate his efforts unilaterally would be disastrous for him. Rationality on the part of each capitalist, however, brings the death of the capitalist class.

The structural similarities between the predicament of the capitalists and that of the proletariat are striking. In each case, there is an interest common to all members of the group. In the case of the proletariat, there is the common interest in winning control over the means of production; for the capitalists, preservation of their control over the means of production and the power and wealth that go with it. Yet in each case, rational assessment by each member of the group apparently leads to inaction. What is rational for each is disastrous for all.

Marx, however, assumes that the needed cooperation will be forthcoming in the case of the proletariat, but not in the case of the capitalists. We have already seen that Marx's confidence in proletarian cooperation may be misplaced—he seems to have simply overlooked the possibility that a public goods problem arises for the proletariat. In the case of the capitalists, however, it seems that Marx has not only identified a public goods problem—he has also made its insolubility a cornerstone of his theory of revolution, since the capitalists' continuing to squeeze more surplus value out of the proletariat is supposed to be a necessary condition for the growth of revolutionary motivation. An adequate response to the public goods objection to Marx's theory of proletarian revolutionary motivation therefore must show either (i) that the problems faced by the capitalists and by the proletariat are dissimilar or, if similarity is admitted, must explain (ii) why the problem is soluble in the one case but not in the other.

The task facing the Marxian here is a strenuous one, especially if alternative (ii) is chosen. As we shall see later, the most common response to the public goods problem is to invoke coercively backed regulation to restructure the individual's preferences by making noncooperation more costly than cooperation. The prospects of a coercive solution, however, seem much brighter for the capitalists than for the proletariat. For on Marx's view it is the capitalists who control the dominant coercive apparatus in society—the state. It can be plausibly argued that, since Marx's day, the capitalist class has in fact effectively used its control over the state to make the condition of workers bearable enough to cool their revolutionary ardor. Indeed the modern welfare state—which alleviates the condition of the propertyless, while preserving a large sphere of private ownership of the means of production—is the ideal candidate for a solution to the capitalist's Hobbesian predicament. Redistributive programs prevent the formation of an impoverished revolutionary mass, while the fact that these programs are financed through *compulsory* taxation diminishes the temptation for the individual capitalist to be a free rider and assures him that his contribution to averting the revolution will be matched by those of his fellows.

There are two types of strategies which might be used to rebut the public goods objection to Marx's account of proletarian revolutionary motivation. The first acknowledges that there is a public goods problem but attempts to show that it can be solved. The second tries to show that there is no public goods problem for the proletariat. If either strategy is to serve as a defense of *Marx's* account of proletarian motivation, it must square both with other features of that account and with Marx's social theory as a whole. In this section, I shall pursue and evaluate the first strategy. In Section VII, I consider the second.

There are three generally recognized types of solutions to the public goods problems. The first relies upon (1) *coercion*, the second upon what I shall call (2) *in-process* benefits, and the third upon (3) *moral principles*. The first solution, as noted earlier, is to use coercion to restructure the individual's preferences by making noncontribution more costly than contribution. The second contends that the individual will gain certain benefits from the process of participation itself, regardless of the outcome of the process, and that these in-process benefits will outweigh her costs of contribution. The third type of solution argues that adherence to certain internalized moral principles will solve the problem by precluding the individual from making those cost-benefit calculations which would lead her to go for a free ride. An example would be a principle requiring one to attempt to overthrow an unjust or inhumane social order. Each of the three types of solution will be examined in detail. I shall argue that for both (1) and (3), even if the proposed solution is promising, it is not available to Marx without significant changes in his theory because it conflicts with some of his most basic ideas on the nature of socialist revolution.

1) Coercively backed penalties for pollution provide a contemporary example of the coercive solution; Hobbes' sovereign, as the dominant coercive power in society, is the classical case in political theory. The coercive solution can be applied to the case of the proletariat in either of two ways, depending upon the time period in which force is to be applied. Force might be applied either during the revolutionary struggle or after it. In the former case, some group would threaten the imminent use of violence against those proletarians who refrain from revolutionary activity. In the latter, some group would threaten to use violence against noncontributors once the proletariat achieves power.

Though both versions of the coercive solution may be descriptively accurate as accounts of revolutions that have actually occurred, neither squares with Marx's views on the role of coercion in socialist revolution. Marx nowhere, to my knowledge, even suggests that the threat of either imminent or post-revolutionary violence plays a role in motivating the proletariat to action. It is, of course, true that Marx predicts that violence will be used during the revolution against the bourgeoisie and against those *lumpenproletarians* whom it hires to fight its battles.[14] Further, his doctrine of the *dictatorship* of the proletariat implies that for some time after it has come to power the proletariat will find it necessary to employ coercion against the remnants of the bourgeoisie or perhaps even against proletarians who are still infected with bourgeois attitudes.[15] But Marx does not say or even suggest that coercion will be needed in order to spur the proletariat to action.

Additional problems arise when one asks: *who* is supposed to use coercion against the proletarians to secure their participation and, more importantly, what motivates these motivators and how does their motivation achieve collective action? If the motivators are themselves proletarians motivated either by the desire to maximize their own utility or that of their class, then the public goods problem reiterates. If, on the other hand, the motivators are not members of the proletariat but, say, nonproletarian intellectuals, then two problems remain for the Marxian. First, some account of their motivation is still needed. If that account holds that these nonproletarians somehow come to identify with the proletariat's interests, then the nature of this identification must be explored. Second, even granted such identification, the public goods problem again reiterates at the level of the cooperation needed to form a convincing group of coercive motivators. The formation of such a group is itself a public good for the persons who wish to form it for purposes of solving the proletariat's public goods problem.

It is important to note that Marx's doctrine that the communist party is the vanguard of the proletariat does *not* provide textual support for any version of the coercive solution.[16] Marx's point is not that the communists are revolutionary police whose function is to bully the proletariat into action; his idea, rather, is that they are the *educational* and *tactical* elite of the movement. They "point out and bring to the front the common interests of the entire proletariat, independently of all nationality,"[17] and they insure that the revolutionary efforts of the masses achieve their most effective expression. The first, educational function assigns a crucial role to the elite in *forming* a revolutionary class, but provides no solution to the public goods problem, since it assumes that the mere recognition of a common interest is sufficient for contribution to its achievement. This, of course, is precisely what the public goods objection denies. The second, tactical function again provides no solution since it assumes the existence of a revolutionary proletariat and addresses only the question of its tactical deployment.

And neither the educational nor the tactical function even suggests the use of coercion by a revolutionary elite against the proletariat. It is important to reemphasize that if the Marxian chooses to revise Marx on this issue by assigning a coercive role to the "vanguard," he must still explain the motivation which produces an effective coercive group.

2) According to the in-process benefits solution, certain goods intrinsic to the process of contribution offset the costs of contribution. Plausible examples of this phenomenon may not be hard to find. Not only revolutionary terrorists but also Red Cross volunteers and peace demonstrators may set great store by the community, fraternity, and solidarity which they experience as participants in a common struggle. There appear to be, however, three rather serious limitations on the force of this solution to the problem.

First, Marx nowhere suggests that such derivative goods of association, rather than the proletariat's interest in the overthrow of the system, are a major factor in the revolutionary motivation of the proletariat.

The following passage from the *1844 Manuscripts* suggests that Marx was, however, aware of what I call in-process benefits.

When communist artisans *[Handwerker]* form associations, teaching and propaganda are their first aims. But their association itself creates a new need—the need for society—and what appeared as a means has become an end. The most striking results of this practical development are seen when the French socialist workers meet together. Smoking, eating and drinking are no longer simply means of bringing people together. Society, association, entertainment which also has society as its aim, is sufficient for them, the brotherhood of man is no empty phrase but a reality. . . .[18]

Nonetheless, he fails to develop an account of how the competitive, egoistic barriers to these goods of association can ultimately be overcome. Nor does he attempt to assign a significant role to them by integrating the idea of in-process benefits into the rational interest theory of revolutionary motivation that dominates the theory of the decline of capitalism in his middle and later works.

The second difficulty with this solution is that a theory of proletarian revolution which did assign such a crucial role to in-process benefits would have to provide an account of the conditions under which such benefits are a sufficient motivating factor. For it is clear that these intrinsic benefits of association are not always forthcoming nor, even if forthcoming, always effective. History provides numerous examples of peoples who failed to achieve effective resistance to their oppressors, even though they shared a common form of life and a common experience of persecution. A Marxian who relies on the in-process benefits solution must explain, for instance, how the case of the proletariat differs from that of the Ghetto Jews in Nazi Europe. On the face of it, one would have thought that the resources of community, fraternity, and solidarity would have been richest in such closeknit ethnic groups.

There is a third, more serious difficulty which is independent of the first and second. Where an ongoing process of common struggle already exists, it is plausible to appeal to in-process benefits to explain the continual existence of cooperation. But the mere possibility of in-process benefits in the future, if the process gets under way, is of dubious merit as an explanation of how the process gets started. This problem is greatly exacerbated by Marx's insistence that the capitalist system fosters competition and egoism in all its members and thoroughly undermines all genuine forms of community. In addition to the general climate of competitive egoism and individualism in capitalism, Marx emphasizes two related barriers to proletarian cooperation: (i) competition for jobs between employed workers and the "industrial reserve army" of the unemployed and (ii) competition between employed workers for managerial positions. At one point he goes so far as to say that relations among workers are even more competitive than among capitalists. Yet Marx provides no adequate account of how these barriers to community and its benefits can be overcome within capitalism, offering instead only the following unenlightening remarks.

Competition separates individuals from one another, not only the bourgeois but still more the workers, in spite of the fact that it brings them together. Hence, it is a long time before these individuals can unite, apart from the fact that for the purpose of this union—if it is not to be merely local—the necessary means, the big industrial cities and cheap and quick communications, have first to be produced by large-scale industry. Hence every organized power standing over and against these isolated individuals, who live in conditions daily reproducing this isolation, can only be overcome after long struggle.[19]

Here the problem is recognized and some *necessary* conditions (concentrations of workers, improved means of communications) for its solution are listed. Yet no solution is offered. We are only comforted with the observation that the solution will take a long time. Marx maintains that the eradication of egoism, competition, and individualism, and the transformation of man into a "communal being" begins with the process of revolution and is completed only when human beings grow up in communism.[20] Unfortunately, the psychological transformation produced by a process of revolutionary cooperation cannot explain how untransformed individuals came to participate in the process in the first place.

In spite of these problems, an attempt to develop a prominent role for the notion of in-process benefits seems to be the most promising approach to remedying the deficiencies of Marx's theory of revolutionary motivation. For one thing, in-process benefits do seem to be one major motivational factor (among others) in a variety of actual revolutionary movements. Further, even if Marx himself was unaware of the proletariat's public goods problem and even if he assigned no specific theoretical role to the notion of in-process benefits, a revised Marxian view might attempt to do so while preserving much of what is most distinctive in Marx's theory of revolution, in particular, the refusal to rely upon juridical principles and the insistence that self- or class-interest is the main motivational factor in successful revolution. My aim in articulating the difficulties that the in-process benefits solution must surmount and in emphasizing that Marx himself does not assign the notion of in-process benefits a prominent role in his scenario for revolution is to help identify more clearly the important tasks of a more adequate Marxian position. Until these tasks are successfully completed Marx's claim that effective revolutionary motivation need not rely on juridical principles (or coercion) will not be adequately supported.

3) It can be argued that a distinctive function of certain moral principles is to provide a solution to public goods problems as well as other problems of social coordination. Among the moral principles to which this function might be attributed are various types of generalization principles, principles imposing a duty to keep promises, and principles requiring us to help establish just or humane or free social institutions.[21] The idea is that adherence to such principles produces cooperation in cases where none would be forthcoming if individuals acted to maximize individual or group utility. In the case at hand, it might be argued that adherence to a principle imposing a duty to help establish humane institutions would serve this needed function for the proletariat.[22]

If we set aside for the moment the question of whether Marx himself could accept such a role for moral principles, there is at least one reason why this solution to the proletariat's public goods problem is more plausible than the coercive solution. As I argued earlier, the proletariat, unlike the capitalist class, does not exert control over an antecedently existing coercive apparatus. Hence, the coercive solution, in the case of the proletariat, simply pushes the public goods problem back to a deeper level—the problem then becomes that of achieving the cooperation needed to create a convincing coercive apparatus. For this reason the moral principles solution is worth considering.

The immediate difficulty in appealing to moral principles as a *Marxian* response to the public goods problem is, of course, that it requires a rejection of Marx's fundamental claim that the proletarian's motive is a self-interest or the interest of his or her class. Before we proceed further, however, it is important to make a distinction which is often neglected in the perennial debate over whether Marx's theory includes moral elements or is "strictly scientific." We must distinguish two questions. (a) Do moral concepts play a significant role in Marx's analysis of capitalism and of history in general? (b) Do moral concepts play a significant role in Marx's theory of proletarian revolutionary motivation? In Chapter 4, I noted that there is evidence for a negative answer to the latter question: Marx repeatedly scoffs at socialists who rely on moral exhortation to move the masses to revolt and asserts that communists preach no morality. The answer to the former question is much more problematic. I have argued that Marx's analysis of capitalism only employs the concepts of *justice* and *rights* in internal criticisms and that these are not his fundamental criticisms. Yet Marx's charges that capitalism is exploitative, that it alienates man from his nature as a communal being, that it is an inhuman system, and a disguised form of slavery all rest upon moral or at least normative concepts—whether they are concepts of justice or not. What solution is available to a consistent Marxian who wishes to preserve Marx's denial of a motivating role for moral principles in his account of proletarian revolution, while acknowledging that Marx's analysis of capitalism employs moral concepts? Such a position would hold that though the moral condemnation of capitalism and the proletarian's self-interest both dictate the overthrow of the system, appeal to moral principles would be superfluous, since self-interest will suffice. Where one's self-interest—indeed one's survival—dictate revolutionary action, the exhortation that one ought morally to revolt is an otiose echo. This way of harmonizing the claim that Marx's analysis of capitalism employs moral concepts with the claim that his account of revolutionary motivation assigns no significant role to such concepts leaves the public goods problem untouched. It simply assumes that the proletarian's recognition of his own interest or of that of his class will itself produce effective revolutionary action. Marx seems to have overlooked the possibility that even where morality and interest seem to speak as with one voice, morality may still have an ineliminable function.

It was noted earlier that there are two main strategies for the Marxian who seeks to rebut the public goods objection. The first is to acknowledge that the problem exists and to attempt to solve it, either by appeal to coercion, in-process benefits, or moral principles. I have just argued that none of these solutions plays a prominent role in Marx's theory of revolutionary motivation.[23] Further, I have argued that with the possible exception of the in-process benefits solution, these solutions to the public goods problems are not available to Marx unless important elements of his theory are rejected. The second main strategy available to the Marxian is to attempt to show that no public goods problem exists for the proletariat. It is this second type of reply we must now examine.

VII

There are, it seems, only three versions of the second strategy worth considering. The first appeals to a certain interpretation of Marx's materialism; the second to an extreme version of the doctrine of the immiseration of the proletariat; and the third to Marx's historicist critique of concepts of rationality.[24]

In briefest form, the first version goes like this: the objection that the proletariat faces a public goods problem is based on a misconception. The misconception is that the revolutionary movement is produced through deliberation and calculation on the part of individual proletarians. But Marx's view—the correct view—is that the individual's participation in the revolutionary struggle is simply a response to changes in the material base of society.[25] To emphasize individual decision-making is to neglect the material forces that shape history—it is to flirt with idealism. Even if individual reasoning about interests is present, it is present only as a reflection, an epiphenomenal overlay: the moving force of history lies in the transformation of a society's mode of production.

A consistent Marxian should be reluctant to embrace this reply because it rests on a very dubious interpretation of Marx's materialism. To emphasize the crucial importance of the processes by which a society produces the material means of life is not to deny that individuals deliberate, calculate, and act on their interests or the interests of their group as they perceive them. Marx never denied that the individual's behavior is a purposive expression of his needs and interests as he perceives them. Marx's thesis, rather, is that the needs and interests an individual has, as well as his awareness of them, are conditioned by his location in the social structure, and that the material processes of production are the foundation of that structure.[26] Marx's materialism, then, is not a substitute for a theory relating the proletarian's needs and interests to his actions. It is an explanation of how those interests and needs come to be and of how the proletarian comes to see them for what they are, without the benefit of ideological cosmetics. More importantly, though I shall not argue the point here, this version of materialism is much more plausible than the epiphenomenalist interpretation, regardless of which version enjoys the strongest textual support. Perhaps the most unattractive feature of the materialist reply to the public goods problem is that it forces one to deny any sense to the question of what reasons there are for a proletarian to become a revolutionary.

A second way of arguing that there is no public goods problem for the proletariat is to deny that condition (iv) above (see p. 89) is satisfied. The Marxian could argue that the proletariat's condition deteriorates until a point is reached at which the burdens of continuing to live under capitalism become so overwhelming that the worker no longer counts his revolutionary effort as a cost. This strategy for avoiding the public goods problem, however, comes at an excessive price. It rests upon the most extreme version of Marx's prophecy of the accelerating immiseration of the proletariat, and that prophecy has so far proved false.

The third, somewhat more plausible attempt to show that there is no public goods problem for the proletariat can be sketched as follows. According to Marx, our most basic concepts, including our concept of rationality, are historically conditioned social products. The concept of rationality as individual or group utility-maximization is the *bourgeois* concept of rationality. The public goods objection makes the mistake of identifying bourgeois rationality with rationality *per se*. Thus even if bourgeois rationality thwarts revolutionary action, it does not follow that rationality *(per se)* requires that the proletarian refrain from participating in the revolution.

There are several reasons why this reply will not do. First, the main force of the public goods objection does not depend upon whether individual or group utility-maximization is accorded the honorific title of "rationality." Call it what you will, the problem is to show either that such maximization will produce the desired cooperation, or, if it will not, to provide some alternative account of effective revolutionary motivation.

Second, it seems most plausible to interpret Marx's claim that the revolutionary action of the proletariat is motivated by the interests of the proletariat as the claim that in revolting, the proletarians seek to maximize their individual or class interests. It is difficult to imagine how else one could interpret the former claim.[27]

Third, the historicist reply can be turned against itself. Suppose we grant that the concept of rationality as individual or group utility-maximization is that historically conditioned concept of rationality which arose and which will fall with the bourgeois mode of production. Suppose also that we grant the further claim, not made explicit in the historicist reply, that there is a different concept of rationality peculiar to the socialist mode of production. Each of these claims requires support—support which I believe is not to be found either in Marx's writings or in those of later Marxians. But let us set that problem aside. Instead we ask, granted these claims about rationality, what is the correct Marxian account of the proletarian's motivation?

If the historicist reply is to be effective, it must establish two theses: (i) that proletarians are rational according to the socialist, not the bourgeois concept of rationality; and (ii) that the public goods problem does not arise for individuals who are rational in the socialist sense.

The latter thesis cannot of course be established until a coherent concept of socialist rationality is articulated. Further, there are important restrictions on what such a concept of rationality could include, if recourse to it is to be compatible with Marx's rejection of a significant role for moral principles in revolutionary motivation. In particular, a socialist concept of rationality cannot include those sorts of principles—for example, principles of justice—scorned by Marx in his attacks on the moralizing socialists.

Whatever the content of the socialist concept of rationality turns out to be, recourse to it as an explanation of proletarian revolutionary activity appears to be illegitimate for Marx. It must be remembered that for Marx the bourgeois concept of rationality would be that concept of rationality which is dominant *throughout* capitalism, not just among the bourgeoisie—as Marx himself emphasizes, "the ruling ideas of each age have ever been the ideas of its ruling class."[28] A distinctive socialist concept of rationality would have to be one, then, which *emerges* in the course of the revolutionary struggle: the process of revolutionary cooperation transforms the proletarian from one who is rational in the bourgeois sense to one who is rational in the socialist sense. Yet the new form of rationality which emerges from the proletarian struggle cannot explain how individuals come to participate in that struggle.

It might be replied that the new socialist form of rational cooperation is emerging within the capitalist factory and that this phenomenon explains how individuals come to participate in the revolutionary process. The following passages from *Capital* might be invoked as rather tenuous support for this view.

When the labourer (in the capitalist factory) cooperates systematically with others, he strips off the fetters of his individuality and develops the capacities of his species. . . . (The working class) is being disciplined, unified, and organized by the very mechanism of the capitalist mode of production.[29]

There are two immediate problems with this reply. First, the notion of a new form of rationality emerging within the capitalist factory must somehow be made to square with Marx's repeated charges that factory work in capitalism turns worker against worker in the competition for jobs, alienates man from his communal nature, mortifies his body, and ruins his mind.[30] This will be no small task. Second, it is not enough to say that a new form of rational cooperation capable of solving the public goods problem will emerge in the capitalist factory—empirical investigation to support this thesis is required. Marx nowhere executed such an investigation.

More recent researchers have studied the processes by which successful union activity emerges within the context of the factory. A Marxian who wishes to use the fruits of such research must do so with care. Granted Marx's rejection of reliance upon coercion and moral motivation, some of the more obvious and common explanations of how unions overcome public goods problems cannot be adopted by the Marxian. Explanations which assign a fundamental role to the coercion of workers (for example, the closed shop) or to the motivational power of the call for a "fair wage" or for a just social order are not available to the Marxian. My point is not that it is impossible to provide an account of how a new form of rational cooperation—one which relies neither upon coercion nor moral principles—could arise in the capitalist factory. I am only urging that such an account must be produced and confirmed by empirical research if it is to serve as an adequate reply to the public goods objection.

VIII

The foregoing analysis may help account for the persistence of two phenomena that adherents of Marx's interest theory of proletarian motivation find difficult to explain but equally difficult to ignore: the revolutionary's use of violence against members of the proletariat and his reliance upon what Marx called "obsolete verbal rubbish" about justice and rights. The use of violence against members of the proletariat is usually explained away as an exception due to the underdeveloped class consciousness of backward countries. But if, as I have argued, there is a public goods problem for the proletariat, coercion of proletarians by a dedicated elite may be needed even where the entire proletariat is convinced that its own interests dictate overthrow of the system. Further, the Marxian who believes that concepts of justice or of the rights of man are muddled, obsolete notions that cannot withstand Marx's ruthless scientific analysis must consider the possibility that appeal to these spurious notions is nonetheless necessary for the success of the revolution. The dedicated revolutionary would then be faced with the prospect of maintaining two contradictory views about moral principles—the one esoteric, the other exoteric.

The Marxian who wishes to rehabilitate Marx's theory of revolutionary motivation by conceding a significant role to moral principles commits himself to an onerous task. He must produce an adequate moral principle or set of moral principles. There is reason to believe, however, that the most broadly acknowledged moral principles are not capable of solving the more serious public goods problems.[31] Consider, for example, a principle requiring one to help establish a just or humane or free social order, granted that one has assurance that others will also put forth effort. On the one hand, it is the assurance clause of this principle that makes it so plausible, yet this same clause makes it ineffective in solving public goods problems without recourse to coercion. Rawls acknowledges this by stating that the duty to help establish and support just institutions applies only where a coercive apparatus assures one that others will reciprocate.[32] On the other hand, if the assurance clause is excised, the resulting principle may be strong enough to solve the public goods problem without recourse to coercion, but its very strength will make it implausible. It is one thing to say that one ought to help establish just or humane or free institutions, if one has reasonable assurance that others will reciprocate. It is quite another to demand that one ought to help establish such institutions no matter what others do and regardless of whether one's own destruction may result. Though I cannot argue the point here, I suspect that many, if not all, of the moral principles a Marxian might plausibly invoke are either too weak to solve the proletariat's public goods problem or too strong to enjoy independent plausibility. At any rate, the Marxian who invokes moral principles must show that they do solve the problem and that they are principles to which a proletarian could reasonably commit himself.

There is, however, yet another serious obstacle for a revised Marxian account to overcome. It is not enough to show that there are moral principles which the proletariat could plausibly embrace and which would solve their problem of coordination. The revised Marxian account must also show that the capitalists are incapable of achieving a similar solution.

The difficulties I have raised for Marx's account of revolutionary motivation are not presented here as decisive objections. However, they do seriously challenge what many have taken to be one of the strong points of Marx's social thought: his claim to have provided a theory of rational self-interested motivation which dispenses with motivation by juridical concepts. More importantly, it is hoped that the reflections of this chapter have helped to identify more clearly the tasks for a more adequate Marxian theory. In the chapter that follows, the perspective for evaluating Marx's thought is reversed: I attempt to gauge the power of Marx's critique of juridical theories by articulating and assessing Marxian objections to what I believe to be the most comprehensive and plausible contemporary theory of justice.[33]

6

Marx and Rawls

I

For almost a decade, John Rawls' book, *A Theory of Justice,* has sustained a rich dialogue between members of disciplines that too often suffer from stifling isolation. Drawn together by a common interest in the issues of social justice which Rawls examines, philosophers, political scientists, economists, sociologists, and lawyers are engaged in an ongoing exploration of exceptional depth and rigor. Rawls' publications since the book promise to stimulate further discussion.

One writer has suggested that *A Theory of Justice* could serve as a kind of philosophical Rorschach Test—and in fact responses to Rawls' rich and sometimes obscure volume often do reveal more about the critics themselves than about Rawls' views.[1] Though *A Theory of Justice* has been criticized sharply from the left, the objections often seem to arise, at least in part, from misunderstandings about Rawls or Marx or both. The analysis presented in preceding chapters provides a more adequate framework for understanding Marx's views on justice. In this chapter, I shall first summarize Rawls' complex view in order that we may have both theories clearly before us. Then I shall articulate and evaluate what I take to be the most important and influential Marxian objections to Rawls' view. Finally, without minimizing the fundamental disagreements, I shall show that Rawls' theory assimilates certain central Marxian elements which enhance its power and depth. The objections to Rawls considered here are labeled "Marxian" to indicate that they are criticisms that have been or could be raised from the perspective of Marx's distinctive contributions to social theory. It is not to be assumed that any of the critics whose objections I consider are, or would refer to themselves as, Marxists or Marxian social theorists. My reasons for using for my point of departure criticisms that have actually been raised in the Rawls literature is two-fold. First, it is these objections which have been and will continue to be influential for the understanding and assessment of both Marx and Rawls. Second, it

103

would be less than responsible to attempt a confrontation between the two theories without an explicit consideration of at least some of the most important writings now available on the subject.

I have elected to devote this much attention to Rawls' work in a book concerned with Marx for the same reason that I undertook a study of Marx in the first place: I regard Marx not just as a great figure in the history of social theory but also as a thinker who has much to contribute to contemporary thought. For this reason, I believe that an adequate evaluation of Marx's ideas on justice requires that they be measured against what I believe to be the best available theory of justice. This chapter, then, provides one major element of my effort to evaluate Marx as a critic of juridical theorizing; the final chapter will provide the other. My analysis cannot be exhaustive but it will, I hope, prepare the way for more fruitful exchanges between Marxian thinkers and non-Marxian thinkers concerned with problems of justice and rights.

II

1. RAWLS' AIMS IN A THEORY OF JUSTICE

Rawls has two basic aims in *A Theory of Justice*. One is to articulate a small set of general principles of justice which underlie and account for the various considered moral judgments we make in particular cases. By our moral judgments, Rawls means the indefinitely large set of moral evaluations we have made and may make about particular actions, laws, policies, institutional practices, etc. Our *considered* moral judgments are those moral evaluations that we make reflectively, rather than in the heat of the moment. They are moral evaluations which we make or would make in circumstances conducive to impartiality and consistency. The judgment that racial discrimination is unjust is an example of one of our most basic, firmly held considered moral judgments concerning justice. An exmaple of a more particular considered moral judgment is the judgment that it would be unjust for a certain employer, Mr. Smith, to refuse to hire a certain applicant, Mr. Jones, simply because Mr. Jones is black.

The second of Rawls' two basic aims is to develop a theory which is superior to Utilitarianism as a theory of social justice. There are several versions of Utilitarianism. Rawls concentrates on two: Classical Utilitarianism and Average Utilitarianism. *Classical* Utilitarianism may be defined as the view that social institutions are just when and only when they serve to maximize aggregate utility. "Utility" is defined as happiness or satisfaction, or in terms of the individual's preferences as the latter are revealed by his choices. The aggregate utility produced by a set of institutional arrangements is calculated by summing up the utility which those arrangements produce for each individual affected by them.

Average Utilitarianism, as a theory of social justice, may be defined as the view that social institutions are just when and only when they serve to maximize average utility per capita. "Utility" here, as in Classical Utilitarianism, is defined as happiness or satisfaction or in terms of preferences revealed through choices. Average utility per capita is calculated by dividing the aggregate utility produced by a given set of institutional arrangements by the number of persons affected by those arrangements. Rawls' second basic aim, then, is to show that the principles of justice he advances are superior to both Classical and Average Utilitarianism.

These two basic aims are closely connected for Rawls. For as we shall see more clearly when we examine Rawls' justifications for his principles, he hopes to show that his view is superior to Utilitarianism by showing that his principles do a better job of accounting for our considered moral judgments about social justice. In other words, if Rawls can show that it is his principles of justice, rather than utilitarian principles, which underlie our considered moral judgments about social justice, then this will be a point in favor of Rawls' view and against Utilitarianism.

2. THE PRIMARY SUBJECT OF JUSTICE

Rawls notes that:

Many different kinds of things are said to be just and unjust: not only laws, institutions, and social systems, but also particular actions of many kinds, including decision, judgments, and imputations. We also call the attitudes and dispositions of persons, and persons themselves, just or unjust.[2]

Thus there are many different subjects of justice—many different kinds of things to which the terms "just" and "unjust" can be applied. Corresponding to the different subjects of justice, there are different problems of justice. Rawls concentrates on what he takes to be the *primary* subject of justice: what he calls the basic structure of society. By the basic structure of a society, Rawls means the entire set of major social, political, legal, and economic institutions. As examples of some of the major institutions of our society, Rawls lists the Constitution, private ownership of the means of production, competitive markets, and the monogamous family. The function of the basic structure of society is to distribute the burdens and benefits of social cooperation among the members of society. The benefits of social cooperation include wealth and income, food and shelter, authority and power, rights and liberties. The burdens of social cooperation include various liabilities, duties, and obligations, including for example, the obligation to pay taxes.

The primary subject of justice is the basic structure of society, according to Rawls, because the basic structure exerts such a profound influence on individuals' life prospects.

The intuitive notion here is that this structure contains various social positions and that men born into different positions have different expectations of life determined, in part, by the political system as well as by economic and social circumstances. In this way the institutions of society favor certain starting places over others, but they affect men's initial chances to life; yet they cannot possibly be justified by an appeal to the notions of merit or desert. It is these inequalities, presumably inevitable in the basic structure of any society, to which the principles of social justice must in the first instance apply. These principles, then, regulate the choice of a political constitution and the main elements of the economic and social system.[3]

Rawls' point here can be illustrated by an example. Due to certain discriminatory features of the basic structure of our society, blacks and Chicanos generally have lower life prospects than white males. Their life prospects are generally lower in the sense that, as a group, their lifetime earnings are lower, their educational and social opportunities are inferior, and their access to health care is restricted. As another example of how the basic structure apparently influences life prospects, consider the fact that children of uneducated parents—regardless of race or gender—have lower prospects of completing an advanced education.

3. THE PRIMARY PROBLEM OF JUSTICE

The primary subject of justice is the basic structure of society because the influences of the basic structure on individuals are present at birth and continue throughout life. The primary problem of justice, then, is to formulate and justify a set of principles which a just basic structure must satisfy. These principles of social justice would specify how the basic structure is to distribute prospects of obtaining what Rawls calls *primary goods*. Primary goods include basic rights and liberties, powers, authority, and opportunities, as well as income and wealth. In *A Theory of Justice*, primary goods are said to be

. . . things that every rational man is presumed to want. These goods normally have a use whatever a person's rational plan of life.[4]

Primary goods are perhaps best thought of as (a) maximally flexible means (or conditions) for the pursuit of one's goals or as (b) conditions of the critical and informed choice of ends and of the formulation of plans.[5] Wealth, in the broadest sense, is a maximally flexible means in that it is generally useful for achieving one's goals, regardless of what one's goals are. Freedom from arbitrary arrest is a condition of the effective pursuit of one's goals. Freedom of speech and information are needed if one is to choose one's goals and formulate one's plans for attaining them in an informed and critical way. A just basic structure will be one which produces a proper distribution of prospects of obtaining primary goods.

When applied to the facts about the basic structure of our society, principles of justice should do two things. First, they should yield concrete judgments about the justice or injustice of specific institutions and institutional practices. Second, they should guide us in developing policies and laws to correct injustices in the basic structure.

4. RAWLS' TWO PRINCIPLES AS A SOLUTION TO THE PRIMARY PROBLEM OF JUSTICE

Rawls proposes and defends the following two principles as a solution to the problem of specifying what would count as a just basic structure.
First Principle:

Each person is to have an equal right to the most extensive total system of equal basic liberties compatible with a similar system of liberty for all.[6]

Second Principle:

Social and economic inequalities are to be arranged so that they are both:

a) to the greatest benefit of the least advantaged, and
b) attached to offices and positions open to all under conditions of fair equality of opportunity.[7]

Rawls calls the First Principle the Principle of Greatest Equal Liberty. The Second Principle includes two parts. The first part is the Difference Principle. It states that social and economic inequalities are to be arranged so that they are to the greatest benefit of those who are least advantaged. The second part is the Principle of Fair Equality of Opportunity. It states that social and economic inequalities are to be attached to offices and positions that are open to all under conditions of fair equality of opportunity. Before we can hope to assess Marxian objections to Rawls' theory, each of these very general principles must be carefully interpreted.

5. THE PRINCIPLE OF GREATEST EQUAL LIBERTY

Rawls' First Principle of Justice is the Principle of Greatest Equal Liberty. It covers the following basic liberties.

a) freedom to participate in the political process (the right to vote, the right to run for office, etc.)
b) freedom of speech (including freedom of the press)
c) freedom of conscience (including religious freedom)
d) freedom of the person (as defined by the concept of the rule of law)
e) freedom from arbitrary arrest and seizure, and
f) the right to hold personal property.[8]

The principle states that each person is to have an equal right to the most extensive total system composed of the liberties listed in (a) through (f), compatible with everyone else having an equal right to the same total system.

6. THE DIFFERENCE PRINCIPLE

The Difference Principle states that social and economic inequalities are to be arranged so as to be to the greatest benefit of the least advantaged. To understand this principle, two key phrases must be interpreted: "social and economic inequalities" and "least advantaged."

For reasons which will become clearer later on, Rawls' First Principle and the Difference Principle must be viewed as distributing two different subsets of the total set of primary goods. The First Principle distributes one subset of the total set of primary goods: the basic liberties listed above. The Difference Principle distributes another subset: this subset includes the primary goods of wealth, income, power, and authority. Thus the phrase "social and economic inequalities" in the Difference Principle refers to the inequalities in persons' prospects of obtaining the primary goods of wealth, income, power, and authority.[9]

The second key phrase in the Difference Principle is also to be interpreted as referring to this same subset of primary goods. The least advantaged are those who are least advantaged in their prospects of obtaining the primary goods of wealth, income, power, authority, etc. In other words, the phrase "least advantaged" refers to those persons who have the lowest prospects of gaining these goods.

We are now in a better position to understand the Difference Principle. The Difference Principle requires that the basic structure be arranged in such a way that any inequalities in prospects of obtaining the primary goods of wealth, income, power, and authority must work to the greatest benefit of those persons who are the least advantaged with respect to these primary goods.

An example will help illustrate how an institution of the basic structure might produce inequalities which work to the advantage of the least advantaged. Suppose that large-scale capital investment in a certain industry is required to raise employment and to produce new goods and services. Suppose that by raising employment and producing these new goods and services such capital investment will ultimately be of great benefit to the least advantaged members of the society. Suppose, in particular, that such capital investment, if it can be achieved, will greatly increase the income prospects of the least advantaged through employing many who are not now employed and by raising the wages of those who are already employed. Suppose, however, that individuals will not be willing to undertake the risks of the large-scale capital investment unless they have the opportunity to reap large profits from the enterprise, should it succeed. In such a case, tax advantages for capital investment and lowered taxes on profits might provide the needed incentives for investment. The Difference Principle would require such tax laws if they were required for maximizing the prospects of the least advantaged. In the case described, the successful investor would enjoy a larger share of the primary goods of wealth and power than other persons in his society. Yet this inequality in prospects of primary goods would be justified, according to the Difference Principle, granted that it is necessary in order to maximize the expectations of the least advantaged. If a different institutional arrangement would do a better job of raising the prospects of the least advantaged, then, according to the Difference Principle, that arrangement would be more just. As a more fundamental example of an inequality in the basic structure which might be viewed as maximizing the prospects of the worst-off, consider the United States Constitution's provisions for special powers for the President. According to the Difference Principle, the inequalities in power which these provisions create are justified only if they maximize the prospects of the worst off.

Though Rawls first introduces the Difference Principle in the form stated above, he quickly proceeds to restate it using the notion of the *representative worst-off man*. Rawls does not offer a detailed account of how the representative worst-off man is to be defined. Instead he sketches two distinct definitions and suggests that "either of [them], or some combination of them, will serve well enough."[10] According to the first definition, we first select a particular social position, such as that of unskilled worker, and then define the worst-off group as those persons with the average income for unskilled workers or less. The prospects of the representative worst-off man are then defined as "the average taken over this whole class." The other definition Rawls suggests characterizes the worst off-group as all persons with less than half the median income, and defines the prospects of the representative worst-off man as the average prospects for this class.

This complication in the statement of the Difference Principle is not a minor point for Rawls. It is one instance of Rawls's emphasis on the notion of procedural justice. Rawls distinguishes several varieties of procedural justice, but for our purposes the main point is that procedural justice utilizes institutional arrangements and conceptions, such as that of the representative worst-off man, which allow us to apply principles of justice without focusing on actual particular persons. According to Rawls, the great advantage of procedural justice "is that it is no longer necessary in meeting the demands of justice to keep track of the endless variety of circumstances and the changing relative positions of particular persons. One avoids the problem of defining principles to cope with the enormous complexities which would arise if such details were relevant."[11]

7. THE PRINCIPLE OF FAIR EQUALITY OF OPPORTUNITY

The Principle of Fair Equality of Opportunity requires that we go beyond formal equality of opportunity to insure that persons with similar skills, abilities, and motivation enjoy equal opportunities.

Again an example may be helpful. Suppose that two individuals, A and B, both desire to attain a certain position which requires technical training. Suppose further that they are roughly equal in the relevant skills and motivation, but that A's family is extremely poor and cannot finance his training, while B's family is wealthy and willing to pay for B's training. Rawls' Principle of Fair Equality of Opportunity would presumably require institutional arrangements for financial aid to insure that the fact that A was born into a low income class does not deprive her of opportunities available to others with similar skills and motivation.[12]

8. THE PRIORITIES OF JUSTICE

Since the Second Principle of Justice contains two distinct principles—the Difference Principle and the Principle of Fair Equality of Opportunity—there are three principles of justice in all.[13] Having advanced these three principles, Rawls offers two priority rules for ordering these three principles. The need for priority rules arises because efforts to satisfy one principle of justice may conflict with efforts to satisfy another. The first priority rule states that the First Principle of Justice, the Principle of Greatest Equal Liberty, is *lexically prior* to the Second Principle as a whole, which includes both the Difference Principle and the Principle of Fair Equality of Opportunity. One principle is *lexically prior* to another principle if and only if we are first to satisfy the requirements of the first principle before going on to satisfy those of the second. So Rawls' first priority rule states that the first priority of social justice is greatest equal liberty. Only after greatest equal liberty is secured are we free to direct our efforts to achieving the requirements laid down by the Difference Principle and the Principle of Fair Equality of Opportunity.

The second priority rule states a priority relation between the two parts of the Second Principle of Justice. According to this rule, the Principle of Fair Equality of Opportunity is lexically prior to the Difference Principle. We are to satisfy the demands of the Principle of Fair Equality of Opportunity before meeting those of the Difference Principle.

The priority on liberty expressed by the first lexical priority rule is one of the most striking features of Rawls' theory. This first lexical priority rule declares that basic liberty may not be restricted for the sake of greater material benefits for all or even for the least advantaged. Where conditions allow for the effective exercise of liberty, liberty may only be restricted for the sake of a greater liberty on balance for everyone. In other words, certain basic liberties may be restricted, but only for the sake of achieving a more extensive total system of liberty for each of us. Freedom of the press, for example, might be somewhat restricted, if this were necessary to secure the right to a fair trial, in situations in which unrestricted freedom of the press would lead to biased trials. Trade-offs among basic liberties are allowed, but only if the resulting total system produces greater basic liberty on balance. Trade-offs of basic liberties for other primary goods such as wealth are not allowed.

9. RAWLS' JUSTIFICATIONS FOR HIS PRINCIPLES OF JUSTICE

Rawls offers three distinct types of justification for his principles of justice: two based on appeals to considered moral judgments and a third on what Rawls calls the Kantian interpretation of his theory.

The first type of justification rests on the thesis that if a principle accounts for our considered moral judgments about what is just or unjust, then this is a good reason for accepting that principle. To say that a principle accounts for our considered judgments about the justice or injustice of certain actions or institutions is to say at least this much: granted that principle and granted the relevant facts about the action or institution, it is possible to derive a statement expressing the considered judgments in question. According to the second type of justification, if a principle would be chosen under conditions which, according to our considered moral judgments, are appropriate conditions for choosing principles of justice, then this is a good reason for accepting the principle. If a principle either accounts for our considered moral judgments about what is just or unjust or would be chosen under conditions which, according to our considered moral judgments, are appropriate for choosing principles of justice, let us say that it *matches* our considered moral judgments.

Though both of these first two types of justification appeal to considered judgments, they may be distinguished according to *what* it is that the considered judgments are about. The first of these matching justifications appeals to our considered moral judgments about *what is just or unjust*, and contends that Rawls' *principles* account for these judgments. Let us call this the *principles matching justification*. The second matching justification appeals to our considered judgments, not about what is just or unjust, but rather about what *conditions* are appropriate for the choice of principles of justice. Let us call this second type of justification the *conditions matching argument*.

Rawls uses the phrase "reflective equilibrium" to refer to the goal of the process of mutual adjustment between considered judgments, on the one hand, and principles or conditions for the choice of principles, on the other. If there is a discrepancy between principles that would be chosen in the original position and our considered judgments about particular cases we may adjust the conditions so as to yield principles that better match those judgments. But the revision may also go in the other direction: reflection on principles and the plausibility of the conditions under which they would be chosen may lead us to revise some of our judgments about particular cases. In the following passage, Rawls envisions what I have called the first two kinds of justification working together.

> By going back and forth, sometimes altering the conditions of the contractual circumstances, at others withdrawing our judgments and conforming them to principle, I assume that eventually we shall find a description of the initial situation that both expresses reasonable conditions and yields principles which match our considered judgments duly pruned and adjusted. This state of affairs I refer to as reflective equilibrium.[14]

The conditions matching argument includes three stages. First, a set of conditions for choosing principles of justice must be articulated. Rawls refers to the set of choice conditions he articulates as "the original position." Second, it must be shown that the conditions articulated are the appropriate conditions of choice, according to our considered judgments. Third, it must be established that Rawls' principles would be chosen under those conditions.

Rawls describes the conditions matching justification in Chapter 1 of *A Theory of Justice*:

> We shall say that certain principles of justice are justified because they would be agreed to in [the original position]. I have emphasized that this original position is purely hypothetical. It is natural to ask why, if this agreement is never actually entered into, we should take an interest in these principles, moral or otherwise. The answer is that the conditions embodied in the original position are ones that we do in fact accept [as appropriate conditions for the choice of principles of justice].[15]

The following caveat, which Rawls offers immediately after the claim that the conditions constituting the original position are the ones that we do accept according to our considered judgments, introduces his third type of justification.

> Or if we do not [accept the conditions of the original position], then perhaps we can be persuaded to do so by philosophical reflections.[16]

In "The Kantian Interpretation" section of his book, Rawls endorses a certain kind of philosophical justification for the conditions constituting the original position—a justification based on Kant's conception of an autonomous agent, or "noumenal self." For Kant an autonomous agent is one whose will is determined by rational principles rather than by particular desires, and it is the mark of rational principles that they can serve as principles for everyone, not merely for this or that agent, depending upon whether he has some particular desire.

> My suggestion is that we think of the original position as the point of view from which noumenal selves see the world. The parties [who choose from the perspective of the original position] qua noumenal selves have the complete freedom to choose whatever principles they wish; but they also have a desire to express their autonomous nature as rational and equal members of the intelligible realm with precisely this liberty to choose, that is, as beings who can look at the world in this way and express this perspective in their life as

members of society . . . the description of the original position interprets the point of view of noumenal selves, of what it means to be a free and equal rational being. Our nature as such beings is displayed when we act from principles we would choose when this nature is reflected in the conditions determining the choice. Thus men exhibit their freedom, their independence from the contingencies of nature and society, by acting in ways they would acknowledge in the original position. Properly understood, then, the desire to act justly [i.e., to act on those principles that would be chosen from the original position] derives in part from the desire to express most fully what we are or can be, namely free and equal rational beings with a liberty to choose.[17]

This passage, like the remainder of "The Kantian Interpretation," is exceedingly condensed and complex, but for our purposes, one central thesis can be extracted from it: when persons such as you and I accept those principles which we recognize would be chosen from the original position we are expressing our nature as noumenal selves, i.e., we are acting autonomously.[18] There are two main grounds for this thesis, corresponding to two features of the original position. First, since the *veil of ignorance*, which we will discuss shortly, excludes information about particular desires, acceptance of the principles does not depend upon the particular desires which an agent may or may not have. Second, since the *formal constraints* on the choice of principles include the requirement that the principles must be universalizable, the principles chosen will be rational principles in Kant's sense.

In *The Foundations of the Metaphysics of Morals*, Immanuel Kant presents a moral philosophy that identifies autonomy with rationality.[19] Thus, for Kant, the answer to the question "Why should one act autonomously?" reduces, ultimately, to the thesis that rationality requires it. *If* Rawls succeeds in establishing that we act autonomously when we accept those principles which would be chosen from the original position, and *if* the Kantian identification of autonomy with rationality can be made, the result will be a justification for Rawls' principles which is distinct both from the principles matching justification and from the conditions matching argument.

Granted the critical fire which Rawls' two matching justifications have attracted, the possibility of developing a third, independent type of justification is extremely important. Those who have rejected the matching arguments have done so for one of two reasons. Some have rejected Rawls' assumption that there is considerable consensus among different persons' considered judgments by arguing that either Rawls' principles or his choice conditions fail to match their own considered judgments. Others have argued that even if there is wide consensus among persons' considered judgments, the mere fact that there is has no justificatory force. If Rawls' Kantian interpretation can be developed into a plausible Kantian *justification*, then even if these objections to the two types of arguments from considered judgments turn out to be sound, they will not prove fatal to Rawls' theory.

We have already touched upon the principles matching justification in Section II, where it was noted that one of Rawls' basic aims is to provide a theory of justice superior to Utilitarianism. Rawls believes that one important respect in which his theory is superior to Utilitarianism (and to other theories he considers) is that it provides a better account of our *most basic* considered judgments about justice. According to Rawls, his principles provide a systematic foundation for these judgments. He also contends that these principles provide a superior guide for extending our considered judgments to new cases which we have not previously encountered.

Rawls argues that his principles of justice are superior to competing principles because, when applied to the relevant facts, they generated our considered moral judgments about what is just or unjust in a straightforward way. The principles he advances are preferable, Rawls concludes, because they provide a *simpler*, more plausible account of our considered judgments about the justice of social institutions.

A salient instance of Rawls' employment of the principles matching justification is his argument to show that his principles provide a better account of our considered judgments about *liberty* than utilitarian principles do. Rawls suggests that among our most basic considered moral judgments is the belief that a basic structure which discriminates among persons in the distribution of basic liberties is an unjust basic structure. It may be possible, he concedes, to derive this basic considered moral judgment from utilitarian principles and thus to give a utilitarian foundation for the belief in question. However, Rawls argues, in order to derive this basic considered judgment about liberty from utilitarian principles, we must make several dubious empirical assumptions, including the assumption that everyone has roughly the same capacity for enjoying the various basic liberties. For unless, as a matter of psychological fact, everyone finds roughly equal satisfaction in the basic liberties, greater utility might be achieved through an unequal rather than an equal distribution of basic liberties. In other words, should it turn out that the empirical assumption of equal capacity for the enjoyment of liberty is false, Utilitarianism would require an unequal distribution of basic liberties. The liberty of those who were judged to have a lower capacity for the enjoyment of liberty would be restricted if this produced greater aggregate or average utility. More generally, Rawls objects that, unless it relies on certain problematic assumptions, Utilitarianism is likely to allow institutional arrangements that systematically disadvantage some individuals for the sake of maximizing aggregate or average utility.

The Principle of Greatest Equal Liberty, in contrast, provides a straightforward and secure foundation for our considered moral judgment that the basic structure should not discriminate among persons in the distribution of basic liberties. Moreover, Rawls' principles, when taken together, are designed to insure that the institutional arrangements will not disadvantage some individuals for the sake of maximizing aggregate or average utility. Thus Rawls concludes that his theory of justice provides the simplest and most plausible account of our most basic considered judgments about social justice: it accounts for our considered judgments while relying on fewer and less problematic empirical assumptions.

The most distinctive feature of Rawls' conditions matching justification is his use of the traditional idea that acceptable principles of political organization can be viewed as the outcome of a mutually binding contract among the members of society. The conditions which together comprise the original position are then viewed as conditions under which suitably described parties make a contract with one another.

The principles of justice for the basic structure of society are the principles that free and rational persons concerned to further their own interests would accept in an initial position of equality as defining the fundamental terms of their association. These principles are to regulate all further agreements; they specify the kinds of social cooperation that can be entered into and the forms of government that can be established. This way of regarding the principles of justice I shall call justice as fairness. [20]

The idea of a social contract has several advantages. First, it allows us to view the principles of justice as the outcome of a *rational collective choice*. Second, the idea of contractual obligation emphasizes that the persons participating in this collective choice are to make a *basic commitment* to the principles they choose, and that compliance with these principles may be rightly enforced. Third, the idea of a contract as a *voluntary agreement* for mutual advantage suggests that the principles of justice should be "such as to draw forth the willing cooperation of everyone" in a society, "including those less well situated." [21]

To utilize the idea of a hypothetical social contract, two things must be done. First, the hypothetical situation in which the agreement is to be made must be carefully described in such a way that it does yield agreement on a determinate set of principles. In other words, the hypothetical choice situation must be so described that it is possible to derive the conclusion that rational persons who found themselves in this situation would choose one set of principles rather than another.

Second, the reasoning from this hypothetical situation must actually be gone through. We must determine exactly which principles of justice would be chosen by rational persons who found themselves in the hypothetical situation described in the first stage. Let us now examine in some detail Rawls' execution of the two stages of the argument, beginning with the first.

Rawls calls his description of the hypothetical choice situation the *original* position to signify that it is the situation of choice from which the principles of justice originate or derive. The original position includes four main elements: (a) the rational motivation of the parties, (b) the veil of ignorance, (c) the formal constraints of the concept of right, and (d) the list of competing principles of justice. To understand the nature of the hypothetical situation of choice as Rawls conceives it, and to see why he thinks it accords with our considered judgments about the conditions which are appropriate for the choice of principles of justice, we must now briefly explicate each of these four elements.

(a) The parties to the contract are motivated to pursue their life plans in a rational way. By a life plan, Rawls means a consistent set of basic goals to be pursued over a lifetime. Each party has a desire to gain as large a share of primary goods as possible, since primary goods are generally useful, whatever one's life plan happens to be. The parties are mutually disinterested in the sense that each thinks of himself as an independent agent with a worthwhile life plan which he desires to pursue.[22]

(b) The parties in the original position are subject to a set of informational constraints which Rawls refers to collectively as the veil of ignorance. The idea is that the parties are deprived of certain information. No one knows whether he (or she) is rich or poor, black or white, male or female, skilled or unskilled, weak or strong. The main purpose of depriving the parties of this information is to avoid a biased choice of principles.

The principles of justice are chosen behind a veil of ignorance. This ensures that no one is advantaged or disadvantaged in the choice of principles by the outcome of natural chance or the contingency of social circumstances. Since all are similarly situated and no one is able to design principles to favor his particular condition, the principles of justice are the result of a fair agreement or bargain. For given the circumstances of the original position, the symmetry of everyone's relations to each other, this initial situation is fair between individuals as moral persons. . . . The original position is, one might say, the appropriate initial status quo, and thus the fundamental agreements reached in it are fair. This explains the propriety of the name "justice as fairness": it conveys the idea that the principles of justice are agreed to in an initial situation that is fair.[23]

The intuitive idea here is that the choice of principles of justice should not be influenced by factors that are arbitrary from a moral point of view. If, for example, a group of persons in the original position knew that they were rich while others were poor, they might choose principles of justice which produced even greater advantages for the rich while further disadvantaging the poor. Similarly, a person who knew that he was a member of the dominant racial majority might choose principles which would discriminate against certain minorities.

(c) The parties in the original position are also described as limiting their choice to principles which satisfy certain formal constraints. The rationale behind these constraints is that they must be satisfied if the principles of justice that the parties choose are to fulfill their proper role. The proper role of principles of justice, according to Rawls, is to provide a public charter which defines the terms of social cooperation by specifying how the basic structure is to distribute rights, wealth, income, authority, and other primary goods. Rawls suggests that if the principles of justice are to be capable of achieving this goal they must be (i) general, (ii) universal in application, (iii) universalizable, (iv) publicizable, (v) adjudicative, and (vi) final.

They must be *general* if they are to cover all or almost all questions of social justice that may arise. They must be *universal in application* in the sense that their demands must apply to all members of society. The principles of justice must also be *universalizable* in the sense that they must be principles whose universal acceptance the parties can endorse. If the principles of justice are to guide our actions and policies and to serve as justifying grounds in particular cases, they must be *publicizable* and understandable by everyone. Since questions of justice arise where different individuals come into conflict over the benefits produced by social cooperation, principles of justice must be *adjudicative* in the sense that they must provide a way of *ordering* conflicting claims and thereby settling disputes. Lastly, the principles of justice must be *final:* they must be principles which provide the *ultimate* court of appeal for disputes about justice.[24]

(d) Rawls' description of the original position also includes a list of competing principles of justice from which the parties are to choose. The main competitors, according to Rawls, are the two versions of Utilitarianism (Classical and Average) and Rawls' principles of justice.

Setting out the conditions listed in (a) through (d) completes the first stage of Rawls' contractarian argument, the description of the original position or hypothetical situation for the choice of principles of justice. We can now turn to a brief outline of the second stage of the contractarian argument—the attempt to show that granted this description of the original position the parties would choose Rawls' principles of justice.

By construing the selection of principles of justice as a problem of rational choice, Rawls is able to enlist techniques developed by contemporary decision theorists. Granted the informational constraints imposed by the veil of ignorance, the problem of choosing principles of justice in the original position is what decision theorists call a problem of rational choice under uncertainty.

The idea is that the parties are to choose a set of principles that will then be applied to the basic structure of the society in which they live. Different sets of principles will produce different distributions of prospects for liberty, wealth, authority, and other primary goods. Since the parties do not know their present status in their society, they are not able to predict exactly how the choice of this or that set of principles will affect them personally. The parties are to choose principles which will profoundly influence their life prospects, but they are to do so in a situation in which the outcome of the alternatives is uncertain.

Decision theorists have proposed various rules for making decisions under uncertainty. Rawls argues that the appropriate decision rule for the parties in the original position to employ is the *maximin rule*. The maximin rule states that one is to choose that alternative which has the best worst outcome. The maximin rule tells one, in effect, to choose the safest alternative.

Rawls' decision-theoretic version of the contractarian argument for his principles of justice consists of two stages. First, Rawls argues that the conditions that make up the original position make it rational for the parties in the original position to employ the maximin decision rule. Second, he argues that if the parties employed the maximin decision rule they would choose his principles of justice over the competitors on the list. According to Rawls, the Principle of Greatest Equal Liberty, along with the Principle of Fair Equality of Opportunity and Difference Principle, insure the best worst outcome of any of the sets of principles on the list.

It is important to understand exactly why Rawls thinks that the worst possible outcome under Utilitarianism would be worse than the worst possible outcome under his principles. As we saw earlier, Rawls argues that Utilitarianism might require or at least allow severe restrictions of liberty for some if this produced greater overall utility. Thus, the worst outcome under Utilitarianism might be slavery or servitude or at least a lesser share of liberty than others have. A person in the original position is to consider the possibility that he might turn out to be a member of the worst-off group in society. Rawls' claim is that since Utilitarianism may sacrifice the interests of a minority to produce greater aggregate utility, the worst-off under Utilitarianism may be very badly off indeed. In contrast, the lexical priority of the Principle of Greatest Equal Liberty eliminates this possible outcome by insuring that no one's basic liberty will be sacrificed for the sake of maximizing overall utility. Further, the Difference Principle requires that inequalities in wealth, income, and authority must work to the greatest benefit of the worst-off, subject to the lexical priority of the Principle of Greatest Equal Liberty and the Principle of Fair Equality of Opportunity. Rawls concludes that parties in the original position would adopt a minimal risk strategy, choose his principles, and reject the alternative conceptions, including Utilitarianism.

Though it has attracted the most attention, Rawls' maximin decision rule argument does not exhaust his contractarian justification for his principles of justice. He sketches several informal contractarian arguments that do not employ decision theory. Among these are (i) the argument from self-respect, (ii) the argument from the strains of commitment, and (iii) the argument from stability. Granted the limitations of this summary, we can only sketch these informal arguments very briefly to emphasize their independence from the maximin decision-rule argument.

(i)　Rawls stresses that "perhaps the most important primary good is that of self-respect" because

Without it nothing may seem worth doing or if some things have value for us, we lack the will to strive for them. All desire and activity becomes empty and vain, and we sink into apathy and cynicism. Therefore the parties in the original position would wish to avoid at almost any cost the social conditions that undermine self-respect. [25]

He then emphasizes the effects of publicity on self-respect. The public knowledge that the basic structure of society is to be arranged according to his two principles of justice would, Rawls contends, support individuals' self-respect in two ways. First, society's commitment to ensuring everyone's greatest equal liberty and fair equality of opportunity would be seen as a public expression of unconditional respect for each. Second, Rawls states that the Difference Principle is a principle of *reciprocity* insofar as it insures that the distribution of social goods is to everyone's advantage. The concept of reciprocity or mutual advantage, he observes, is consonant with the assumption that each person's pursuit of the good as he conceives it is to be respected. Thus the common knowledge that the distribution of wealth and income is to be regulated by a principle of mutual benefit also provides social support for the individual's self-respect. Rawls concludes that the parties to the hypothetical contract would recognize that his conception of justice "gives more support to [self-respect] than other principles and [that this] is a strong reason for them to adopt it."[26]

(ii) The strains of commitment argument[27] capitalizes on the fact that it is a condition of the original position that the parties know they are to make a *contract*, a *sincere agreement*, not just a unanimous choice.

The argument from the strains of commitment has an important place in justice as fairness and its concept of contract (agreement) is essential to it. . . . In general, the class of things that can be agreed to is included within, and is smaller, than, the class of things that can be rationally chosen. We can decide to take a chance and at the same time fully intend that, should things turn out badly, we shall do what we can to retrieve our situation. But if we make an agreement, we have to accept the outcome; and so to give an undertaking in good faith, we must not only intend to honor it but with reason believe we can do so.[28]

So the parties are actually to make a contract: they are to make a binding agreement, not simply to say that they agree. But if they are to make a binding agreement, then they are to consider whether they will be able to keep it—to comply fully with the principles chosen. And if they are to consider whether they will be able to keep the agreement, they must consider whether the facts about human motivation make such compliance possible. Further, it is not even enough to determine that compliance with a certain set of principles is motivationally *possible*. The parties must also determine whether the psychological costs of compliance are excessive. Rawls refers to these psychological costs as "the strains of commitment" and argues that the parties would conclude that the strains of commitment associated with his principles are less serious than those associated with competing principles. Again, the case of Utilitarianism provides a central illustration of this contractarian argument. Rawls contends that, because it might require that certain individuals' interests be sacrificed for the sake of maximizing overall or average utility, Utilitarianism involves greater strains of commitment than his own conception of justice.

(iii) Rawls' third informal contractarian argument, the argument from stability, depends, at least in part, upon the success of the argument from self-respect and the argument from the strains of commitment examined above. He contends that the parties in the original position will choose that conception of justice which, if successfully implemented, will produce a social order that enjoys the greatest stability, other things being equal.[29] A conception whose implementation will produce excessive strains of commitment, or one which will undermine self-respect, will be unstable. Rawls concludes that since (as he believes he has shown) his conception minimizes strains of commitment and best supports self-respect, it would be chosen in the belief that it is more stable than competing conceptions.

What is perhaps most striking about *A Theory of Justice* is the diversity of particular arguments and types of justification it contains. Any adequate evaluation of the theory must carefully distinguish and critically evaluate each of the various lines of support which Rawls offers.

10. RAWLS' MODEL FOR A JUST BASIC STRUCTURE

Having articulated and argued for his principles of justice, Rawls then provides a brief account of how the basic structure of *our* society could be arranged so as to satisfy those principles. This account does not purport to be a detailed blueprint for the just society, but it is intended to serve two important functions. (1) It helps to specify further the content of Rawls' principles of justice by examining their practical implications. (2) An attempt to apply the principles of justice to the basic structure of our society is necessary if we are to evaluate Rawls' arguments from considered moral judgments. For to see whether Rawls' principles provide the best account of our considered moral judgments about justice, we must perform two tasks. First, we must determine what particular judgments about justice Rawls' principles yield when applied to the facts about the basic structure of our society. Second, we must see whether those particular judgments which the principles yield match our considered judgments about what is just or unjust. A fairly concrete plan of how Rawls' principles could be satisfied in our society is crucial for executing the first task and hence also for the second.

In sketching a model for a just basic structure Rawls concentrates mainly on the institutional arrangements he thinks would satisfy the Difference Principle. The requirements of the Difference Principle in our society could best be met, Rawls believes, through the creation of four branches of government: (a) the allocation branch, (b) the stabilization branch, (c) the transfers branch, and (d) the distribution branch.[30]

Rawls contends that, granted fair equality of opportunity and greatest equal basic liberty, the Difference Principle would be satisfied by an institutional arrangement exhibiting the following features, corresponding to the four branches of government listed above. (1) There is private ownership of capital and natural resources. A free market system is maintained by the *allocation branch* of government. (2) There is a *stabilization branch* whose function is to "try to bring about reasonably full employment . . . ." (3) The *transfers branch* of government "guarantees a social minimum [i.e., a minimum income for all] either by family allowances and special payments for sickness and unemployment, or more systematically by such devices as a graded income supplement (i.e., a negative income tax)." (4) There is a *distribution branch* whose "task is to preserve an approximate justice in distribution shares by means of taxation and the necessary adjustments in the rights of property." There are two aspects of the distributive branch. "First, it imposes a number of inheritance and gift taxes, and sets restrictions on the rights of bequest." Second, it establishes a scheme of taxation "to raise the revenues that justice requires."[31]

Now what is notable about this model for a just society is that, with the possible exception of the "reasonable" full employment measures mentioned in (2), it purports to satisfy the Difference Principle through purely redistributive measures in the narrowest sense. Rawls assumes, that is, that the Difference Principle can be satisfied in our society at this time or in the foreseeable future simply by redistributing income and wealth through taxing the better-off and transferring the proceeds to the worst-off. He assumes, then, that the representative worst-off man's prospects of wealth, powers, authority, etc. can be maximized by boosting the wages earned on the free market with an income supplement. The idea, roughly, is that the market will do part of the job of satisfying the Difference Principle and that taxation and income transfers will do the rest. What is crucial to note here is that Rawls believes that his principles of justice could be satisfied in our society without the abolition of competitive markets and the adoption of socialism. He contends that justice could be attained without a transition to public ownership of the means of production. Nonetheless, Rawls also emphasizes that in some circumstances, satisfaction of the Difference Principle might allow or even require socialism in the sense of public ownership of the means of production. His principles of justice themselves, as distinct from his assumptions about how they could be satisfied in our society, are in this sense silent on the issue of public versus private ownership. It is only when the principles are applied to empirical data about a given society that they are capable of settling the question of property rights in the means of production.

III

Now that we have the main lines of Rawls' theory before us, we can consider what appear to be the most serious Marxian objections to it. They are, I believe, the following.

1) Rawls focuses on distribution to the neglect of production, failing to see that the former depends upon the latter.
2) Rawls wrongly assumes that the existence of social classes is a permanent feature of human society.
3) Rawls' method of reflective equilibrium fails to recognize that even the most basic considered moral judgments are class-relative. If a proletarian and a bourgeois each work through the process of reaching reflective equilibrium and each achieves a coherent theory of justice, they will be different, and indeed incompatible, theories. Both a person's firmest considered judgments and his attempts to achieve a match between these judgments and a set of moral principles or a set of conditions for choosing moral principles are determined by that person's class consciousness.
4) Rawls unwittingly (and uncritically) assumes a liberal-bourgeois or individualistic-utilitarian conception of human nature, according to which man is a mere "consumer of utilities" rather than a being whose nature is creative, social activity.
5) While claiming to rely only upon a "thin" or "morally neutral" theory of the good, Rawls in fact employs a substantive conception of the good for man (or a normative ideal of the person) thereby arbitrarily excluding, among others, those conceptions of the good which give preeminence to the Marxian virtues of community and solidarity.
6) Rawls' hypothetical contract approach neglects class conflict: it assumes a common interest which does not exist in the class-divided society in which we live. The knowledge of class conflicts precludes any agreement in Rawls' original position.
7) Rawls lacks a theory of transition from current society to the Rawlsian well-ordered society—his theory is thus utopian. In particular, he provides no account of how the sense of justice can serve as an effective motivation for social change.
8) Rawls' theory suffers from a failing that is characteristic of liberal theories: it accords priority to civil and political rights without adequately acknowledging the problem that social and economic inequalities produce inequalities in the effectiveness with which equal rights can be exercised.
9) Rawls offers what he takes to be universal principles of justice, but as Marx's analysis of the relation of base to superstructure shows, there can be no one set of principles of justice which are even applicable to, much less valid for, all societies at all times. Any given set of principles arises out of and can only be sensibly applied to a certain mode of production, and different modes of production exist in different societies during different periods of history.
10) Rawls' statement that justice is the first virtue of social institutions signals his failure to understand that the very need for a theory of justice reveals deep though ultimately eliminable defects in the mode of production. Rawls assumes that the circumstances of justice are an inevitable feature of the human condition. He fails to see that the problems of justice cannot be solved but only dissolved, through the transition to a new mode of production which eliminates both the subjective and objective components of the circumstances of justice.

1. In *Understanding Rawls*, Robert Paul Wolff states the first objection as follows:

Looked at more broadly . . . Rawls' failure grows naturally and inevitably out of his uncritical acceptance of the socio-political presuppositions and associated modes of analysis of classical and neo-classical political economy. By focusing exclusively on distribution rather than on production, Rawls obscures the real roots of that distribution. As Marx says in his *Critique of the Gotha Program*, "Any distribution whatever of the means of consumption is only a consequence of the distribution of the conditions of production themselves. The latter distribution, however is a feature of the mode of production itself." Has Rawls sought the principles of justice in the right way? No, for his theory, however qualified and complicated, is in the end a theory of pure distribution.[32]

Wolff does not clarify what he means by "a theory of pure distribution," though his citation of the passage from the *Critique of the Gotha Program* implies that he means a theory of the distribution of the "the means of consumption." This criticism is off the mark. Rawls' theory is not concerned exclusively or even primarily either with the distribution of the means of consumption or, more broadly, with distribution in any sense which contrasts profitably with production.[33]

First of all, Rawls' Principle of Greatest Equal Liberty and his Principle of Equality of Fair Opportunity are not principles for the distribution of the means of consumption. The former specifies an array of equal civil and political rights, which are to be understood as constitutionally protected liberties to perform certain actions and participate in certain processes, without being interfered with in certain ways. The latter specifies conditions of access to offices and positions. Further, it must be remembered that the Principle of Greatest Equal Liberty and the Principle of Equality of Fair Opportunity are lexically prior to the Difference Principle. So even if the Difference Principle were a principle of the distribution of the means of consumption, it would still be incorrect to say that Rawls focuses exclusively on distribution of the means of consumption, since to do this would ignore the two principles of justice which are lexically prior to the Difference Principle.

Second, the Difference Principle is not a principle of the distribution of the means of consumption either. What the Difference Principle "distributes," if anything, is life prospects of an index of certain social primary goods, including not only wealth and income, but also powers and opportunities, and what Rawls calls the social bases of self-respect. But, strictly speaking, the Difference Principle is not a distributive principle of any kind, if by this is meant a principle that parcels out goods among individuals or groups. Instead, the Difference Principle requires that institutions of the basic structure be designed in such a way that a certain array of life prospects of certain social primary goods exists.

Indeed none of Rawls' three basic principles is an exclusively distributive principle, even if what is distributed is not confined to the means of consumption, for the simple reason that *any of these principles may require changes in basic productive processes.* This comes out most clearly in the case of the Difference Principle. As I noted earlier, Rawls explicitly leaves open the possibility that satisfaction of the Difference Principle will require a change from private to public ownership of the means of production. Further, if we take seriously Rawls' insistence that in determining what arrangements would maximize the life prospects of the representative worst-off man we include self-respect, and if "meaningful work" is, as many Marxians maintain, a necessary condition of self-respect, it again appears that the Difference Principle may require changes in the mode of production.

There is an explanation of the confusion to which Wolff and other proponents of the first Marxian objection have succumbed. We must distinguish between what Rawls' principles would require in various circumstances and what Rawls himself thinks they would require, on the basis of his factual estimates of the current state of our society. As I noted in my summary of Rawls' theory, Rawls' discussion of how his principles could be applied to our society focuses primarily on institutional arrangements for satisfying the Difference Principle and concludes that this could be achieved through the creation of the four branches of government.

If one focuses on this rather conservative scheme for the implementation of the Difference Principle, one will be tempted to conclude, as some Marxian critics have, that Rawls' theory of justice is concerned exclusively or primarily with distribution in a narrow sense, namely, the distribution of income. But it is essential to note that Rawls apparently uses the taxation and transfer scheme because he makes the dubious empirical assumption that increasing the income prospects of the worst-off will maximize their prospects of the whole range of other social primary goods included in the scope of the Difference Principle.

Consider how strong this assumption is. It is the claim that in our society at the present and for a period extending into the future, the overall prospects of the worst-off, including their prospects of self-respect, can be maximized by supplementing their wages through the use of tax revenues. It is not simply that Rawls fails to marshall any empirical evidence to show that this can be done, though this is bad enough. There is the more serious problem that there is a good deal of empirical evidence against the assumption that self-respect (and authority) are correlated with income in this simple fashion even in our society at the present time.[34]

Suppose, for example, that a person's self-respect depends significantly on his belief that his work is meaningful or important, or that it involved the exercise of some of his higher capacities. As already noted, Rawls does include self-respect in the scope of the Difference Principle. So to the extent that self-respect is dependent upon meaningful work, the Difference Principle will require institutional arrangements that take the need for meaningful work into account. However, it is wishful thinking to assume without evidence that Rawls' simple and rather conservative taxation and transfer scheme will come to grips with the difficult task of increasing the worst-off's prospects of meaningful work or of self-respect through meaningful work. To assume that these problems can be solved even in our society at the present time simply by redistributing income through the familiar taxation and transfer measures of the welfare state is to make the same error for which Marx took the French socialists of his day to task. It is to assume that problems which intimately involve persons' productive activities can be solved by purely distributive measures in the narrow sense.

Though my purpose here is to examine Marxian objections to Rawls, it is worth noting that an attempt by Rawls to reply to the objection just raised may make it *more difficult* for him to fend off certain familiar libertarian criticisms. Libertarians such as Robert Nozick have charged that the Difference Principle would require frequent and intolerable interferences with individuals' liberty to use and transfer their goods.[35] Now if the Difference Principle could be satisfied through supplementing the mechanism of the market by raking off income from the better-off and transferring it to the worst-off, then the force of this libertarian objection would be greatly diminished. For if satisfaction of the Difference Principle were merely a matter of redistributing income through taxation, then there would be no need for forced labor or for other direct restrictions on freedom of occupational choice. And since well designed tax laws would provide a stable, predictable framework for legitimate expectations, the libertarian need not fear frequent or unpredictable appropriations of his holdings. Further, so long as individuals or private associations meet their predictable tax responsibilities there would be no need for further government restrictions on the development of new life styles or cooperative ventures. Finally, taxation and transfer policies—as opposed to direct intervention with production—would not mandate the cancerous growth of government power which direct control requires and which libertarians rightly see as one of the greatest threats to individual freedom.

I shall not attempt here to assess the adequacy of this Rawlsian reply to the libertarian objection. Instead, I wish only to emphasize that if it is to afford a conclusive rejoinder to the libertarian, Rawls must narrow the scope of the Difference Principle so drastically that it will then leave him exposed to the Marxian charge that he has focused on distribution to the neglect of production. On the other hand, if Rawls refuses to weaken the Difference Principle by restricting its scope to prospects of income (to the exclusion of self-respect, powers, and authority), then he will not be able to blunt the force of libertarian objections by reassuring us that the Difference Principle can be satisfied through a taxation and transfer scheme, with a minimum of disruption and interference with individual liberty.

It seems clear that his theory—as distinct from his speculations about its application—requires that Rawls refuse to restrict the scope of the Difference Principle by limiting it to income prospects. For if, in order to meet more effectively the libertarian objection, Rawls restricts the scope of the Difference Principle, he thereby undercuts the supporting role of the theory of primary goods. That theory was employed to provide content for the principles of justice. The parties in the original position were described as desiring the whole range of goods, not a severely restricted subset of them. To solve the problem by paring down the theory of primary goods would rob that theory of plausibility. It appears, then, that Rawls can effectively reply to the Marxian charge that his theory concentrates on distribution to the neglect of production, but only if he admits that it is gratuitous to assume that the Difference Principle could be satisfied by the distributive arrangements he sketches. The price of this reply to the Marxian, however, is that it precludes what might otherwise be a simple and decisive reply to one libertarian objection. The theory of primary goods requires that the price be paid.[36]

A related objection, also available to the Marxian, is much more serious. It arises when we reflect upon the difficulty of specifying the set from which we are to choose that institutional arrangement which maximizes the prospects of the worst-off. To apply the Difference Principle we must rank alternative institutional arrangements as to their contributions to the prospects of the worst-off. But how are we to construct the set of alternatives? Rawls faults Utilitarianism for requiring us to make imponderable interpersonal utility comparisons, but it appears that his own theory is vulnerable to a similar objection: the Difference Principle requires comparisons among an unlimited number of possible institutional structures.

Rawls would presumably reply that we are not required to consider all *logically possible* institutional arrangements (compatible with satisfaction of Greatest Equal Liberty and Fair Equality of Opportunity). Presumably we are to narrow the range of alternatives by attending to the possibilities for change present in our own society as it now exists. Rawls may have this in mind when he considers whether maximizing the prospects of the worst-off would be achieved by public or private ownership of the means of production.

Which of these systems and the many intermediate forms most fully answers to the requirements of justice cannot, I think, be determined in advance. There is presumably no general answer to this question, since it depends in large part upon the traditions, institutions, and social forces of each country, and its particular historical circumstances. The theory of justice does not include these matters. But what it can do is to set out in a schematic way the outlines of a just economic system that admits of several variations. The political judgments in any case will then turn on which variation is most likely to work out in practice. A conception of justice is a necessary part of any such political assessment, but it is not sufficient.[37]

Rawls' idea seems to be that we arrive at a manageably small set of alternatives by including only those institutional arrangements that are in some sense feasible granted certain empirical features of our society. But *which* features are relevant and how exactly are they to constrain what counts as a *feasible* arrangement? Constructing a set of alternatives that are feasible relative to "the traditions, institutions, social forces, and particular historical circumstances" of one's society makes the task of determining what would maximize the prospects of the worst-off much less imponderable, but this gain may be achieved at an unconscionable price. For now it appears that what maximizes the prospects of the worst-off—and hence what is just—will depend too heavily upon *existing injustices*. Depending upon how "compatibility" or "feasiblity" are interpreted, the alternative institutional arrangements that are compatible with or feasible relative to the traditions, institutions, social forces, and historical circumstances of an extremely unjust inequalitarian society may not include a just institutional structure nor one which maximizes the prospects of the worst-off in any significant sense. Suppose, for example, that we now live in a society in which a minority enjoys great wealth, power, and educational advantages, and that many of these persons would not enjoy these benefits had they not been born into favored social positions. Suppose that the institutions, traditions, and social forces of this society reinforce their expectation that the terms of productive social cooperation allow or even require great inequalities. More specifically, suppose that it is part of the "tradition" that gross inequalities, including those based on inheritance of wealth, are necessary as incentives for greater productivity. In such "historical circumstances," the "political judgment" as to what is feasible relative to the traditions, institutions, and social forces of our society will tend to legitimize current inequalities in the name of justice. Indeed, granted the prevalence of such inegalitarian assumptions about the need for incentives, especially among those in positions of power, it may be true that the arrangement which maximizes the prospects of the worst-off will be extremely inegalitarian. Where a sufficient number of persons in positions of power believe that large incentives are necessary to elicit effort, sufficient effort may not be forthcoming when incentives are decreased. Productivity may decline, and the prospects of the worst-off may be lowered. Under such conditions, the Difference Principle may become a recipe for reaction.[38]

It is important to note that this objection poses a problem for the Difference Principle as an element of what Rawls calls *ideal theory*. The difficulty is with how we are to take current arrangements—including current motivational structures and their effects on productivity—into account in determining what justice ideally requires. This is distinct from the subsequent problem of determining how to move toward the ideal once it is ascertained. It appears, then, that Rawls is faced with a dilemma: either we place no restrictions (other than logical possibility) on the feasible set in determining what would maximize the prospects of the worst-off or we follow his suggestion and consider only those alternative arrangements that are feasible relative to the traditions, institutions, social forces, and historical circumstances of existing society. The former strategy leaves us with no nonarbitrary way of determining which of the innumerable possible arrangements to try to achieve. The latter threatens to legitimize the most dubious inequalities in the name of justice.

The Marxian would plausibly contend that the materialist theory of the development of consciousness and motivation is indispensable at this juncture. According to that theory, both the prevalence of the *belief* that private gain is a necessary incentive for productive effort and the fact that private incentives *are* currently necessary are to be explained by the existence of the system of private property. That system, according to Marx, includes an ideology that mistakes the motivational structure characteristic of persons in capitalism for the human motivational structure *per se*. And capitalist society reinforces this ideological distortion by producing persons who are motivated largely by private incentives. Further, Marx's theory purports to show that where private property is abolished high productivity can be achieved without private incentives. It also claims to provide an explanation of the process by which the existing system of private incentives is replaced by a system of nonprivate or communitarian incentives.

Now if the materialist theory of consciousness and motivation could be adequately developed in these ways, then it would be possible to say, as Rawls does, that what will maximize the prospects of the worst-off depends upon existing social conditions, including current motivational structures and current beliefs about them, *without* thereby simply legitimizing current unjust inequalities. Such a theory would allow us to take the nature of current motivational structures and the limitations they place on productivity into account, while at the same time explaining how these limitations can and will be transcended. Rawls, however, neither proposes a theory of consciousness and motivation which would do this job nor even acknowledges the need for one. Instead, he seems to assume that what justice requires can be determined without the aid of an ideological critique of the limitations of current motivational structures and without an account of the development of new motivational structures which do not suffer from these limitations. To put it simply, Rawls erroneously assumes that an adequate theory of justice can do without a theory of ideology. We may conclude, then, that Rawls' view that the Difference Principle must take into account the particular features of existing society may lead to unacceptably conservative results unless that view is supplemented with a theory which Rawls currently lacks.

2. A second Marxian objection, advanced by C. B. Macpherson among others, is that Rawls' theory uncritically assumes the permanence of social classes. According to this objection, Rawls mistakes a feature of societies at one stage of historical development for an inevitable feature of human society as such:

He [Rawls] proposes and defends his principles of justice as criteria for judging the moral worth of various distributions of rights and income only within a class-divided society. His explicit assumption is that institutionalized inequalities which affect men's whole life-prospects are "inevitable in any society"; and he is referring to inequalities between classes by income or wealth. It is with these supposedly inevitable basic inequalities that "the two principles of justice are primarily designed to deal." Or, as he puts it again, "differences in life-prospects arising from the basic structure are inevitable, and it is precisely the aim of the second principle [the Difference Principle] to say when these differences are just."[39]

One immediate difficulty in assessing this objection is the fact that the term "class" has no single meaning in social theory. Marx uses the term primarily to pick out not just any inequality, but rather to refer to the relationship of various groups to the means of production. The main class-division for Marx is between the capitalists, who control the means of production, and the proletarians, who do not. In general, Macpherson appears to operate with this Marxian conception of class, though he is not explicit about doing so in the passage cited.[40] Since we are concerned here primarily with Marxian objections to Rawls we will begin by seeing whether the applicability of Rawls' Difference Principle presupposes the existence of class-divisions in Marx's sense. Later we shall examine the objection interpreted more broadly, where "classes" can refer to groups which differ in income.

In the passage cited above Macpherson misinterprets the Difference Principle. Like those who accuse Rawls of focusing exclusively on distribution to the neglect of production, Macpherson writes as if the Difference Principle were limited to distributing "income and wealth." I have already argued that it is not. But there are other, more serious confusions in Macpherson's criticism. First, he fails to observe that the Difference Principle refers not to social classes in Marx's sense but to distinctions among individuals according to their life prospects of a complex index of social primary goods. Rawls does use the term "class"[41] in his sketchy discussion of how we are to define the representative man position for the various group-divisions according to the index of primary goods; but he never says that these classes are to be defined exclusively or even primarily according to the criterion of control over the means of production. Second, Rawls makes it clear that he is *not* assuming the inevitability of classes in Marx's sense when he leaves open the possibility that the Difference Principle may require the abolition of private ownership of the means of production and hence of classes in Marx's sense. Third, once again the Marxian objection is based on a failure to distinguish between what Rawls' theory, in this case the Difference Principle, implies and Rawls' rather speculative remarks about the conditions under which it will be applied. Rawls is of the opinion that the basic structure will lead to significant inequalities in a person's life prospects (regardless of whether the means of production are privately or publicly controlled), but contrary to appearances the Difference Principle does not itself logically presuppose inequalities, whether they be inequalities of class in Marx's sense or not.

Rawls is not always as clear as he might have been in formulating the Difference Principle and this may have led Macpherson and others astray. Macpherson apparently fixes on passages in which Rawls formulates that principle as follows:

D. The basic structure is to be arranged so that social and economic inequalities (in prospects of wealth, income, powers, etc.) maximize the prospects of the worst-off group.

However, the very nature of Rawls' main argument for the Difference Principle requires that it be interpreted in a way which is compatible with strict equality. For according to that argument, the parties choose that principle which maximizes the minimum—that principle which requires the highest minimum share of prospects of the social primary goods in question. This principle is not D; it is

M. The basic structure is to be arranged so as to maximize the prospects (of wealth, powers, etc.) of the worst-off group.

In an article published after his book, Rawls confirms this interpretation by referring to the Difference Principle as "the maximim criterion." M, not D, is a criterion which demands that we maximize the minimum.

To see why D, unlike M, does not require that the minimum be maximized, it is important to note that D places *no* conditions on equal distributions. As Rawls himself observes, each person's share under an equal distribution may be smaller than the worst-off's share under some unequal distribution. Thus D, which allows any equal distribution, no matter how small the equal shares may be, does not require that the minimum share be maximized.

It is true that M refers to a worst-off group or, strictly speaking, a representative worst-off position, but even this locution does not logically commit Rawls to the assumption that inequalities are inevitable, because under an equal distribution the phrase "worst-off group" (or "representative worst-off position") still has a referent. Under an equal distribution the maximum and minimum shares coincide: the minimum one can receive in an equal distribution is the same as what everyone else gets, but it is the minimum nonetheless, i.e., the smallest share one can get. If we define the representative worst-off group as that group which is such that no group has lower prospects and if we define the best-off group as that which is such that no group has higher prospects, then under an equal distribution the worst-off and best-off groups are identical. Thus the fact M refers to a worst-off group (or position) does *not* show that that principle presupposes inequalities, much less Marxian class inequalities.

The argument may now be summarized. Principle D, which puts no constraints on equal distribution, does not require that the minimum share be as high as possible; but the maximin strategy requires that the parties choose M, the principle which demands that the minimum share be maximized. Therefore, if, as Rawls contends, the parties employ the maximin strategy, they do not choose D but rather M, since it is only M which requires the minimum to be maximized. Principle M, the Difference Principle, does not presuppose the existence of any inequalities nor, *a fortiori*, Marxian classes. Though I shall not argue the point here, I believe that Rawls' other arguments for the Difference Principle are also arguments for M, not D.

We can now explain why Rawls sometimes misleadingly suggests that the Difference Principle is D, rather than M, and hence why Macpherson and others might conclude that the Difference Principle presupposes inequalities or class inequalities. Rawls advances M, the Difference Principle, which does not itself presuppose inequalities, but he also holds the empirical hypothesis that

E. (At least in the circumstances of justice) inequalities are inevitable or, even if not inevitable, needed to provide incentives for maximizing the prospects of the worst-off.[42]

Since M and E together imply D, it is not surprising that Rawls should sometimes refer to D when discussing the Difference Principle. If this account is correct, then Rawls may have encouraged misinterpretation by failing to distinguish clearly between the logical presuppositions of the Difference Principle (which do not include inequality, much less Marxian classes) and his own empirical judgment that maximizing the prospects of the worst-off will require or at least allow inequalities. Nonetheless, he has not offered a principle that assumes the inevitability of social inequalities. Nor do his arguments commit him to such a principle.

Finally, there is a deeper reason why it is wrong to assume that Rawls believes that class divisions, whether of the Marxian sort or otherwise, are inevitable in human society. To attribute this belief to Rawls is to overlook the fact that he is offering a theory of *justice*—a theory which applies to and only applies to societies in the circumstances of justice. The main point of Rawls' discussion of the circumstances of justice—and of Hume's account upon which it draws—is to distinguish those conditions which together result in the need for principles of justice and to leave open the possibility that some human societies may not find themselves in those circumstances. So even if, as Marx seems to have thought, the circumstances of justice include class-divisions and will disappear with them, and even if it turns out that Rawls erroneously assumes that we shall as a matter of fact always find ourselves in the circumstances of justice, it would still not follow that Rawls' principles presuppose the inevitability of classes. All that would follow is that Rawls is wrong about the range of application of his principles. Even if Rawls mistakenly believes we shall always need principles of justice, this itself does not show that his principles are inadequate for the job for which they are intended. What it shows is that they will not always be needed. I shall consider the significance of this possibility in Section 9.

3. A third Marxian objection is directed against Rawls' most fundamental methodological tool: the notion of reflective equilibrium. According to Rawls, considered moral judgments are brought to bear in the search for an adequate theory of justice in two ways. (i) We strive for a match between our firmest considered judgments about justice and a small, powerful set of principles of justice which can explain those judgments and even extend them to previously intractable cases. We achieve a state of reflective equilibrium between principles and considered judgments of justice by revising and qualifying principles in the light of judgments and judgments in the light of principles, until a coherent, self-consistent theory emerges. (ii) Using the hypothetical contract approach, we appeal to considered judgments about the appropriate conditions for choosing principles of justice. Again, the process of revision and qualification extends in both directions. Our judgments about justice in particular cases may lead us to revise some of the conditions of the original position if we recognize that those conditions, unless modified, would generate principles which conflict with our judgments about particular cases, and we may revise particular judgments to bring them in line with principles which would be chosen under what we believe to be the appropriate conditions of choice.

As we saw earlier, Rawls' employment of the method of reflective equilibrium includes both (i) and (ii). Further, he suggests that we may appeal not only to our prephilosophical judgments about appropriate conditions for the choice of principles, but also to explicitly philosophical considerations, including, presumably, our judgments about the adequacy of competing theories of the person or competing theories of rationality.[43]

The Marxian objection, stated most simply, is that the method of reflective equilibrium is incapable of yielding a single set of principles of justice. The difficulty is not just that persons living in different cultures or in different historical periods may differ on particular judgments of justice, on principles, or on conditions for the choice of principles, and that these differences may remain no matter how long the process of reflection and revision continues. The more radical difficulty is that even in our own society at this time differences in class consciousness insure that if a proletarian using Rawls' method ends up with a coherent theory of justice it will be quite different from—and in conflict with—any theory which could result from a bourgeois' use of the same method. For individuals of either class, initial differences in particular judgments about justice may be revised in the light of reflections on principles or *vice versa*, just as conditions on the choice of principles and principles derivable from those conditions may be mutually adjusted. But at each stage of the process the adjustments will be controlled by the perspective peculiar to the person's social class, and even if the proletarian and the bourgeois each arrive at a coherent theory of justice, they will not be the same theory.

Stated in this rather abstract fashion, this Marxian objection is difficult to assess. Rawls might first of all reply that the method of reflective equilibrium as he employs it in his treatment of justice is "not peculiar to moral philosophy"[44] but is in fact essential for scientific theorizing as well. He might then argue that there is no more reason to worry about the possibility of unresolvable disagreement over theories of justice than about the possibility of unresolvable disagreement over competing scientific theories.

At this point the objector, building upon Marx's suggestive but incomplete views on class consciousness, might argue that the problem is in fact much greater in the case of theories of justice than, say, in the case of physical theories. The individual's class interests play a more important controlling role in his beliefs about moral matters and his assessment of social theories than in his assessment of theories about phenomena which are not so closely related to class struggle. In other words, even if the method of reflective equilibrium can produce significant convergence of belief in the natural sciences, the irreducible opposition of class interests will preclude members of different social classes from arriving at the same theory of justice or the same social science theory.

If it is to carry much weight, this objection must still be made much more concrete. It is not enough to declare that differences in class consciousness produce differences in considered judgments about justice, since the method of reflective equilibrium can acknowledge this without difficulty. It must be shown that differing class perspectives *permanently* block convergence on a single theory of justice. The Marxian must show how it is that differences in class consciousness produce *unresolvable* disagreements in considered judgments or philosophical views about principles or conditions for choosing principles. In particular, he must show *which* elements of Rawls' theory reflect class perspectives. It will be especially important for the Marxian to show that unresolvable differences in class attitudes and beliefs undercut Rawls' attempts to give adequate philosophical support for his specification of the conditions of the original position, including his characterization of the parties, and for his derivation of principles from the original position. Further, the Marxian must determine how serious the problem of unresolved disagreement is for Rawls' overall project. We should not assume that a theory is inadequate unless it commands the allegiance of everyone, regardless of his position in society and regardless of how his interests are related to injustices which currently exist.[45]

There is a reply which does much to neutralize this Marxian objection by turning it against itself. It appears that Marx himself, whether self-consciously or not, was a practitioner of the method of reflective equilibrium. Therefore to deny the efficacy of that method in social philosophy is to deny the value of Marx's work. Marx began (as must we all) with a store of more or less unsystematic evaluations and factual beliefs about history and his own society. His intellectual life was a process of mutual adjustment between philosophical principles inherited from Hegel and Feuerbach, economic concepts gleaned from the work of the classical political economists, socialist ideas borrowed from the French, and his own experience of contemporary political events. In both his explanatory and his evaluative efforts, Marx sought an accommodation between a relatively small but powerful set of principles and his considered judgments. He appropriated and refined some concepts (such as the labor theory of value, from Ricardo) because he believed they did the best job of accounting for a multitude of facts, including some of the most important facts.

When inherited ideas proved inadequate he developed new ones, such as the distinction between labor and labor power, both to explain otherwise unintelligible data and to provide the basis for criticisms not expressible within the framework of classical political economy. Because he believed that juridical concepts did not adequately capture the most profound evils of capitalism, he developed non-juridical evaluative concepts in his theories of alienation and exploitation. Indeed it appears that the idea of reflective equilibrium is needed, not only to show what Marx's work has in common with other instances of scientific theorizing, but also to explain how bourgeois intellectuals like Marx, Engels, and Lenin were able to transcend the narrow horizons of their class and develop a revolutionary theory designed to overthrow the capitalist order. This reply can be recast as a dilemma: either the constraints of class consciousness are weak enough that the method of reflective equilibrium can operate successfully or they are so strong that the development of Marx's thought (as well as that of Engels and Lenin) becomes inexplicable.

The Marxian might concede that *the method* of reflective equilibrium is capable of overcoming the bias of class perspective, at least at those propitious moments in the history of capitalism when socio-economic crises begin to rend the veil of ideology. Nonetheless, the Marxian might argue that *Rawls' application* of the method has not in fact been successful, perhaps because Rawls' theorizing has not been informed by a penetrating study of political economy.

Mainly for economy of exposition, I shall explore this quite different version of the Marxian objection to Rawls' use of the method of reflective equilibrium no further at this point. Instead, I shall approach it indirectly by examining several distinct Marxian objections which focus either on Rawls' principles of justice, his conditions for the choice of principles, or his arguments from the conditions of choice to the principles. Only after these objections have been thoroughly explored will it be possible to assess the charge that Rawls' employment of the method ignores the importance of class consciousness and class interests.[46]

4. Several of Rawls' critics, including Macpherson and Wolff, have raised what purports to be a fundamental objection to Rawls' whole approach. Rawls, they contend, has fallen into a trap that Marx laid bare long ago. He has founded his theory on an historically parochial conception of man. More specifically, Rawls is guilty of the same error Marx exposed in the classical political economists and liberal philosophers of the eighteenth and early nineteenth centuries. He mistakes characteristics of man in capitalist society for the essential features of man. Marxians variously label this historically parochial conception of man the liberal conception, the bourgeois conception, the liberal-bourgeois conception, the individualistic conception, or the conception of man as a mere consumer of utilities. There is some disagreement as to just what is included under this conception, but the following items are usually stressed.

i)   Individuals' basic ends are given and (more or less) fixed independently of the social institutions within which they find themselves. There are certain basic ends which all human beings seek (e.g., power over others, according to Hobbes), regardless of their social position or place in history, and which are permanent features of the human constitution.

ii) A person acts rationally when and only when he maximizes his utility (rationality as egoistic utility maximization).

iii) Social arrangements (particular associations and society as a whole) are valuable to the individual solely or primarily as means to the individual's ends.

Macpherson vividly labels this the conception of man as a mere "consumer of utilities" to contrast it with Marx's view that man essentially is free, conscious, social activity.[47]

We must try to see whether Rawls assumes that some or all of the three items listed are features of human beings as such. The first thing to notice is that it will not suffice to show that Rawls attributes these characteristics to the parties in the original position, since, as Rawls himself insists,[48] we must keep the characterization of the parties distinct from descriptions of actual persons. The original position, including the characterization of the parties, is a highly abstract construction, a specialized methodological device with a definite and limited role to play in the theory. Therefore it is dead wrong to extract Rawls' statements about the parties and read them as if they were his generalizations about human beings.[49] Unfortunately, those who accuse Rawls of uncritically assuming the bourgeois or liberal or individualistic conception of man have tended to overlook this distinction between what Rawls says about the parties and what views about the nature of human beings he is committed to. Instead, they simply point to his characterization of the parties as conclusive evidence that he holds what they take to be a distorted and outmoded conception of human nature.[50]

Further, even if one could read Rawls' characterization of the parties as constituting his conception of man, this would still not show that he subscribes to any of the three theses which comprise the liberal or bourgeois or individualistic conception of man because Rawls' description of the parties includes none of these three theses. First of all, in *A Theory of Justice* and in several subsequent papers, Rawls explicitly states that the parties in the original position are *not* rational egoists—they are not maximizers of their exclusively self-regarding preferences.

[The parties] have their own plans of life. These plans, or conceptions of the good, lead them to have different ends and purposes, and to make conflicting claims on the natural and social resources available. Moreover, although the interests advanced by these plans are not assumed to be interests in a self, they are the interests of a self that regards its conceptions of the good as worthy of recognition and that advances claims in its behalf as deserving satisfaction.[51]

Those who claim that Rawls' parties are rational egoists have overlooked the distinction between interest *in* the self and interests *of* the self. In the passage just cited, Rawls draws this distinction to emphasize that the parties are conceived of as having their own conceptions of the good, though it is not assumed that those conceptions are egoistic, i.e., exclusively or primarily self-regarding. All the parties know is that they have their own conceptions of the good—whether these conceptions turn out to be egoistic, altruistic, or something in between is a fact shielded from them by the veil of ignorance.

In "Fairness to Goodness" Rawls again emphasizes that the parties are not egoists.

A further cause of misunderstanding is the nature and scope of the motivation assumption. That the parties are mutually disinterested is sometimes taken to mean they are self-interested individuals with individualistic aims. The relation between self-centered economic competitors or seekers after power is then regarded as a suggestive paradigm. But a more helpful case is the relation between members of different religions; for while they are mutually disinterested under the circumstances of justice, they are neither self-interested nor necessarily engaged in the pursuit of individualistic plans of life.[52]

It is clear, then, that the parties are *not* described as rational egoists—as maximizers of their self-regarding preferences—because they are not described as beings whose conceptions of the good are exclusively or even primarily self-regarding or individualistic. So even if it were legitimate to infer Rawls' views about human nature from his description of the parties, he would still not be committed to (ii), the thesis that rationality is egoistic utility maximization.

Further, it follows that the Marxian cannot argue that since Rawls characterizes the parties as rational egoists, he is committed to (iii), the thesis that social arrangements are valuable to individuals solely or primarily as means to achieving the individual's ends. There is, in addition, another reason to reject the Marxian charge that Rawls' conception of man includes (iii). In his discussion of the good of social union—where he is talking not about the parties but real human beings—Rawls emphasizes the inadequacy of that view of human nature according to which social institutions and social relations are only of instrumental value.

The social nature of mankind is best seen by contrast with the conception of private society. Thus human beings have in fact shared final ends and they value their common institutions as good in themselves.[53]

In sum, neither Rawls' description of the parties in the original position, nor his explicit remarks about human nature commit him to the view that human beings are rational egoists nor to the view (ii) that rationality is egoistic utility-maximization, nor to the thesis (iii) that social arrangements are valuable only as means, whether to egoistic or nonegoistic ends.

There is a deeper reason why neither (ii) nor (iii) can correctly be attributed to Rawls, and articulating it will show that Rawls also explicitly rejects thesis (i). Especially in the papers published after the book, Rawls makes it clear that the parties in the original position are not to be conceived of as having ends which are fixed and which are independent of the formative influence of social institutions. In "Reply to Alexander Musgrave," for example, he says:

The parties regard themselves as having a highest-order interest in how all their other interests, including even their fundamental ones, are shaped and regulated by social institutions. They do not think of themselves as inevitably bound to, or as identical with, the pursuit of any particular complex of fundamental interests that they may have at any given time. . . . Rather, free persons conceive of themselves as beings who can revise and alter their final ends and who give first priority to preserving their liberty in these matters. Hence, they not only have final ends that they are in principle free to pursue or to reject, but their original allegiance and continued devotion to these ends are to be formed and affirmed under conditions that are free. Since the two principles [of justice] secure a social form that maintains these conditions, they would be agreed to. Only by this agreement can the parties be sure that their highest-order interest as free persons is guaranteed.[54]

This passage attributes the highest-order interest in preserving one's freedom to revise one's ends, and hence in choosing institutions that will shape our ends, to the parties *insofar as they are free persons*. Thus Rawls attributes this highest-order interest not just to the parties but to actual human beings, insofar as they are free persons, agents who are motivated by considerations of their own autonomy. Later (in Section 7) I shall raise the question of whether Rawls has given us any reason to believe that our concern for our autonomy can serve as an effective motivation for the transition to a just society. For now, suffice it to note that according to Rawls neither the parties nor actual persons so far as they are *free* rational persons are mere utility maximizers, for in neither case does Rawls limit rationality to the maximization of whatever preferences one happens to have. Hence even if (ii) were revised so that "utility" covered both egoistic (i.e., exclusively or primarily self-regarding) and nonegoistic preferences, it could still not be attributed to Rawls, either as a statement about the parties or about actual persons.

At this point the inappropriateness of Macpherson's characterization of Rawlsian man as a mere "consumer of utilities" becomes apparent. The parties are not passive slaves to unalterable preferences of any kind, much less to preferences for "consumables." Instead, Rawls describes the parties, and ourselves so far as we are free moral persons, as active choosers, as beings who criticize and revise, and take responsibility for their conceptions of the good over time, as they confront the world of experience. As I have argued elsewhere,[55] Rawls' theory of justice is a theory of justice as fairness to critical choosers of ends, not justice as fairness to satisfaction maximizers, beings who strive to maximize given preferences, whatever they happen to be.[56]

In fairness to Rawls' critics, it should be said that in *A Theory of Justice* (as opposed to the later papers) there are passages[57] which support the view that the parties in the original position are simply utility maximizers (egoistic or otherwise). There is, I think, an explanation of why such passages occur in *A Theory of Justice*, and more frequently in earlier papers such as "Distributive Justice" and "Justice as Fairness," but not in papers written after the book. It may be that Rawls' failure to make it entirely clear in *A Theory of Justice* that the parties are critical choosers of ends rather than utility maximizers reflects a deep methodological ambivalence which was finally resolved in the later papers. In his early papers and perhaps to a lesser extent in *A Theory of Justice*, Rawls is attracted by the power and rigor of the conceptual tools of economics and in particular of decision theory, including the austere and apparently unproblematic notion of rationality as utility maximization. But, even in *A Theory of Justice*, there is another current that prevents Rawls from unreservedly embracing the economic notion of rationality, namely the Kantian conception of autonomy which surfaces from time to time in the book, especially in the section on the Kantian interpretation. In developing the argument for the priority of liberty in *A Theory of Justice*, Rawls seems to rely implicitly upon the idea that at least some of the basic liberties are valuable not only as means toward given ends, but as conditions for the rational criticism and revision of ends.

Now it seems that equal liberty of conscience is the only principle that the persons in the original position can acknowledge. They cannot take chances with their liberty by permitting the dominant religious or moral doctrine to persecute or suppress others if it wishes. Even granting (what may be questioned) that it is more probable than not that one will turn out to belong to the majority (if a majority exists), to gamble in this way would show that one did not take one's religious or moral convictions seriously, or *highly value the liberty to examine one's beliefs*. (italics added)[58]

Similarly, in the Kantian interpretation section, Rawls says that the parties are to be characterized in such a way "as to allow for freedom in the choice of final ends."[59] Later in this section, Rawls breaks away from any pretense that the parties in the original position are the simple utility maximizers of economic theory.

> My suggestion is that we think of the original position as the point of view from which noumenal selves see the world. The parties qua noumenal selves have complete freedom to choose whatever principles they wish; but they also have a desire to express their nature as rational and equal members of the intelligible realm with precisely this liberty to choose. . . . They must decide, then, which principles when consciously followed and acted upon in everyday life will best manifest this freedom in their community, most fully reveal their independence from natural contingencies and social accident. [60]

In the passages from his later papers cited earlier in this section, Rawls explicitly states that the parties in the original position are not beings who strive to maximize *given* ends, but autonomous agents who have an overriding commitment to insuring that they will live their lives in conditions that allow for the critical choice and revision of ends. [61]

My hypothesis, then, is that in his early papers, Rawls tended to describe the parties as rational economic agents—maximizers of given, fixed preferences—on the assumption that this characterization alone would permit the use of the formal tools of decision theory. In later papers and to a lesser extent in the book, Rawls placed increasing emphasis on the Kantian notion of autonomy by making it clear that the parties, and each of us so far as we are free moral agents, are critical choosers of ends, not mere utility-maximizers. This shift is reflected in the difference between Rawls' treatment of the theory of primary goods in *A Theory of Justice,* on the one hand, and in later papers such as "Reply to Alexander and Musgrave," "A Kantian Conception of Equality," and "Responsibility for Ends," on the other. [62] In *A Theory of Justice,* the primary goods are presented chiefly, if not exclusively, as maximally flexible assets, that is, as effective means toward realizing a very broad range of preferences, and hence as being attractive to beings who do not know what their given preferences will turn out to be once the veil of ignorance is lifted. In the later papers, however, the primary goods are seen not only as effective means towards realizing a broad range of preferences, but as providing conditions for the critical formation and revision of basic preferences themselves. [63]

The importance of this shift away from the characterization of the parties as utility-maximizers to a conception of them as critical choosers of ends should not be underestimated. Though my purpose here is only to examine distinctively Marxian criticisms of Rawls, I should like to note that this shift casts a new light on two central features of Rawls' work. First, it raises the question of whether, granted Rawls' rejection of the characterization of the parties as utility-maximizers, he can still rely upon a decision-theoretic argument for his principles, since that argument may require such a characterization. Second, Rawls' dispute with Utilitarianism now takes on an entirely different look. If, as the later papers stress, the parties in the original position are not utility-maximizers and the primary goods are not to be understood simply as goods for utility-maximizers, then it looks as if the deck has been more heavily stacked against Utilitarianism from the start than Rawls admits. If the characterization of the parties represents a radically nonutilitarian conception or ideal of the person, then the main dispute between Rawls and Utilitarianism comes very early, at the level of argument as to how the parties are to be characterized, rather than at the level of the choice of principles. Indeed, once this characterization of the parties is granted, it is difficult to see how a principle of utility can even be a serious contender. While Rawls will find it easier to generate principles suitable for autonomous choosers of ends, once we grant him the characterization of the parties stressed in the later papers, this gain comes at the price of shifting the burden of his argument. He must now show why the original position should incorporate the conception of persons as autonomous choosers of ends rather than as utility-maximizers.

Even if he concedes that the parties are autonomous choosers of ends rather than utility-maximizers, the Marxian critic might argue that there is still something basically individualistic about Rawls' conception of the parties which is not captured by theses (i), (ii), or (iii) above (p. 135): Rawls sees each person as an individual who is concerned to advance his own conception of the good and who is willing to press *his claims* against others with differing or competing conceptions of the good. Rawlsian persons are beings who assume that there will be not only divergences but conflicts of interests among persons—conflicts serious enough to make necessary the establishment of rights-principles to serve as standards for adjudicating claims which they press against one other. The conception of human interaction as essentially conflictual or adversarial, the Marxian continues, is individualistic as opposed to the communitarian conception found in Marx's writings. Rawls reveals his bourgeois prejudices when he assumes that an individualistic characterization is appropriate.

This version of the charge that Rawls has assumed a temporally parochial conception of human nature is based on two errors. First, it wrongly assumes that the relevant contrast is between individualistic and communitarian conceptions rather than between individualistic and *pluralistic* conceptions. It is true that both Rawls' characterization of the parties and his remarks about actual persons (in the circumstances of justice) show that he rejects what may be called the communitarian conception. This rejection of the communitarian conception, however, does not commit him to individualism, but only to pluralism.

Now each of the foregoing terms has been used in a variety of ways by different writers and I shall not attempt to sort them out here. By "communitarian" I mean, roughly, a view of human society as a thorough-going community of interests or, more strongly, an identity of interests. In society, as the communitarian envisions it, there is no significant divergence among particular interests, or between particular interests and the common interest, to serve as a basis for serious conflict nor, hence, for one person or one group pressing claims against another. By "pluralism" I mean, again roughly, the denial of communitarianism. According to the pluralist conception, there are serious divergences of interests among individuals and groups and these divergences issue in situations in which individuals may find it necessary to press their claims against others. "Pluralism" so understood is more inclusive than "individualism," since the latter suggests a situation in which divergence and conflict of interest have reached an atomistic zenith. In rejecting the communitarian conception, pluralism leaves open the possibility that the major conflicts may be between groups rather than between individuals *qua* individuals and that most individuals may share or even identify with the interest of some others.

Both Rawls' characterization of the parties and his remarks about actual persons in the circumstances of justice reveal a pluralistic rather than an individualistic conception. The parties in the original position are said to accord priority to the Principle of Greatest Equal Liberty in order to protect their freedom of association with others, in particular, their freedom to participate in moral or religious communities. Similarly, as we also saw earlier, Rawls' discussion of the good of social union stresses the importance of the individual's sharing in or identifying with the interests of some group or groups, while also emphasizing that the just society provides a framework for a plurality of groups.

Suppose that the Marxian concedes that the more accurate statement of his objection is that either Rawls' characterization of the parties or his conception of actual human beings is noncommunitarian, i.e., pluralistic. At this point, the Marxian's second error comes clearly into view. The objection, even in this revised form, neglects the fact that both Rawls' characterization of the parties and his discussions of actual human beings are tied to the *circumstances of justice*. It is because the parties are in, and recognize themselves as being in, the circumstances of justice that they are concerned to establish principles that will achieve a proper assignment of fundamental rights and duties that will serve as a final court of appeal in adjudicating claims they may press against each other, either as individuals or as members of communities. Similarly, when Rawls discusses the plurality of religious and moral communities that can coexist within the framework of the just society, he is only committed to the claim that human societies in the circumstances of justice are pluralistic, not the much stronger claim that no human society in any circumstances whatsoever could exist as a single, thorough-going community or identity of interests.

Indeed it seems that granted we restrict ourselves to human society in the circumstances of justice, Rawls is correct in assuming that pluralism, rather than individualism or communitarianism, is the conception with which the theorist of justice should work.

As we saw in Chapter 4, Marx seems to be committed to the thesis that the circumstances of justice will eventually wither away and hence to the prediction that human society will eventually become so much more harmonious that neither individuals as individuals nor as members of communities will find it necessary to press (general) claims of right against one another. In that sense, Marx believes that neither individualism nor pluralism is a permanent feature of the human condition. However, there is no basis for the charge that Rawls' principles commit him to the permanence of pluralism. He only assumes pluralism in the circumstances of justice and this assumption is trivially true insofar as the circumstance of justice are those circumstances in which there is a need for principles for adjudicating claims among persons or groups, under conditions of (moderate) scarcity. In Section 10 of this chapter, I shall explore in some detail the disagreement between Rawls and Marx concerning the nature and persistence of the circumstances of justice. Even if it should turn out that Rawls has uncritically assumed that the circumstances of justice, like the Gospel's poor, will always be with us, this is quite different from the erroneous allegation that he assumes an individualistic (or pluralistic) conception of *human nature*.

5. Several of Rawls' critics on the left have argued that the characterization of the parties in the original position as desiring primary goods is not morally neutral among competing conceptions of the good because it insures that the principles chosen will undervalue or even rule out certain conceptions of the good, including Marx's, which place great importance on the values of community or solidarity.[64] It is important to understand what the objectors should not be construed as saying; namely, that something is amiss in Rawls' theory because his *principles of justice* are not neutral among competing conceptions of the good. Rawls would, of course, agree that the principles do exclude certain conceptions of the good, since principles of justice that ruled nothing out as unjust would be toothless. The objection, instead, is that Rawls has violated his own methodological assumptions that the *theory of the good* he employs in the original position is to be a "thin" theory, one that does not assume a substantive conception of human good or a normative ideal of the person, but rather is neutral among such conceptions or ideals.

Adina Schwartz has suggested that the preoccupation with wealth as a primary good embodies values that may be incompatible with the existence of genuine community in Marx's sense. However, the notion of wealth Rawls employs is so broad that this version of the objection seems less plausible than it might first appear. Rawls explains that, when he lists wealth as a primary good, he is defining it so broadly as to include virtually any socially recognized form of acccess to goods and services, including wealth in "non-individualistic" forms, such as access to public facilities such as libraries.[65] Perhaps a more convincing example would be this: some of the alleged primary goods, such as freedom of religion or freedom of expression, may in certain circumstances be incompatible with the uniformity of values and beliefs that are required for the flourishing or even the existence of certain forms of community. But if this is so, then the assumption that the parties in the original position place a preeminent value on these primary goods is not neutral among conceptions of the good.

Those who have raised this type of objection may have done so on the assumption that the parties are individual utility-maximizers who desire primary goods because they believe these things are useful regardless of what their conception of the good may be. I have argued in the preceding section that, most clearly in the later papers, Rawls sees the inadequacy of this characterization and describes the parties not as utility-maximizers but as autonomous choosers of ends—beings who have a highest-order interest in securing conditions for the critical formulation and revision of their conceptions of the good. I have also suggested that this characterization implies a different definition of primary goods: they are to be understood as being attractive not only because they are flexible assets for the successful pursuit of a wide range of conceptions of the good, but also because they provide conditions for the critical formulation and revision of conceptions of the good. This second feature is especially plausible in the case of freedom of religion and freedom of expression. On this characterization, Rawls is *not* committed to the thesis, which Rawls' critics have correctly attacked, that the primary goods are useful for or even compatible with *all* coherent conceptions of the good.

However, this shift in the characterization of the parties and in the definition of primary goods threatens to confirm rather than rebut the charge that the parties' preference for primary goods is not based on a thin, morally neutral theory of the good. For now Rawls' critics will complain that the Kantian conception of persons as autonomous choosers of ends which Rawls emphasizes in the later papers clearly is a substantive conception of human good or a normative ideal of the person—and that its adoption arbitrarily excludes competing conceptions or ideals.

Rawls might, of course, reply that the adoption of this conception of the good or ideal of the person is not arbitrary because it is the one that best matches our considered judgments about the appropriate conditions for choosing principles of justice. Those who feel the attraction of competing conceptions of the good or ideals of the person will not, however, find this convincing since they will sincerely protest that their considered judgments are quite different.

There is another, much more ambitious reply that Rawls might make. He might argue that the conception of persons as autonomous choosers of ends is an element of, or is at least supported by, the correct theory of *rationality*.[66] If this connection with rationality could be made out, then Rawls could argue that though the characterization of the parties is not neutral among competing conceptions of the good, that

144 MARX AND RAWLS

characterization is not itself based upon the arbitrary adoption of one conception of the good among others. A theory of rationality rich enough to support the claim that rational persons have a highest-order interest in critically formulating and revising their conceptions of the good would far exceed the thin economic conception of rationality with which Rawls claims to be operating in *A Theory of Justice*. So far, at least, Rawls has not taken up the task of providing a broader theory of rationality, but unless he does it appears that his contractual argument for principles of justice will rest ultimately upon an unsupported normative ideal of the person or an unsupported conception of human good.

The attempt to develop a richer theory of rationality must come to grips with a further Marxian objection. There is the problem that different individuals or classes may have irreconcilably different ideas about what is rational. But an even deeper difficulty becomes apparent if we take seriously the Marxian thesis that conceptions of rationality are historically limited social products.

The force of this potentially grave objection, however, is difficult to assess unless the historicist thesis about conceptions of rationality is clarified and supported. Further, even if the thesis is granted, its implications are not clear, since if all conceptions of rationality are historically limited it does not seem to be a criticism of a particular conception to point this out, unless the conception is being applied beyond its appropriate historical range. If the Marxian can show that the enriched Rawlsian conception of rationality is becoming as obsolete as the society which engendered it gives way to a new society with its own distinctive conception of rationality, this would render the Rawlsian conception of rationality useless as a basis for principles of justice intended to apply to future social arrangements. But as we saw in Chapter 5, Marx did not develop a socialist or communist conception of rationality; nor did he provide an explanation of just how such a new conception comes to replace the old one. This much, however, does seem clear: if the richer conception of rationality which Rawls' theory requires is a historically limited one, then it cannot serve as the basis for principles of justice unless the range of application of those principles is correspondingly limited. In Section 9, when we explore other versions of the objection that Rawls' principles are of much more restricted application than he claims, we shall see that though Rawls does recognize some limitations on the scope of his principles he does not consider those which arise from the choice of a particular conception of rationality.

In its most general form, the objection I have been exploring in this section is not peculiarly Marxian. But as both Teitleman and Schwartz suggest, Marx's theory of ideology can be used to deepen the objection by providing an explanation of why a theorist in a capitalist society might be expected to rely tacitly upon a normative ideal of the person or a conception of human good that excludes or undervalues communitarian ideals, while purporting to use an uncontroversially "thin," "morally neutral," theory of the good.

6. Rawls distinguishes between two tasks which his theory of justice is to perform: it must enable us to ascertain what the principles of an ideally just society are and it must also provide a basis for what he calls the Natural Duty of Justice, the obligation to promote institutions which satisfy the principles of justice, at least where we can do so without excessive costs to ourselves. Richard Miller has argued that if certain Marxian claims about the extent of class conflict are correct, Rawls has failed in the second task even if he succeeds in the first.[67]

Miller argues very plausibly that Rawls is committed to the claim that both the correct principles of justice for an ideally just society and the commitment or obligation to promote those principles in less than ideal circumstances are supposed to emerge *from the hypothetical contract in the original position*. Miller's objection relies upon Rawls' assertion that the parties in the original position will know the general facts about society, though the veil of ignorance precludes them from knowing a host of particular facts. Thus the parties will know, if Marx's hypotheses are correct, that all nonprimitive societies have been class-divided, that the interests of the ruling class are opposed to those of the ruled class, and that members of the ruling class characteristically have great needs for wealth and power. According to Miller, if the parties in the original position believe these to be general facts about society, they will realize that they may turn out to be members of a ruling class. Consequently, they will not be able to commit themselves to promoting the Difference Principle in less than ideal circumstances, because this might be incompatible with the satisfaction of their greater (and distorted, we would say) needs.

If Marxist social theory is right [in particular, if members of the ruling classes have great needs for wealth and power], at least when applied to some societies, someone in the original position would foresee that the difference principle may be intolerable for him if he turns out to be a typical member of a dominant exploitative class. Thus he would not accept, as grounds for a commitment to help realize the difference principle, an argument that this commitment, unlike its rivals, will be one he can live up to, no matter what social position he turns out to occupy.[68]

Miller deepens the objection by suggesting that the parties' knowledge that most (or even some) societies include a dominant class with exhorbitant needs would preclude their commitment to not only the Difference Principle but any competing principle as well.[69] The idea is that if Marx's thesis of the fundamental incompatibility of class interests states one of the general facts known by the parties, then no commitment to support a principle for the distribution of wealth and power (in unjust societies) will emerge. The parties will realize that what they can accept if they turn out to be members of the dominant class in an unjust society will be unacceptable to them if they turn out to be members of the dominated class and *vice versa*. So consideration of what Rawls calls the strains of commitment makes the contractual derivation of a duty to support justice in unjust circumstances impossible, in spite of the fact that the parties do not know which class they belong to.

This objection, however, seems to rest on a misunderstanding of the form which Rawls' ideal contractualist argument for the duty to support the Difference Principle should take. The argument would presumably go like this. The parties in the original position assess those strains of commitment to promoting the Difference Principle in non-ideal circumstances that would be incurred by individuals occupying the various representative social positions, *from the perspective of the attitude toward primary goods attributed to the parties, not from the perspective of the attitudes that persons actually occupying those various positions would have*. For it must be recalled that Rawls' characterization of the parties is supposed to play a crucial and ineliminable role in the contractualist approach, both in the task of ascertaining the principles of justice for an ideally just society and in the task of deriving a commitment to support justice in less than ideal circumstances. Miller seems to overlook this fact insofar as he assumes that what is relevant to assessing the strains of commitment to promoting the Difference Principle in unjust societies depends upon the actual needs and attitudes of persons occupying the various social positions.

According to the interpretation of Rawls I am advancing, the parties reason that *they*, having the preference they have for primary goods and having a highest-order interest in forming and revising their conceptions of the good in conditions that are free, would find the strains of commitment to promoting the Difference Principle acceptable when compared to the strains of commitment to the alternative principles they are to consider, regardless of which social position they should find themselves in. A party in the original position is to consider, for instance, whether he or she—having the attitudes Rawls attributes to the parties—could fulfill the obligation to promote satisfaction of the Difference Principle in an exploitative capitalist society, should he or she turn out to be a member of the ruling class. But a party in the original position must also consider the strains of commitment of promoting the Difference Principle in capitalist society, should he or she turn out to be a member of the exploited proletarian class. In both cases, the strains of commitment are to be assessed from the perspective of the attitude or preferences, not of an actual proletarian or capitalist, but rather of the parties as Rawls describes them, were they to find their access to primary goods and hence their opportunities for living the life of an autonomous chooser of ends limited by the various social positions. What is important for assessing the strains of commitment, then, is whether a person who conceives himself as an autonomous chooser of ends, and who values primary goods as extremely important for that reason, would find it possible to support the Difference Principle.

At one point in his argument, Miller does acknowledge an element of Rawls' characterization of the parties, or rather what Rawls takes to be a consequence of that characterization: their unwillingness to risk a guaranteed minimum of primary goods for the possibility of gains in primary goods beyond that minimum. But Miller contends that this conservative attitude is inappropriate once the parties consider the possibility that they may turn out to be members of a ruling class, since such individuals would not be satisifed with the minimum guaranteed by the Difference Principle. This argument, however, is again based on a failure to appreciate the fundamental role which the characterization of the parties plays in Rawls' theory. As we have already seen, Rawls makes it clear, at least in the later papers, that the conservative attitude toward risk is supposed to be a consequence of the parties highest-order interest in securing social conditions required by an autonomous chooser of ends. But if this is so, then whether actual members of an exploitative ruling class have this conservative attitude is quite irrelevant to the questions of whether the parties—who do conceive themselves as autonomous choosers of ends—would commit themselves to promoting the Difference Principle.

On my interpretation, Rawls would argue that the characterization of the parties as having this highest-order interest does imply a conservative attitude toward risking the conditions most conducive toward fulfilling this interest, and that granted that they have this attitude the parties would be more concerned to avoid a social order in which they might turn out to be exploited than to have a chance at being exploiters. Whether or not this argument is convincing, it is not vulnerable to Miller's objection because it is quite compatible with the parties having knowledge of the hypotheses about conflicting class interests and needs that Miller attributes to Marx. One indication that Miller's objection is based on a misinterpretation of Rawls is that on his reading of the strains of commitment argument the characterization of the *parties'* preferences (as autonomous choosers of ends) simply drops out of the picture—it plays no role in the argument.

However, this way of avoiding Miller's objection comes at a price. The gap between the characterization of the parties as autonomous choosers of ends and the actual features of members of an unjust society raises serious problems about whether enough real people will be sufficiently motivated to promote the Difference Principle where it is not already satisfied. In other words, even if, contrary to Miller, Rawls' ideal contract does generate a duty to promote justice, there remains the question of whether enough people will act on that duty. I will address this important objection later (in Section 7). I mention it here only to emphasize that it is distinct from Miller's and does not rest upon a misunderstanding of the role which the characterization of the parties is supposed to play in Rawls' ideal contractualism.

7. Perhaps an equally serious Marxian objection to Rawls is the charge that his theory is utopian: it includes no adequate account of

how the transition from our unjust society to a Rawlsian well-ordered society will or even can be made.[70] So far as Rawls provides even the barest elements of such an account, his approach is "idealistic"—it relies exclusively upon the individual's sense of justice, ignoring the dominant influence of material interests and, above all, of class interests. Marx's scathing criticism of utopian socialists, who rely on the motivating power of moral ideals, applies with undiminished force to Rawls.

Before exploring this objection further, I should like to note that its force depends in part on whether competing theories are also vulnerable to the charge that they lack an adequate theory of transition, including a plausible account of motivation for social change. In Chapter 5, I argued that Marx's claims to a unique and workable solution to the problem of transition, what I call his simple rational interest theory of motivation, may be ill-founded. Once it is admitted that Marx's own theory of the transition to communism is defective or at least seriously incomplete and may even need to be supplemented by an account which assigns a major motivational role to moral principles, the force of the Marxian objection that Rawls' theory is utopian and idealistic may be significantly diminished. Nonetheless, even if Marx also failed to provide it, it seems reasonable to require that a theory of justice or of the ideal society should include, or be supplemented by, a theory of transition. We cannot simply dismiss the charge against Rawls by noting that it may also apply against Marx.

The Marxian could argue that even if our class interests do not prevent us from performing the feat of abstraction required by the veil of ignorance and from working through the argument to Rawls' principles, there is no reason to believe that our sense of justice will be strong enough to overcome our allegiance to the existing order, especially if we profit greatly from its injustices. The occasions on which we soberly adopt the perspective of the original position will be like those ecstatic spiritual episodes that occur when the *bourgeois* briefly becomes a *citoyen* as he steps into that holy of holies, the voting booth.[71] Unfortunately, as with transubstantiation, everything will still look and taste the same, in spite of an alleged miraculous inner metamorphosis. Even if we acknowledge that Rawls' principles would be chosen by beings concerned to express their nature as free and equal moral beings, the motivational structure imposed by our social position will continue to govern our conduct. Rawls provides neither a theory of moral education nor a theory of how socio-economic transformations will produce, or at least make possible, the needed motivational shift.

It is important to note that the force of this objection does not depend upon whether one adopts a "materialist" theory of the source of social change, and in particular, of the motivation for social change. One need not require that Rawls provide an account of how changes in the "material base" produce changes in the "ideological superstructure." Instead, the objection can be formulated in terms of Rawls' broader, more cautious notion of the *basic structure*. Rawls' own emphasis on how our interests and even our deepest values are shaped and regulated by the basic structure demands an account of how the sense of justice can become an effective force for social change.

An adequate theory of transition would include two main components: (a) a descriptive component, including a theory of motivation that at least specifies the conditions under which a transition to the just society is possible and (b) a normative theory that specifies what we ought to do and what we may or may not do to achieve the transition. Rawls' theory at present lacks the first component and includes only the beginnings of the second. The lexical priority of liberty does place moral restrictions on how we may strive for a just society, but these restrictions are only operative after an *unspecified* threshold of material well-being and political culture has been reached, since it is only then that the priority of liberty obtains. Similarly, the lexical priority of fair equality of opportunity places moral restrictions on the transition toward a just society only after the requirements of the Principle of Greatest Equal Liberty have been fully satisfied. The only other normative principle for transition which Rawls articulates is the contentless Principle of the Natural Duty of Justice, which says simply that we are to help establish and preserve just institutions, at least if we can do so without great cost to ourselves.

Once we recall that Rawls' principles of justice are presented, not as normative principles which apply in any *direct* way to the transition to the well-ordered society, but rather as principles for the well-ordered society itself, a surprising result emerges. The very feature that makes Rawls' view vulnerable to the charge of utopianism, namely, the lack of a developed theory of transition, tends to weaken another standard Marxian objection. Marxians often charge that the liberal's priority on civil and political rights, especially the right of free speech and the right to vote, can serve as a barrier to the revolutionary transformation of society because it may be necessary to violate these rights temporarily, during the transition to a classless society. But because Rawls lacks a developed theory of transition, he is not explicitly committed to a well-defined prohibition on the abridgment of civil and political rights. Indeed Rawls' condition on the priority of his first principle explicitly recognizes that such abridgement may be necessary, while only stating in an extremely vague way the circumstances under which it may be abridged.

8. Rawls' theory appears to share with traditional liberal theories a simple assumption which Marx relentlessly attacked: the assumption that civil and political equality is compatible with significant socio-economic inequality. This dogma seems to be reflected in Rawls' distinction between the Principle of Greatest Equal Liberty and the Difference Principle. While the former requires strict equality of civil and political rights, the latter permits socio-economic inequalities, so long

as they maximize the worst-off's prospects of certain social primary goods. As we saw in our discussion of his internal criticisms of capitalism (in Chapter 4), Marx emphasized the limitations of political emancipation by noting that even where all possessed equal civil and political rights, inequalities in wealth and power produce severe inequalities in the effectiveness with which different individuals can exercise those equal rights. Individuals with greater wealth and the power it brings can exercise their rights of free speech and political participation much more effectively than others, even without recourse to illegal acts such as coercion, bribery, or election fraud. It seems that Rawls' theory, by sharply distinguishing between equal civil and political rights and socio-economic inequalities, and by placing an absolute priority on the former while allowing the latter, may incorporate the same defect which Marx thought characteristic of liberal theories in general.

Norman Daniels has made a serious and penetrating attempt to apply this Marxian criticism to Rawls' theory.[72] According to Daniels, once we take seriously what Marx calls the limitations of political emancipation, we must conclude that there may be a fundamental incompatibility between Rawls' Principle of Greatest Equal Liberty and his Difference Principle. The socio-economic inequalities allowed by the Difference Principle may not be compatible with the equal liberty required by Rawls' first principle. Daniels then suggests that Rawls introduces the distinction between liberty and worth of liberty in an attempt to render compatible the incompatible.[73]

The worth of a liberty L (or freedom F) to a person P, according to Rawls is "proportionate to [his] capacity to advance [his] . . . ends within the framework the system defines."[74] The system in question is the complex of institutions that establish a definite set of rights understood as legally guaranteed freedoms. Though Rawls is not always explicit about this, when he refers to freedom of speech or political liberty, he means the legally guaranteed freedom to engage in certain activities without being interfered with in certain ways. Consequently, I shall understand his distinction between liberty and worth of liberty in the context of his discussion of the lexical priority of his first principle, as a distinction between having a legal right R to a liberty L or a freedom F and the effectiveness with which one can exercise that right in the pursuit of one's ends whatever they happen to be.

According to Daniels, Rawls invokes the distinction between equal rights and unequal effectiveness in the exercise of rights in an unsuccessful attempt to "circumvent the problem" of the incompatibility of his first principle and the Difference Principle.[75] Rawls' idea, says Daniels, is that "Unequal wealth and unequal power no longer cause inequality of liberty itself [i.e., of civil and political rights], only inequality in the worth of liberty [i.e., in the effectiveness with which the rights can be exercised]. . . ."[76]

Daniels then shows that this strategy fails by arguing that the very reasons which, according to Rawls, lead the parties in the original position to choose the principles of equal civil and political rights would be equally strong reasons for not allowing inequalities in the effectiveness of the exercise of those rights.

There are two features of Rawls' theory which may provide some of the material for an effective response to Daniels' objection. First, it appears that Daniels has underestimated the significance of the fact that Rawls' lexical priority on equal civil and political rights is *conditional*. Rawls states that

[T]he idea underlying the lexical ordering is that *if the parties assume that their basic liberties* [i.e., the civil and political rights specified by the first principle] *can be effectively exercised*, they will not exchange a lesser liberty [i.e., a less extensive system of civil and political rights] for an improvement in economic well-being. *It is only when social conditions do not allow the effective establishment of these rights* that one can concede their limitation; and these *restrictions can be granted only to the extent that they are necessary to prepare the way for a free society.* . . .[77] (emphasis added)

What this passage suggests is that, strictly speaking, the parties do not choose a principle of equal civil and political rights. Instead, they choose to accord lexical priority to civil and political rights *granted* that conditions permit the effective exercise of those rights, while making a commitment to strive for the establishment of those conditions. Hence resources for a reply to the problem of the disparity between equal rights and inequalities in the conditions for their effective exercise are already built into the argument for the priority of the first principle, though as we noted in the preceding section there is the serious difficulty of the vagueness of Rawls' characterization of the conditions for priority.

It is true that Rawls does not say that the parties would choose, as the condition on lexical priority, the requirement that rights can be exercised with strictly *equal* effectiveness by all, but in fact this more stringent condition may be implausible. For one thing, whether different individuals can exercise their rights with *equal* effectiveness (i.e., whether their rights will be of equal worth) will depend in part upon what their respective conceptions of the good are and upon the abilities and other personal characteristics of the individuals in question. In other words, whether a given right will be of equal effectiveness or worth for different individuals will depend upon many different factors, some of which it is neither possible nor desirable to subject to social control or regulation. Consequently, the goal of *equal* effectiveness (or worth) is unattainable and inappropriate and likely to encourage serious infringements of liberty. Instead, what is needed is an explanation of what counts as unacceptable inequalities on effectiveness or worth, and this may be what Rawls is gesturing towards in the phrase "fair worth."

On the other hand, the notion that equal civil and political rights have lexical priority only when they can be "effectively" exercised or have a "fair value" for all is vague, and the question of the degree or range of acceptable inequalities in effectiveness or worth must sooner or later be faced. Nonetheless, it at least has the virtue of leaving open the possibility that at some level short of strictly equal effectiveness it may be reasonable to forgo further increases toward equal effectiveness for the sake of greater socio-economic gains of the sort covered by the Difference Principle.

A second reply to Daniels would be based on Rawls' description of the functions of the distribution branch of his model for the implementation of his principles. Among these functions are various taxation measures and "adjustments in the rights of property" for "*preventing concentrations of power detrimental to the fair value of political liberty . . .*" (emphasis added).[78]

Rawls then notes that the appropriate policies for maintaining the "fair value" of political liberty would include restrictions on rights of bequest and inheritance and perhaps a scheme of progressive taxation. Though again he fails to clarify further the notion of the fair worth or value of political liberty it seems clear enough that he is attempting to provide materials for a solution to the problem Daniels raises without espousing the implausible goal of *equal* effectiveness in the exercise of political rights.

It may be, then, that Rawls' condition on the priority of the first principle and his remarks about the need for property rights restrictions to prevent concentrations of power can be developed into an effective reply to the Marxian objection that Rawls, like other liberal theorists, has inflated the importance of civil and political rights without attending to the socio-economic conditions of their effective exercise. But even if these Rawlsian replies can be successfully developed, Daniels' argument still establishes an important and surprising conclusion. Rawls is wrong in assuming, as he seems to, that the Difference Principle will require the most significant restrictions on inequalities of wealth and power. Instead, the strongest egalitarian thrust of Rawls' theory may come from the first principle or rather from the commitment to establish the conditions in which that principle enjoys lexical priority. If, as a matter of empirical fact, the effective exercise of equal civil and political rights is incompatible with inequalities of wealth and power which would otherwise be allowed by the Difference Principle, then the Difference Principle may never come into play.

We have here yet another instance where it is crucial to distinguish between what Rawls' theory commits him to and how he thinks his principles would apply, granted his empirical judgments about society. It appears that even if Rawls has underestimated what will be required for the effectiveness of political rights, the fact that his theory acknowledges that the effectiveness and hence the value of such rights depends upon socio-economic factors is extremely important. It leaves the door open for attempts to develop Rawls' theory in ways that avoid what Marxians rightly take to be a major defect of liberal political theory.

9. Regardless of whether Rawls' theory rests upon a historically limited conception of rationality, Marxian social theory provides another challenge to the scope of Rawls' principles. Though he sometimes seems to be concerned only with articulating "our" sense of justice,[79] Rawls elsewhere claims to be presenting universally valid principles of justice.[80] But Marx's analysis of the relationship between the material base and the ideological superstructure shows that there can be no universally valid principles of justice, for two related reasons.

(i) First, since a given conception of justice only arises with and serves as an ideological support for a particular mode of production, and since modes of production are transient historical products, any given conception of justice will not even be available to all persons, or even to all rational persons, in all societies at all times. It is absurd to say, for example, that the lack of an equal right to free speech was an injustice of Aztec society or that Alexander the Great violated a principle of justice by failing to establish a system that maximized the prospects of the worst-off. The claim that certain principles are universally valid implies that it is possible for at least some persons in any given society to at least try to act in accordance with them. But it is clearly not possible for persons even to try to act in accordance with a given set of principles of justice if those principles are, due to the historical limits of their situation, beyond the comprehension of those persons. Yet for any given set of principles of justice, including Rawls', there will be some societies in which those principles will not even be available for consideration, much less for adoption. Consequently, Rawls' claim to have provided a universally valid theory of justice is false.

Indeed the problem for Rawls goes even deeper. The very idea that principles of justice are objects of human *choice*—an idea fundamental to Rawls' whole approach—would be incomprehensible to members of more traditional societies which preceded capitalism. In such societies, what Rawls calls the basic structure is seen as a part of the natural or divine order—unalterable and beyond human manipulation. To such persons, the idea of choosing principles for the basic structure would make as little sense as the notion of choosing the laws of celestial mechanics would to us. Moreover, for persons living in precapitalist societies, the notion of an overriding commitment to be a critical chooser of ends who takes responsibility for his own conception of the good and for his fundamental values would be equally alien.

This first reason for rejecting Rawls' claim of universality can be met if a distinction is granted. We can distinguish between two ways in which a principle of justice *J* could be said to be valid for a given society *S*.

a) *J* is valid for *S* only if it is psychologically possible for persons in *S* to understand *J* and at least consider it as a normative principle for regulating their interactions or, more generally for regulating the institutions of their society.

b) *J* is valid for *S* only if *J* can be coherently used to evaluate the interactions or institutions in *S* by those who understand *J* and know the relevant facts for applying it to *S*.

A principle of justice could fail to satisfy condition (a) and yet satisfy condition (b). There seems to be nothing incoherent in saying, for example, that slavery in ancient Greece was unjust, even if it is the case the slaveholders in ancient Greece were incapable of comprehending a principle of justice which required equal rights for both "barbarians" and Greeks. If, for reasons beyond their control, the members of a given society would be incapable of comprehending or taking seriously certain principles of justice, then it may be incorrect to fault them for violations of that principle. Nonetheless, there seems to be nothing wrong with using a normative principle to criticize or evaluate a society while acknowledging that it may be inappropriate to use that principle as a criterion for assigning moral blame to persons in that society.

Indeed Marx himself seems to employ the distinction in question when he uses the non-juridical, normative ideal of autonomous, socially integrated communist man to criticize earlier class-divided societies. Marx thinks it appropriate to condemn the religious alienation of the Middle Ages and the exploitation of ancient slavery without assigning blame to *individuals* in such societies and without implying that *they* should have attempted to overcome alienation and end exploitation.

(ii) The second form of the objection is not so easily answered. It turns on the thesis that any given conception of justice, including Rawls' suffers the limitations of specialization: any conception of justice is adapted to and only adapted to a particular mode of production. This adaptation consists in its playing a certain role which contributes to the functioning of the distinctive mode of production in question. For example, the conception of justice which was dominant in the capitalism of Marx's day could serve only to explain and justify the distinctive social institutions of that mode of production, in particular, the all-important institution of wage-labor. There can be no nontrivial conception of justice that applies to all societies because there is no one conception that could play the needed justifying role in all societies.

Perhaps this Marxian objection can be made more concrete by focusing on features of Rawls' principles which might be thought to be inapplicable to some societies. Michael Teitleman has attacked the universality of Rawls' principles by arguing that some of the primary goods those principles cover are valuable only in certain sorts of societies. In applying this objection to the Difference Principle, Teitleman notes that "wealth and power may be essential for the attainment of a person's ends in some kinds of societies but not in others."[81] Similarly, the Marxian might argue that Rawls' first principle cannot be valid for all societies since some societies lack the political and legal institutions which are presupposed by the right to political participation and the various due process rights which Rawls includes under the first principle.

At this point the Rawlsian might reply that the objection is based on a series of misinterpretations. First, as we saw earlier, Rawls points out in "Fairness to Goodness," that the charge that the Difference Principle reveals a culturally bound preoccupation with wealth and power is unfounded because wealth as a primary good is to be understood in the broadest sense possible, which is not restricted to "individualistic" socially recognized access to goods and services.

Further, Rawls suggests that those who charge that the Difference Principle is of limited validity may be confusing the broad concept of wealth exhibited above with the comparative notion of being wealthy. The desire to be wealthy in the sense of enjoying a relative advantage of buying power over others may be a temporally parochial aspiration, but that is irrelevant since the Difference Principle does not range over prospects of being wealthy anyway. Similarly, even if Hobbes and others wrongly assumed that the desire for power over others is a feature of human nature rather than of bourgeois man, this objection cannot be raised against Rawls' view. For as Rawls points out in "Fairness to Goodness," the Difference Principle takes into account powers as in "powers and opportunities" or "powers and preroga-tives," where the term merely denotes capacities which can serve as means toward fulfilling one's plans, not the narrower capacity to force one's will upon others.[82]

The charge that Rawls' first principle cannot be universally valid because some of the rights it specifies presuppose institutions not present in all societies seems also to be based on a misinterpretation. Rawls does not claim that the Principle of Greatest Equal Liberty is universally valid. His condition on the priority of that principle explic-itly recognizes that some societies may lack the requisite conditions for a system of equal civil and political rights. In such circumstances, justice only requires that efforts be made to create conditions in which the equal rights can be effectively exercised.

There is, however, a deeper reason to reject the charge that Rawls has claimed universal validity for principles which are in fact at best valid only for certain societies in certain circumstances. This charge ignores Rawls' distinction between societies which are in the circum-stances of justice and those which are not. Rawls' acknowledgement that principles of justice are only needed in certain circumstances clearly implies that no principles of justice are universally valid for all possible societies, but at most only for all societies in the circumstances of justice. It is true that Rawls himself can be faulted for obscuring this important limitation on his principles when he declares that "justice is the first virtue of social institutions"[83] *simpliciter*, rather than "justice is the first virtue of social institutions in the circumstance of justice." Nonetheless, a charitable reading demands that we give Rawls credit for leaving open the possibility of human societies which, like Marx's communism, are beyond the circumstances of justice.

It appears, then, that taken strictly, the charge that Rawls makes a false claim of universality rests on a false presupposition. Rawls' view that the Principle of Greatest Equal Liberty is the first priority of justice only under certain social conditions and his recognition that the circumstances of justice may not be ineliminable features of human existence are explicit disclaimers of universal validity. In addition, attempts to show that specific features of Rawls' principles further restrict their applicability to a proper subset of the set of societies which exist in the circumstances of justice seem less than convincing. The primary goods covered by Rawls' principles are so broadly conceived that further argument is needed if the Marxian is to make good his claim that those principles can only be applied to evaluate some but not all societies in the circumstances of justice.

Nonetheless, even if Rawls acknowledges the possibility that the circumstances of justice may not obtain in all human societies, he apparently assumes without argument or discussion that all actual human societies existing now and in the foreseeable future are or will be in those circumstances. It is because of this assumption—which Rawls never examines—that he takes the major task of social philosophy to be the construction of a theory of justice. However, if Marx is correct in thinking that the circumstances of justice are approaching obsolescence and that obsession with questions of justice only impedes our progress toward a society of greatly increased abundance and harmony in which principles of justice are not required, then Rawls' assumption is far from innocuous. On the contrary, it serves ideological purposes by focusing our attention upon the insoluble problems of justice while blinding us to the possibility of changes in production which will dissolve them. The force of this version of the objection depends, of course, upon the plausibility of Marx's views about the obsolescence of justice. The bearing of these views on Rawls' project will be considered in more detail in the next and final section.

10. All of the previous Marxian objections except the last are compatible with the thesis that there is a distinctively Marxian theory of justice, as opposed to a Marxian critique of all theories of justice.[84] In that sense, they are not the most radical Marxian objections which could be raised against Rawls' theory. As I argued in Chapter 4, Marx's most radical criticisms are the following. (i) The need for principles of justice as basic prescriptive principles of social organization is symptomatic of deeper but remediable defects in the mode of production; once these defects are remedied through the emergence of the communist mode of production, the problem of justice will disappear. (ii) The problem of justice cannot be solved by the use of principles of justice: the very circumstances which give rise to the need for such principles ensure that they cannot do the job for which they are intended. (iii) Principles of justice will not play a major motivational role in the transitional period between capitalism and the society that will replace it. The success of the revolutionary struggle depends upon changes in the material base and the corresponding recognition on the part of proletarians that their own interests require the overthrow of the

system, not upon the motivational appeal of juridical concepts. At best internal criticisms of bourgeois principles of justice can prepare the way for self-interested proletarian action by sweeping aside the ideological support which such principles lend to the existing order. At worst, the appeal to principles of justice is confusing and devisive and obscures the radical character of the contrast between capitalism and communism.

In the following chapter, each of these three most radical Marxian objections against theories of justice in general will be examined in detail. I argue that none of them is, as it stands, persuasive. Here I will only sketch very briefly the main reasons for not accepting (i), (ii), and (iii) as sound criticisms of Rawls' theory.

The difficulty with (i) lies in its assumptions about the nature of the circumstances of justice. First, Marx apparently believes that reliance on principles of justice is necessary only because of egoistic interaction rooted in the conflict of classes over unnecessarily scarce resources. Second, he believes that scarcity will be greatly reduced with the abolition of classes and that egoistic strife will give way to communal harmony. Both of these claims are dubious at best. The first apparently ignores the fact that there can be conflicts of interest or of ideals, which, though nonegoistic, are nonetheless serious enough to require the use of principles of justice, even in the absence of class conflict. Even a society of perfect altruists or of perfect utilitarians may have throat-cutting disagreements over what the common good is or over the means by which the greatest happiness is to be obtained. Indeed Marx seems to ignore two key functions of conceptions of rights-claims which have no necessary connection with egoism whatsoever. In addition to serving as boundary lines between hostile egoists or as instruments of class-oppression, rights-claims can function (a) as constraints on our efforts to further the good of others (i.e., as constraints on paternalism) and (b) as restrictions on what may be done to maximize social welfare, or well-being in the aggregate. Rawls, in contrast, recognizes that the circumstances of justice presuppose neither egoism nor class-conflict.

It is also important to reemphasize briefly the dubiousness of Marx's assumptions about problems of scarcity. Even if a system of common control over the means of production proved more efficient than the current system, it is not clear problems of scarcity would be greatly diminished. If current needs for basic goods such as nourishment and shelter were met for all, there would still presumably be competition for time and resources needed for the pursuit of other ends, and such competition need not be egoistic. Medical research to lengthen and improve human life appears capable of absorbing almost limitless resources, as does space exploration, to take only two examples. Further, even if the members of society could at some given time reach accord on how to employ social resources without appeal to principles of rights, there is the matter of our obligations to future generations. Nothing Marx says indicates that he appreciated the enormously complex set of issues we now refer to as "the problem of justice to future generations," nor that he considered the plausible hypothesis that coping with them will require juridical conceptions.

To determine whether Rawls can meet objection (ii) and (iii), two questions must be answered. First, has Rawls provided principles which, if effectively implemented, would provide a nonarbitrary assignment of basic rights and duties and a fair adjudication of competing claims? Second, has Rawls provided an adequate account of how the principles of justice can be effectively implemented?

To answer the first question, nothing less than an exhaustive evaluation of Rawls' theory of the just society is required. Such a task cannot even be approximated here. It seems, however, that this much can be said. Rawls' well-ordered society may be immune to some of the most fundamental Marxian criticism of class-divided society. The satisfaction of the Difference Principle, which requires that the prospects of the worst-off be maximized, and of the Principle of Equality of Fair Opportunity, which requires fair access to offices and positions regardless of one's social position, seems incompatible with the exploitation of the majority by the minority. If the Difference Principle were interpreted narrowly to cover only income, one could argue that its satisfaction would not rule out exploitation of the worst-off group, just as Marx argued that increases in wages are compatible with continued exploitation. But once the Difference Principle is understood to range over a much broader set of social primary goods and is combined with the Principle of Equality of Fair Opportunity, this objection becomes much less plausible.[85] There remains, however, the problem discussed in Section 1: Rawls' claim that what the Difference Principle requires will depend on the traditions, institutions, social forces, and historical circumstances of the given society raises the possibility that existing injustices may play a disproportionate role in determining what would maximize the prospects of the worst-off.

The answer to the second question, as I argued earlier, is that so far Rawls has *not* provided anything like an adequate account of how the transition to the just society can be achieved. It is at this point that the requirement of feasibility draws the reluctant philosopher into the alien realm of empirical psychology and sociology. Though Rawls, more so than most Anglo-American philosophers, admits that the theorist of justice must rely on empirical generalizations about human motivation and political processes, he has so far not taken up the empirical burden of providing a theory of transition. If, as seems reasonable, the Marxian objection of utopianism expresses a basic feasibility condition for normative theories, then a key element in the case for Rawls' theory is presently missing.

IV

We have seen that Marx's more radical criticisms of conceptions of justice and rights are based on assumptions about the nature of conflict and on predictions of increased abundance and social harmony which Rawls does not espouse. In spite of these basic disagreements, there are striking similarities. To emphasize these, I shall now review briefly two Marxian themes at the core of Rawls' work. One is a particular conception of the relationship between autonomy and the formative influence which social institutions exert on individuals' beliefs and values. The other is a rejection of what Nozick calls historical principles of justice. Rawls brings these two Marxian themes together in his account of the importance of the basic structure.[86]

Like Marx, Rawls has a conception of the relationship between autonomy and the formative influence of social institutions that is neither determinism nor voluntarism but which combines elements of both. Rawls accepts Marx's thesis that the individual's beliefs and values depend upon the social framework which surrounds him and he insists that a theory of justice must somehow take this basic fact into account.

A theory of justice must take into account how the aims and aspirations of people are formed . . . . [T]he institutional form of society affects its members and determines in large part the kinds of persons they want to be as well as the kinds of persons they are. The social structure also limits people's ambitions and hopes in different ways; for they will with reason view themselves in part according to their position in it and take account of the means and opportunities they can realistically expect. So an economic regime, say, is not only an institutional scheme for satisfying existing desires and aspirations but a way of fashioning desires and aspirations in the future. More generally, the basic structure shapes the way the social system produces and reproduces over time a certain form of culture shared by persons with certain conceptions of the good.[87]

Both Marx and Rawls have suffered the onslaught of critics who take this view in isolation, ignore the qualifying phrase that individuals' ends depend "in part" on social forces, and then launch the accusation of socio-economic determinism. Both Marx and Rawls believe, however, that autonomy *can* be achieved—and only achieved—through conscious control over the social structures which shape our aims and aspirations. In Rawls' theory, we achieve autonomy through subjecting the basic structure to principles that would be chosen in the original position. For Marx, human beings attain full emancipation by collectively mastering the productive forces which form the foundation of their social environment.

A second fundamental Marxian theme emerges most clearly in Rawls' criticism of contemporary libertarian theory's emphasis on "historical" principles of justice. According to Nozick, the only valid principles of justice are historical principles.[88] These specify which holdings of goods are just and which are not. There are only two historical principles: (i) the principle of justice in acquisition (original appropriation) and (ii) the principle of justice in transfer. The first states that individuals are entitled to whatever unheld goods they appropriate, so long as the appropriation does not involve force or fraud and so long as, in some relevant sense yet to be determined, the appropriation does not "worsen" the situations of others.[89] The second principle states that individuals are entitled to whatever goods they receive as a result of voluntary transfers from others (exchanges or gifts) so long as those others are entitled to what they transfer.

Nozick then says that granted these and only these principles, justice can be defined recursively.

1) A person who acquires a holding in accordance with the principle of justice in acquisition is entitled to that holding.
2) A person who acquires a holding in accordance with the principle of justice in transfer, from someone entitled to the holding, is entitled to that holding.
3) No one is entitled to a holding except by (repeated) applications of (1) and (2).

The principles of justice in acquisition and transfer are said to be historical in that they make what is just or unjust depend on the historical sequence of appropriations and transfers that has actually occurred: "Whatever arises from a just situation by just steps is itself just."[90]

Rawls observes that according to this view "[t]he only way injustice is thought to arise is from deliberate violations of these principles or from error or ignorance of what they require and the like."[91] He then attacks this position for the same reasons that Marx attacked the view that the exchange between worker and capitalist is just because both parties enter it "voluntarily."

[S]uppose we begin with the initially attractive idea that social circumstances and people's relationships to one another should develop over time in accordance with free agreements fairly arrived at and fully honored. Straightaway we need an account of when agreements are free and the social circumstances under which they are reached are fair. In addition, while these conditions may be fair at an earlier time, the accumulated results of many separate and ostensibly fair agreements, together with social trends and historical contingencies, are likely in the course of time to alter citizens' relationships so that the conditions for free and fair agreements no longer hold. The role of the institutions that belong to the basic structure is to secure just background conditions against which the actions of individuals and associations take place. Unless this structure is appropriately regulated and adjusted, an initially just social process will eventually cease to be just, however free and fair particular transactions may look when viewed by themselves.[92]

It is true that Rawls rejects the exclusive concern with the sequence of individual transactions as an inadequate conception of justice, while Marx attacks it from the perspective of an ideal of human freedom and fulfillment that he tries strenuously to dissociate from the concept of justice. But inspite of this difference, both Marx and Rawls emphasize that historical principles of justice ignore the fact that the cumulative result of "free" individual transactions over time can be a social system which imposes intolerable limitations on individuals' opportunities for autonomous living.

As we have seen, some critics on the left have tended to view Rawls' work as simply another version of liberalism—a political theory which they believe to be irremediably defective. However, attempts to show that Rawls is vulnerable to the standard Marxian objections to liberalism, I have argued, are in some cases based on misunderstandings of Rawls' theory. In several prominent instances, those who assume that Rawls is in the thrall of liberal ideology have themselves been blind to the fact that Rawls' work incorporates basic Marxian themes.

Nonetheless, at least four of the Marxian criticisms considered above raise extremely serious problems for Rawls' theory: (1) the objection that Rawls' contractual derivation of principles of justice assumes one substantive conception of human good or one normative ideal of the person, arbitrarily excluding, among others, those which give preeminence to the Marxian virtues of community and solidarity; (2) the complaint that Rawls' theory is utopian because it lacks a theory of transition to the just society; (3) the charge that Rawls' system underestimates the dependence of civil and political equality upon economic equality; and (4) the objection that efforts to determine what arrangements would maximize the prospects of the worst-off will either require imponderable comparisons among indefinitely many alternatives or will be unduly constrained by existing inequalities. It is difficult at this point to know whether these objections, when elaborated in their most telling form, are fatal to Rawls' theory. What does seem clear enough is that Marx's thought presents a serious challenge to Rawls' system.[93]

7

Further Critical Conclusions

I

In the preceding chapters, I have articulated Marx's evaluative perspective and reconstructed his position on justice and rights, placing the latter within the framework of his response to Hegel, his theories of alienation and exploitation, and his theory of revolutionary motivation. I have argued that Marx is committed to a very radical position on rights and justice that includes three main theses: (i) conceptions of justice or of rights will not play a major motivational role in the revolutionary transition from capitalism to communism; (ii) communist society—the society of autonomous, socially integrated individuals—will not be a society in which (general) conceptions of rights or justice play any significant or major role in structuring social relationships; (iii) the circumstances which produce the need for conceptions of justice and rights are precisely those circumstances in which the demands of such conceptions cannot be adequately satisfied.

I also distinguished a less radical interpretation, which also enjoys considerable textual support, according to which Marx left open the possibility that conceptions of rights or justice will play an important role in communist society, and was concerned only to reject *bourgeois* conceptions of rights and justice and to make it clear that even if juridical conceptions emerge in communism they will not require coercive sanctions, and that they will play no major motivational role in achieving the transition to communism.

In Chapter 4, I opted for the radical interpretation, arguing that at least some of Marx's attacks are directed against what he takes to be the notions of rights and justice as such, not merely against bourgeois notions of justice and rights, nor merely against coercively backed rights. The task of evaluating Marx's critique of juridical concepts was begun in Chapter 6. There my strategy was to assess the power of Marx's critique by leveling it against what I believe to be the most comprehensive and plausible theory of justice available, Rawls' theory as it is expounded in *A Theory of Justice* and developed in several later papers. The main conclusion of that chapter was that while many of the objections that have been advanced against Rawls from a Marxian perspective are not cogent, Marx's work does provide material for several serious objections to which Rawls has not satisfactorily responded and which, if they can be answered at all, may require important changes in his theory. I shall argue in this chapter that Marx's views on both the radical and moderate interpretations, are vulnerable to serious objections, and that until these objections are answered by providing needed support for Marx's beliefs about the sources of social conflict, his critique of juridical conceptions will rest on precarious foundations.

II

According to the radical interpretation, Marx thought of rights exclusively as boundary markers which separate competing egoists in circumstances of avoidably severe scarcity, which absolve them of responsibility for each other's good, and which, through the coercive guarantees of the state, keep class conflict from erupting into outright war, while at the same time helping to preserve the dominant class's control over the means of production. Marx apparently thought that these are the defining functions of rights and hence that a conception of rights is needed only to cope with such egoistic conflict in class-divided societies. As we shall see shortly, he failed to consider the need for a different—and more attractive—conception of rights, grounded in a broader understanding of the sorts of conflicts which are to be dealt with by the invocation of rights and which admits the possibility that there are different rights in different socio-historical circumstances.

Setting aside the issue of what rights there are or of what rights there are in which circumstances, we must again consider the rather formal concept of a right discussed earlier. This concept, as we saw in Chapter 4, includes three key elements.

a) To claim something as a right is to demand it as one's due, as something one is entitled to, rather than to request it as something one desires; and the violation of a right constitutes an injury to the right-bearer, to whom apologies or compensation or excuses are owed.

b) Justified claims of right take precedence over mere considerations of welfare, whether social welfare or the welfare of the right-bearer him- or herself.

c) Rights may be backed by appropriate sanctions, such as peer pressure or public censure, or where necessary, by coercion (force or the threat of force).

Though Marx provides no explicit statements of the elements of this formal conception of rights—but instead concentrates on criticizing rights as boundary markers which separate egoists, provide a license for ignoring the plight of others, and preserve class dominance—he would not, I believe, disagree with the preceding three-part analysis of the concept. In the German tradition which nurtured Marx, along with Kant and Hegel, the first and third elements are generally recognized. The second element is present in Kant[1] and in the notion of a right to which Marx responded in his criticisms of Locke and in his denunciation of the rights of man as declared in the French and American Constitutions. Here rights are thought of as bases for claims by the individual against the state or society when they threaten to restrict the individual's freedom or appropriate his goods in the name of his own good or the common good. Further, our interpretation of Hegel's analysis of civil society indicates that he thought of rights, in particular the right to private property and the right to choose one's occupation, as taking precedence over other ends, such as the maximization of welfare or even objective freedom. Finally, as we saw in Chapter 4, Marx, like some others in the German tradition, though unlike Hegel, may have thought of the notion of rights as also implying strict universality, since he often attacked the claim that a given conception of rights is valid for all times and places. But, as we also saw, important elements of his attack are directed toward what he takes to be the function of rights and the historical circumstances in which they are needed, not just against the claim of strict universality.

Those who remain unconvinced that Marx held the radical thesis that communism will not rely upon rights may view the criticisms of the present chapter as directed toward the more moderate thesis that *coercively backed* rights are only needed in a society characterized by egoism and class divisions and will not be needed in the democratic form of social organization Marx calls communism.

It is important to emphasize that whether or not its attribution to Marx is plausible, even this more moderate view that coercive sanctions for rights are needed only to cope with egoism and class conflict is still a very strong generalization. The burden of proof, it seems, is on the Marxian who acknowledges that there may be important roles for rights-principles in communist society, but who contends that there will be no need for backing the rights (ultimately) with the threat of force. If rights may be needed to cope with problems that are not rooted in egoism and class struggle, then there is no reason to assume that the need for coercive sanctions for rights only arises because of egoism and class conflict. Whether coercive sanctions will be needed in situations not influenced by egoism or class struggle is an empirical question that cannot be answered in the absence of a confirmable theory capable of specifying the circumstances in which noncoercive sanctions will suffice. But as I noted earlier, Marx does not consider the roles that rights might play in coping with problems of coordination and conflict that do not presuppose egoism or class struggle, nor does he provide a theory of the conditions under which coercive sanctions are not needed. Nor does he sketch possible mechanisms of noncoer-

cive sanctions and address the question of the scope and limits of their
efficacy. What is needed is a theory of communist social organization
to explain why (general) rights-conceptions either will not be needed
or why, if they are needed, they will not require coercive sanctions.

Put most simply, the main defect of Marx's attack on rights is that he
fails to see that there can be a vital need for a concept which includes
elements (a), (b), and (c), even where egoism and class divisions are
not the only or even the main sources of conflict. The conditions which
make a concept embodying these three elements needed are not so
narrowly circumscribed as Marx assumed. There are at least five different types of functions that rights satisfying the formal concept could
serve which do not presuppose either egoism or class conflict. Further,
none of these functions presupposes that rights are strictly universal or
"eternal," i.e., valid for all times and conditions. Rights, understood
according to the formal concept, may serve:

   i) as constraints on democratic procedures (e.g., for the protection of
      minorities) or as guarantees of access to participation in democratic
      procedures;
  ii) as constraints on paternalism, i.e., as limits on when and how we may
      interfere with a person's liberty for the sake of benefiting that person
      (where benefit is understood as welfare or freedom or some combina-
      tion of these);
 iii) as constraints on what may be done (and how it may be done) to
      maximize social welfare, or some other specification of the common
      good, such as freedom;
 iv) as safeguards constraining the ways in which coercion or other penal-
      ties may be used in the provision of *public goods* (in the technical sense)
      and
  v) as a way of specifying the scope and limits of our obligations to provide
      for future generations.

As I noted earlier, whether or not rights-principles that serve these
functions will require coercive sanctions will depend upon particular
circumstances, and absent a developed theory of noncoercive social
coordination in communism, the assumption that these functions can
be successfully achieved without coercive sanctions is unwarranted.

(i) These functions of rights will be considered in Section III when we
examine Marx's conception of democratic social coordination.

(ii) Even if, in the tradition with which Marx was familiar, rights had
not been invoked as constraints on what we may do for the sake of
benefiting another, this is now recognized as one of the most important functions of the notion of a right. Yet the need for rights as
constraints on paternalism does not presuppose either egoism or class
divisions. It is true that paternalistic justifications often mask egoistic
behavior, and that the exploitation of one class by another is frequently
rationalized by paternalistic arguments. But even so there can be and
are many cases in which there is a need to restrict *genuinely* paternalistic behavior—cases in which the idea that there are things that may not

be done to or for a person even for his own good is extremely useful if not indispensable. Indeed in a society in which concern for others was much stronger than it is in our society, the threat to individual autonomy posed by paternalism, might be even greater. And whether such rights will require coercive sanctions will depend upon the efficacy of noncoercive alternatives.

A Marxian might reply that paternalism will not be a serious problem in communism because individuals will be concerned about each other *as autonomous agents* and hence will not restrict a person's freedom to maximize his welfare. This reply is unconvincing because it falsely assumes that paternalistic behavior is always directed toward maximizing a person's welfare, where welfare is interpreted so narrowly as to contrast with freedom or autonomy. In a Marxian communist society, or any society which values autonomy, the most dangerous instances of paternalism might be those in which an individual's freedom is restricted for the sake of enhancing his overall autonomy or his future autonomy. Indeed both Hegel's account of objective freedom and the Fascist theories of which it is an ancestor make it quite clear that persons' liberties may be gravely curtailed not just in the name of their welfare but also their freedom. Further, some of the most stringent and questionable interferences with the freedom of minors and the "mentally ill" in our society are allegedly imposed for the sake of their future autonomy. Perhaps even more importantly, persons may disagree both as to their understanding of the ideal of autonomy and as to what the pursuit of this ideal requires in particular circumstances, even where egoism and class conflict are not present.

(iii) According to Marx, social decisions in communism will aim at the common good (or, just as vaguely, at the good of society as a whole), where the common good is no longer opposed to the individual's good. Our analysis of Marx's vision of the unalienated society in Chapter 2 showed that the common good attained in communism is not to be identified with the maximization of social *welfare*, if the latter is distinguished from autonomy as Marx conceives it. For Marx believes, as we have seen, that a certain level of welfare, i.e., satisfaction of basic desires for food, shelter, etc., is a necessary condition of the sort of freedom which is fitting for human beings and which human beings will prefer, once they have achieved undistorted consciousness. In that sense, his conception of the common or social good is not identifiable with the utilitarian conception though it includes a welfare component.

Communism, Marx believes, will be a society in which "the development of each is a condition of the development of all." From this and similarly sketchy remarks, it is perhaps not clear whether Marx predicts a thorough-going congruence or harmony of interests or, more radically, an identity of interests. Since the former is the weaker and more plausible prediction, and since Marx does say that there will be individual differences in communism, it seems best to read him as

holding that in communism there will be such a congruence or harmony of interests that there will be no need for a notion of rights to
place juridical constraints on what may be done to maximize the
common good.

There is no compelling reason to believe that significant divergences
between the good of the individual and that of others or of society as a
whole occur only as the result of egoistic interaction under conditions
of class struggle for control over the means of production. Even in a ⌐
society of thorough-going altruists in which no group has exclusive
control over the means of production, there may be violent disagree-   *yes*
ments over what the common good is and over how it is to be achieved.
And insofar as different individuals support or even identify with
competing conceptions of the common good and of the path to its
attainment, the interests of individuals will conflict, even though the
conflict will not be egoistic or class-based.   ⌟

On the other hand, if we grant Marx the much stronger premise that
there will be an identity, rather than a harmony, of interests in communism, it would still not follow that there would be no need for rights-
principles understood as constraints upon what may be done to maximize the good which all share as their own good. For even here there
may be nonegoistic disagreements as to how to fill out the concrete
content of the shared good and on the best means of attaining it.
Whether or not juridical principles (or coercively backed juridical principles) would be needed to cope with such disagreements cannot be
determined *a priori*.

(iv) As I argued in Chapter 5, coercion may be needed for the
provision of public goods even in a society in which egoism and class
division are absent or minimal. Granted that coercion or other penalties may be needed in communism to secure certain public goods such
as population control or the conservation of natural resources or energy, there are two ways in which a conception of rights might prove
indispensible.

First, a conception of rights might be needed for delimiting the   *1.*
subset of public goods whose provision may be secured through coercion or other penalties. For any given society, the set of public goods
may be indefinitely large, and a blanket warrant for coercion or penalties to secure anything that qualifies as a public good would be extremely oppressive. In our own society we recognize that coercion may
be justified if it is necessary to secure public goods such as national
defense or conservation of natural resources, but that it is not
justifiable simply on the grounds that it is needed to provide what
some would regard as more frivolous public goods. Even where a
public goods problem is not rooted in egoism and class divisions, a
conception of rights could serve to pick out those public goods or those
sorts of public goods which are important enough to warrant the use of
coercion or penalties. A conception of rights could serve this function
in either of two ways. On the one hand, rights to be provided with

certain public goods could serve to identify those public goods for the sake of which coercion or other penalties may be employed and to exclude by omission those for which such measures may not be used. On the other hand, rights could specify the sorts of public goods for the sake of which individuals may *not* be coerced or otherwise penalized. In the first case, the rights would be conceived as rights of the individual to be provided with certain public goods, where the rights serve as warrants for coercion or penalties. In the second, the rights would be conceived as rights of individuals not to be coerced or penalized for the sake of securing certain public goods.

Second, a conception of rights might prove indispensable for specifying the appropriate types of coercion or other penalties and for defining the procedures by which these measures may be applied for the sake of providing public goods. In our own society, procedural rights are recognized as crucial safeguards on the use of institutionalized coercion. Granted, as Marx emphasized, that unrestricted authority to devise and apply coercion or other penalties is a key element of class domination, a system of rights constraining the use of coercion or penalties for the provision of public goods might prove indispensable both for achieving and for preserving the classlessness of Marx's ideal society.

It is open to the Marxian to argue, of course, either that public goods problems can only occur in egoistic, class-divided society or that communist man will inevitably develop ways of solving public goods problems without recourse to coercion or other penalties. In the light of the argument of Chapter 5, the former Marxian strategy is implausible because public goods problems can arise for nonegoistic, classless individuals, while the latter is unsupported due to Marx's lack of a theory of social coordination in communism.

(v) The task of specifying the scope and limits of our obligations to provide for future generations is one of the most awesome problems facing contemporary moral philosophers and policy makers. Some have held that our obligations to provide social resources for the future, or at least not to destroy essential natural resources, are to be understood as correlatives of rights of possible persons or future persons, or as rights which persons who will exist in the future will have when they exist. Others, contending that rights accrue only to existing persons, strive to purge the debate of talk about *rights* of future generations. If the former approach is chosen, then the need for a conception of rights, again without the presupposition of egoism or class conflict, is obvious. But even if we opt for the latter and eschew talk of rights of future generations, a conception of rights will still, it seems, be needed to specify the limits of our obligations to constrain our present use of resources. In other words, in a society which took the needs of future generations seriously, a conception of rights of the *present* generation would serve to place limits on the sacrifices which the present generation is required to make. And again, since the need for such limits does not seem to presuppose either egoism or class divisions the question of whether coercion will be needed to make these limits effective cannot be answered negatively by repeating the hypothesis that egoism and class divisions are no longer present. It seems, then, that regardless of which of the two main approaches to the problem of our obligations to provide for future generations is taken, rights may play an important role.

Marx's responses to the problems of overpopulation illustrate both his lack of appreciation for public goods problems and his failure to recognize the perplexing issue of our obligations to provide resources for future generations. His scattered comments on the Malthusian controversy indicate that he believed that the problem of scarcity due to overpopulation is an artifact of the egoism and irrationality of capitalism and hence will not arise in communism.[2]

Some recent analyses plausibly contend, however, that overpopulation is, or includes, a classic public goods problem and that as such its existence presupposes neither irrationality nor even egoism and is not limited to capitalist or even class-divided societies.[3] Since an adequate theory of our obligations to future generations will include a plausible analysis of and response to the problem of population control, Marx's unsupported assumption that communist society will be able to control population growth without the aid of juridical principles or coercion constitutes a serious and revealing lacuna in his social theory.

III

Marx emphasizes that communism will be a *democratic* form of social coordination; each will have an equal share in controlling the means of production. So a Marxian might reply to the objections of the preceding section that the transition to *democratic control* (or "common direction") of production will eliminate the circumstances of justice in general and render otiose the particular functions of juridical conceptions listed above in (i) through (v) or at least eliminate the need for coercively backed juridical principles. According to the more extreme interpretation of this claim, Marx predicts that democratic control will eliminate the need for coercion, and for juridical conceptions by *abolishing* scarcity. On the less extreme interpretation, democratic control will so greatly *diminish* scarcity, and along with it the conflict of interests, that neither juridical conceptions nor coercion will be needed.

If Marx espoused the extreme view, which I think he did not, then he not only misunderstood the concept of scarcity but also contradicted his own admission in *Critique of the Gotha Program* that even in the higher stage of communism there will be a need to save for future generations, since the need to save implies scarcity. The concept of scarcity relevant to the comparison of social systems and to the idea of the circumstances of justice is the most general one imaginable. Scarcity exists wherever the choice of one line of individual or joint action precludes the pursuit of alternatives which are in any way valued. In this sense, not only coal and oil and foodstuffs are scarce but also cooperative activity and time itself. Hence so long as an individual or a group must decide to use some natural and social resources rather than others in pursuit of some ends rather than others, there is scarcity. In a word, the need to choose implies scarcity. The question then is not whether communism will abolish scarcity, but rather whether the problems of scarcity in communism will be radically different.

It seems both more charitable and more fruitful, then, to interpret Marx as advancing the less extreme thesis that democratic control over the means of production will so greatly diminish the problems of scarcity and conflict that whatever interpersonal conflicts remain will not require coercion or the use of (general) juridical conceptions. On this reading, Marx is committed to the prediction not only that a democratic form of social cooperation will emerge but also that it will be much more productive and harmonious than capitalism. We have already noted the difficulty with the first part of this prediction—the fact that capitalism as Marx knew it has been replaced by new forms of collective minority control in the shape of state socialism, rather than by communism. Now let us examine the second part of the prediction in more detail.

It is important to emphasize its comparative nature. It will not do simply to say, as Marx and later Marxians often do, that capitalism is extremely *wasteful* and then conclude straightaway that the destruction of capitalism will bring an increase in productivity because this waste will be eliminated. When Marx and later Marxians condemn the wastefulness of capitalism they often point to certain recurrent economic upheavals, such as so-called underconsumption crises: people need goods but the goods perish or are destroyed or lie idle because those who need them lack the money to purchase them. It should be clear, however, that the mere existence of such phenomena does not itself show that capitalism is to be condemned for inefficiency or wastefulness. For it may not be possible to eliminate all such discrepancies between the supply of goods and the effective demand for them without producing a system less efficient overall in the long run. Whether or not it is possible is a question which must be answered by a detailed comparative economic analysis of the overall efficiency of alternative systems, not by an immediate inference from the existence of "wasteful" phenomena such as underconsumption crises. In other words, we must somehow compare the productivity or efficiency of *total systems over time*. Similarly, Marx's frequent charge that capitalism squanders human resources must be understood as an implicitly comparative claim about the inferiority of capitalism as a system relative to communism as a system. And again, unless the standard for comparison is a system which is at least attainable if not inevitable, these criticisms would be utopian according to Marx's own pejorative use of that term.

To show that capitalism is a wasteful or inefficient system of social coordination as compared to communism one must know quite a lot about communism *as a system of social coordination*. Yet as we have seen, Marx tells us remarkably little. And aside from the statement that it will be a system of democratic control of production, much of what he does say is extremely unhelpful in understanding the structure and work- ings of communism as a system of social coordination. To say that communism will be a society of socially integrated, creative, autono- mous producers tells us absolutely nothing about how a multiplicity of human actions will be coordinated in such a way as to achieve even the productivity of capitalism, much less a staggering increase in produc- tivity. Nor do such characterizations of communism explain how this gain in productivity is to be achieved and preserved without recourse to coercion or to juridical principles or to unacceptably oppresive informal sanctions of the sort which Marx attributed to primitive societies. It seems, then, that we are led to the conclusion that if there is support for Marx's comparative condemnation of capitalism as inefficient and for his prediction that communism will achieve greatly increased abundance and harmony and thereby transcend the circum- stances of justice, it must lie in his beliefs about the nature of demo- cratic control over the means of production.

Before we explore the question of whether Marx's writings provide material for a theory of democratic social coordination capable of supporting his complex critique of juridical concepts, it is important to understand clearly why such a *theory* is needed. It will not do for the Marxian to say that a harmonious and bountiful system of democratic social coordination will evolve simply because it must—i.e., because the continued existence of capitalism is incompatible with the preser- vation of civilized life. This reply overlooks the fact that capitalism is not the only form of nondemocratic control over the means of produc- tion, as we saw earlier. Further, it commits an evolutionist fallacy of the crudest sort. From the fact that the well-being or even the survival of a species requires certain changes it by no means follows that those changes will successfully be made.

Nor would it be helpful to pretend that no *theory* of democratic social coordination is needed because it is already sufficiently clear that highly efficient, noncoercive, non-juridical social coordination can be achieved through democratic procedures. On the contrary, there is a vast literature which demonstrates numerous difficulties of inefficiency and domination involved in even the most limited forms of democratic decision-making, while not even a rudimentary account of the democratic provision of all major goods and services is available.[4] Further, to say as Marx does in the *German Ideology* and the *Critique of the Gotha Program*, that communism will overcome the division of labor, makes the task more, rather than less, onerous granted Marx's own acknowledgment of the fact that the great gain in productivity in capitalism over preceding modes of production was due in large part to the development of the division of labor. The difficulty is that Marx's assumption that the communist individual will enjoy tremendous freedom and flexibility in choosing and scheduling his own particular activities greatly enhances the problems of efficiently coordinating large numbers of individuals' activities through the use of democratic, nonoppressive planning techniques, in the absence of even a limited role for the market as a coordinating device.

Marxians sometimes reply that the amazing flexibility and freedom of individual activity that Marx attributes to communism will be possible because "socially necessary production" will be reduced to a small part of the day's activities. The idea, roughly, is that when scientific, rational production techniques replace the irrational wastefulness of capitalism, the business of satisfying everyone's needs for food, shelter, etc. can be done very quickly, and that in the remainder of the time available individuals will be free to do virtually as they please when they please. This reply, however, begs the question. It assumes that there is available a Marxian theory of social coordination capable of supporting the claim that the new system will be so much more efficient than the old that those tasks requiring planned, large-scale cooperation can be successfully performed in a minimum of time (and that this reduction in the time required for participation in "socially necessary production" can be achieved without the use of juridical conceptions or at least without coercively backed juridical principles).

Perhaps the most promising place to look in Marx's writings for the materials for a theory of democratic social coordination capable of supporting his critique of juridical conceptions is in his discussion of the Paris Commune in *The Civil War in France*. Marx approvingly emphasized the following aims of the Commune, which he believed to be the prototype of the transitional socialist state: (1) the replacement of a standing army (as a separate coercive force) by the armed people; (2) universal suffrage; (3) unification of the executive and legislative in the "working body" of the Commune, and abolition of the judiciary as a separate, nonelective branch of government; (4) replacement of political officials by elected agents of the people, who are payed "workingmen's wages" and who are "responsible and revocable at short terms;"[5] and (5) "united cooperative societies [which] are to regulate national production upon a common plan. . . ."[6]

The Marxian who wishes to glean materials for a theory of democratic social coordination in communism from Marx's discussion of this list of goals must do so with caution. For it must be remembered that, for Marx, the main significance of the Commune and its aspirations was that he took it to be the harbinger of "the *political form* . . . under which to work out the emancipation of labor"[7] [emphasis added]. The Commune for Marx was not itself a small and incomplete version of the noncoercive, non-juridical, democratic form of social organization, he called communism. It was an instrument, ". . . a lever for uprooting the economical foundations upon which rests the existence of classes, and therefore of class-rule."[8] We cannot, therefore, assume that Marx believed that all or most of the features he focuses on would survive after this instrument for destroying class rule had done its job. It is only the fifth feature—the idea that cooperative societies of producers are to unite to regulate national production according to a common plan—that Marx explicitly identifies as a characteristic of *communism*, rather than as a feature of the transitional socialist political form.

The function of "the people in arms" is presumably to smash the state apparatus and to protect the revolution from the forces of reaction (as Lenin emphasized in *The State and Revolution*). There is no suggestion that this generalized coercive force is to play a role in communism itself, much less that it is to serve as a coordinating device for heightened productivity, whether through the enforcement of juridical principles or in some other way. It is more plausible to look to the ideas of universal participation in decision-making and the emphasis on arrangements to insure the accountability of those in positions of authority, as building blocks of a Marxian theory of democratic social coordination in communism.

It should be obvious, however, that Marx's brief and rather abstract remarks on these arrangements, even if they are taken as keys to understanding communism rather than as features of a stage of development that precedes it, do not provide adequate materials for a theory of democratic control over production capable of supporting Marx's claim that communism will bring heightened productivity, much less the stronger claim that this increase in productivity can be achieved without a significant role for juridical principles or coercion. To say that those in positions of authority are to be responsible and revocable tells us nothing about what sorts of positions of authority are needed for an efficient and non-oppressive democratic process of formulating and executing a comprehensive plan for the economy, nor how the existence of positions of authority is compatible with the freedom and flexibility of individual activity that Marx says will replace the current strictures of the division of labor. Moreover, the actual official positions of agents of the Commune which Marx lists are for the most part positions in a newly created political apparatus designed to cope with the peculiar predicament of a revolutionary movement in a city under seige. They are not constitutive elements of a new mode of production.

To say that, in communism, there will be a "non-political" analogue of universal suffrage conveys only the idea that everyone is to have access to the decision procedures for formulating and executing plans without saying anything at all about what those procedures are or how it is possible for there to be such universal participation without great costs in efficiency. Granted the background of a class society in which production is controlled by nonproducers, the statement that it will be the associated producers who regulate production has some import simply by way of contrast. But when applied to a classless society it is only the uninformative claim that everyone will participate in the process of regulation; unless the *forms* of association—the concrete social arrangements and procedures for participation—are specified. And it is important to note that the limited successes of democratic procedures in the Paris Commune are of little help here, since there was no attempt at democratic planning for the whole economy of that part of Paris that the Commune controlled, much less for the whole of the national economy.

It is not my aim to provide even the rudiments of a comparative analysis of democratic and nondemocratic systems for the allocation and distribution of goods and services in large-scale, industrial societies. Nonetheless, it is worth pondering for a moment how wide the gap is between Marx's sketches of communism as a form of democratic control over production and his reflections on the Commune, on the one hand, and his predictions about communism's increased harmony and abundance, on the other. To support these predictions, and the critique of juridical concepts that depends upon them, would require an elaborate theory of social coordination—a theory of the allocation and distribution of social and natural resources comparable in explanatory power to the market theory which Marx wholly rejected. In particular, such a theory would have to respond successfully to well-known objections concerning the enormous time and information costs of genuine, large-scale planning in the absence of a role for markets in pricing, where "pricing" is understood in the broadest sense, as any effective means for measuring the social costs of a possible allocation or distribution in lost opportunities.[9] Though some of these difficulties may be reduced under the mixed systems known as "market socialism," this does little to support Marx's predictions of increased abundance and harmony in communism and the consequent obsolescence of juridical principles and coercion. For even if we assume that such systems can achieve higher productivity than predominantly capitalistic systems, Marx's position is not thereby vindicated for the simple reason that all existing versions of "market socialism" rely upon massive coercive juridical structures, money, markets (both legal and "black"), and bureaucratic elites who enjoy a grossly disproportionate share of control over production.

Further, even if we possessed a theory of social coordination capable of supporting the prediction that democratic control would achieve levels of productivity hitherto undreamt of, this would still not be sufficient, since it would not follow that this gain in productivity could be achieved without a major role for juridical concepts in defining institutional roles, procedures, and procedural safeguards to prevent the accumulation of power in the hands of a minority. Neither Marx's reflections on the Commune nor his scattered characterizations of communism do much to support this much stronger claim about the stability of a democratic system.

It may be that Marx failed to take seriously the need for rights-principles for defining positions of authority and for specifying procedures and procedural safeguards because he assumed that dangerous concentrations of power arise only from egoism or where class interests already exist. Yet in his early critique of bureaucracy Marx himself acknowledges that those in positions of authority tend to develop a special interest in preserving and augmenting their power. He did not explore the possibility that this phenomenon was not limited to bureaucracies operating within the framework of a society based on private (individualistic) property.[10] Unlike Plato and Rousseau, Marx never addressed the problem of how to prevent the ideal society from degenerating. Consequently he never considered the plausible hypothesis that procedural or role-defining juridical principles, perhaps even with coercive sanctions, would be needed for establishing the classless society in such a way that its classless character would be preserved.

A Marxian might reply that even if concentrations of power do develop in the communist mode of production, these will not have the pernicious consequences of concentrations of power in capitalism, because in communism, as opposed to the system of private ownership of the means of production, those in authority will use their power for the common good. This reply is defective for two reasons. First, it begs the question by assuming that rights or principles of justice are needed only to avoid or adjudicate conflicts of egoistic interests. It thereby ignores the fact that nonegoists and even perfect altruists can be in serious conflict over what the common good is or how to achieve it, and that those who are committed to achieving the common good as they perceive it, and by the means they deem appropriate, are often willing to use their authority to do so. Second, this reply also begs the question by appealing to a difference between concentrations of power in capitalism and in communism. For Marx, private property in the means of production just *is* one group's control over productive resources to the exclusion of control by others. Hence the issue of whether a system of rights or principles of justice will be needed to establish and preserve democratic control over production cannot be finessed by replying that concentrations of power in communism would not be dangerous. The question is whether genuinely democratic control over an enormously complex system of industrial production can be initially achieved and maintained without using procedural and jurisdictional rights to specify institutional roles, to serve as mechanisms for conflict resolution, and to do so in a way which prevents dangerous concentrations of power.

IV

One of Marx's most important theses on the moderate as well as the radical interpretation is that juridical concepts will not play a major motivational role in the revolutionary transition to communism. At most, bourgeois juridical concepts will be invoked in *internal* criticism designed to demolish the juridical ideological support which capitalist institutions enjoy. We already encountered, in Chapter 5, a serious objection to this thesis, namely, the weakness of the rational interest theory of revolutionary motivation upon which it rests. Now another difficulty is also apparent: once we realize the diverse roles which conceptions of rights may play, including that of establishing the individual's right to participate in the direction of social production and to share the fruits thereof, the thesis that rights-conceptions have no positive motivational role to play in communist revolution becomes much less plausible. If communism itself will require juridical principles, juridical conceptions may be needed to guide the revolutionaries' efforts towards its attainment.

Due to the tremendous influence of this social theory as a whole, Marx's thesis that juridical conceptions will play no major role in revolutionary motivation has been a tragic self-fulfilling prophecy. The cumulative result of Marx's attack on the use of juridical concepts in effecting the transition to communism and his failure to limit his criticism to bourgeois juridical conceptions, has been a profound lack of appreciation for the importance of rights in the theory and practice of Marxists. Even if Marx himself espoused only the less radical critique of juridical concepts, granted what he actually says about rights, it should not be surprising that his followers have tended to be at best confused about, and at worst contemptuous of, rights and justice. By his scathing criticisms of attempts to assign a major role to juridical concepts in the revolutionary transformation of society and by his failure to acknowledge that communism may require juridical concepts, Marx discredited the very notions of justice and rights and undermined their motivational force among adherents of his theory.

It would be implausible—and, one might say, quite undialectical—to reply that the tremendous influence of Marx's attacks have not impeded the emergence of new juridical conceptions which are needed in revolutionary struggles or which would be needed in communism. To defend Marx in this way is to reject his repeated insistence that the new society develops organically out of the revolutionary struggle and to underestimate the ideological success which Marx's assault on juridical concepts has actually enjoyed. It would be quite surprising if a theory that scorns the notions of justice and rights as ideological nonsense and outdated verbal rubbish, or at best tolerates them as tactically useful confusions, that describes the rights of man as boundary markers to separate warring egoists, and that offers no alternative conception of rights of its own or even hints that there is a need for one, contributed to the development of more adequate juridical conceptions.

The blindness to the function and value of rights that Marx's writing encouraged reaches its apogee in the legal system of the Soviet Union. In the new Soviet Constitution (1977) we find a declaration of the powers of the totalitarian state that ritually invokes rights while systematically robbing the concept of all of its distinctive and valuable content. Numerous rights of the citizen are soberly listed, but each is "qualified" with the condition that it may be overridden for the sake of the common good, where the latter is equated with the power of the state. Such a declaration of "rights" betrays either profound cynicism or profound ignorance or both. By reversing the relationship of priority between social goals and rights, it subverts the very concept of a right. The Marxian charge that rights are merely formal and empty then becomes all too true. The withering away of rights is accompanied by the rank growth of unrestrained coercive power.

V

I have argued that key elements of Marx's critique of juridical concepts and institutions are inadequately supported due to deficiencies in his theory of revolutionary motivation, on the one hand, and his lack of a theory of non-juridical, noncoercive, but highly productive and harmonious social coordination, on the other. In neither case have I attempted to show that Marx's views are incoherent or even to demonstrate that they are false. Similarly, though I have argued that at least one contemporary theory of justice, Rawls' theory, has the resources to meet some of the potentially devasting objections that have been advanced against it from the distinctive perspective of Marx's critique of juridical concepts and institutions, I do not pretend to have achieved a decisive settling of accounts between Marx and contemporary juridical thought. Instead, I have endeavored to articulate the complexity of Marx's thought on justice and rights, to discover or reconstruct the assumptions about the sources of social harmony and conflict on which they rest, and then to determine whether his social theory supplies sufficient support for those assumptions. Put more positively, my aim has been to delineate more sharply the tasks which the most plausible and challenging Marxian critique of juridical concepts and institutions must fulfill and to define more adequately the terms of the debate over whether these tasks can be successfully completed. In particular, it has not been my goal to show that highly efficient democratic social coordination is impossible without coercion or juridical principles. My point, rather, is that whether or not it is can only be ascertained on the basis of a genuine *theory* of democratic social coordination and that while Marx's more interesting and foundational criticisms of juridical conceptions and institutions presuppose such a theory, his writings do not supply it. In spite of its deficiencies, Marx's critique of juridical concepts is of great theoretical and practical importance. His work provides a systematic and powerful challenge to the most sacred dogmas of moral and political philosophy. Though some of his criticisms are based in part on dubious and unexamined assumptions about the sources of conflict and harmony, they nonetheless force us to articulate and defend theses which we previously regarded as self-evident—if we were conscious of them at all. The most important of these is the twin dogma that justice is the first virtue of social institutions and that respect for rights is the first virtue of individuals. Even if we ultimately reject much of what Marx has to say against these theses, the attempt to come to grips with his position impels us toward a better understanding of the nature and value of juridical concepts.

The thesis that any society that requires juridical concepts is defective should temper our enthusiasm for juridical principles with the depressing thought that our preoccupation with rights and justice implies that our relations with one another are marked by deep suspicion and pervasive conflict. Even if we reject the thesis that the best feasible human society would be wholly or predominantly non-juridical, we should be much less confident about the currently popular assumption that identifies social progress with the steady extension of the juridical sphere. Too often we assume that all serious social issues are problems of rights, and by casting the parties to conflict in the narrow and unyielding roles of rights-bearers we render the problems intractable. By invoking rights we acknowledge the inevitability of conflicts without examining their sources. Even if an extensive juridical framework is necessary, we should not assume that it will be adequate for all human relations nor that it can stand alone without the support of deeper affective structures which are not themselves informed by conceptions of justice or rights.

For those who find the bonds of mutual respect among right-bearers too rigid and cold to capture some of what is best in human relationships, Marx's vision of genuine community—rather than a mere juridical association—will remain attractive in spite of its unsatisfying vagueness and the frailty of its theoretical foundations. By executing a systematic critique of capitalism without relying primarily on conceptions of rights or justice and by articulating the ideal of a free and humane society that is essentially non-juridical, Marx achieved the most radical challenge imaginable to the conceptual framework of traditional moral and political theory.

Marx's historicist criticisms make it impossible for the political theorist to pass off claims about "universal" rights or "eternal" principles of justice without eliciting skeptical challenges from her audience. After Marx we can never be wholly confident that our alleged eternal verities about human nature are anything more than overblown generalizations about a particular expression of human nature at a certain stage of history in our form of society. And these skeptical qualms remain even if Marx's own use of a concept of human nature transgresses the epistemological bounds laid down by his criticism of bourgeois theorists.

Marx's brilliant critique of the limitations of political emancipation is as important today as it was when he wrote *On the Jewish Question* in 1843. Any serious normative political theory must face the issue of whether it is possible to go beyond equal rights toward equality in the effectiveness with which rights can be exercised by different individuals. Indeed Marx's challenge to the basic liberal assumption that political equality can coexist with socio-economic inequality has not been seriously addressed, though, as we have seen, one recent theory (Rawls') may provide some of the material for coping with the problem.

After Marx no serious theory of distributive justice can neglect the interdependence of distribution and production, and no reform that focuses exclusively on redistribution can escape the charge of superficiality.

Marx's analysis of man's estrangement from and domination by his own products challenges the political theorist who purports to value autonomy yet assumes that autonomy is threatened only by deliberate acts of interference by other human beings. For one of the central theses of Marx's theory of alienation is that heteronomy comes in varied and subtle forms and that the institutions we create but are unable to control place profound restrictions on our consciousness and thereby on our wills, even in the absence of overt interference from others.

Finally, even if Marx's own account of how the new society emerges from the old proves irreparably defective, his efforts impose a simple but stringent condition of adequacy on any normative social theory that deserves to be taken seriously—the requirement that the realization of its ideals must be more than logically possible. In the case of theories which articulate juridical ideals, appeals to the "sense of justice" will not suffice unless they are accompanied by an empirically supported theory of social change.

Notes

Chapter 1

1. For what may be the best available attempt at this Herculean task, see Charles Taylor's *Hegel* (London, 1978), pp. 3–214, 365–427.

2. *Hegel: Selections*, edited by J. Lowenberg (New York, 1957), p. 363.

3. *Ibid.*, pp. 364–65.

4. *Ibid.*, pp. 360–61.

5. My reconstruction of Hegel's contrast between *Moralität* and *Sittlichkeit* is mainly from the following passages: Lowenberg p. 389, 391; Hegel, *The Philosophy of Right*, edited by T. M. Knox (London, 1973), pp. 34–36, 103–4, 133–34, and 319.

6. Knox, pp. 33, 253–55.

7. This becomes especially troubling in the case of Hegel's criticisms of Kant. Hegel raises problems for Kant's Categorical Imperative and suggests that the moral agent must rely upon social norms; but at the same time he wishes to preserve something of the ideal of autonomy. It is hard to see, however, how *Sittlichkeit* leaves any room for a principle like the Categorical Imperative, since the latter is supposed to function as the supreme standard by which all other principles, including the accepted principles of one's society, are to be judged. Yet Hegel seems to be correct in claiming that a principle so formal as the Categorical Imperative cannot by itself yield a unique set of substantive moral principles. For a brief discussion of how a theory of rational ends (or objective goods) might provide content for Kantian formalism, see my review-article on Onora O'Neill's *Acting on Principle, Journal of Philosophy*, vol. LXXV, no. 6, 1978, pp. 325–40.

8. I use the terms "subjective willing" and "objective willing" rather than "subjective will" and "objective will" because the substantive "will" in this context is ontologically pretentious and encourages unhelpful hypostasization. For Hegel's more detailed discussions of willing and of the distinction between subjective and objective willing, see Knox, pp. 21–32, 232, 233.

9. This is what Hegel means when he says that the objective will is that "in which the truth lies." (Knox, p. 232).

10. Knox, p. 232.

11. In this respect the person of *Sittlichkeit* is like the slave or the child. See Knox, pp. 232, 233.

12. I would like to thank W. D. Falk for making this point clearer to me. Indeed, my overall approach to Hegel in this chapter owes a great deal to Falk's unpublished lectures.

13. Knox, pp. 189, 267

14. *Ibid.*, pp. 128, 129.

15. *Ibid.*, pp. 131, 270–71.

16. *Ibid.*, pp. 148, 149, 277.

17. *Ibid.*, pp. 151, 152, 178.

18. *Ibid.*, pp. 267, 280.

19. *Ibid.*, p. 22.

20. *Ibid.*, p. 128.

21. *Ibid.*, p. 38.
22. *Ibid.*, p. 235, 256.
23. On p. 236, Knox (Paragraph 46), Hegel suggests a very unconvincing argument to show why the property must be private property.
24. Knox, p. 123.
25. *Ibid.*, pp. 148, 149, 277.
26. *Ibid.*, p. 123.
27. *Ibid.*, pp. 131, 132, 196, 197, 291.
28. *Ibid.*, pp. 190, 191, 287.
29. My sketch of Hegel's response to the distinctive problems of civil society focuses upon the role of the bureaucratic elite to the neglect of Hegel's discussion of the monarch. There are two reasons for this emphasis. First, it is generally agreed that what is most original and prophetic in Hegel's scheme of government is his conception of the bureaucratic elite and that his preoccupation with finding a place for monarchy is of very limited interest. Second, Hegel's discussion of monarchy is far from clear and difficult to integrate with the more obviously important elements of his political theory.
30. Knox, p. 276.
31. *Ibid.*, p. 277.
32. *Ibid.*, p. 147.
33. Marx and Engels, *The Holy Family*, cited on p. 46 of Avineri, *The Social and Political Thought of Karl Marx* (Cambridge, 1968).
34. For a fascinating contemporary examination of this Hegelian theme see D. Gauthier, "The Social Contract as Ideology," *Philosophy and Public Affairs*, vol. 6, no. 2, 1978, pp. 130–64.
35. Knox, pp. 262, 265.
36. See Chapters 2 and 3 of this book. Note also that Marx charges that Proudhon is guilty of "petty-bourgeois sentimentality" when he "sings the glories of . . . the miserable patriarchal amorous illusions of the domestic hearth." (Marx in a letter to P. V. Annenkov, Dec. 28, 1846, *Marx and Engels: Selected Correspondence*, translated by I. Lasker, edited by S. W. Ryazanskaya (Moscow, 1975), p. 28.
37. Marx, *Capital*, vol. I (New York, 1967), p. 79.

Chapter 2

1. I am especially indebted to David Brink for his insightful comments on an earlier draft of this chapter.
2. See, for example, J. Seigel, "Alienation" (a review-article on B. Ollman's *Alienation*), *History and Theory*, vol. XII, no. 3, 1973, pp. 329–42.
3. See *Grundrisse*, translated by M. Nicolaus (New York, 1973), pp. 157–58, 162, 196, 197, 652, 831.
4. For a more detailed explication of these terms, see "Translator's and Editor's Note on Terminology," *The Economic and Philosophic Manuscripts of 1844*, edited by D. Struik, translated by M. Milligan (New York, 1964), pp. 58–59.
5. *Ibid.*, pp. 108–9. A more complete account of Marx's theory of alienation would require an examination of its relation both to Hegel's and Feuerbach's use of the concept. For the former, see S. Avineri, *Hegel's Theory of the Modern State* (Cambridge, 1972), pp. 87–98, and Taylor, *Hegel* (London, 1978), pp. 3–214. For the latter, see S. Avineri, *The Social and Political Thought of Karl Marx* (Cambridge, 1968), pp. 65–124. Carol Gould, in *Marx's Social Ontology* (Cambridge, Massachusetts, 1978), pp. 41–56, provides an interesting discussion of the relationship between Marx's notion of species being and the distinction between alienation and objectification. These passages also include interesting remarks concerning differences and similarities between Marx's and Hegel's views of objectification.
6. Marx, *Capital*, vol. I (New York, 1967), pp. 69–83.
7. G. Lukács, "Reification and the Consciousness of the Proletariat," in *History and Class Consciousness*, translated by R. Livingstone (Cambridge, Massachusetts, 1971), pp. 83–222.

8. My preliminary discussion of Marx's concept of species being draws on B. Ollman's treatment in *Alienation*, especially pp. 75–83. While Ollman's exposition is in many respects illuminating, it fails to examine sufficiently the normative or evaluative aspects of Marx's concept of species being and is almost wholly uncritical. (*Alienation: Marx's Conception of Man in Capitalist Society*, Cambridge, 1971).

9. Marx, *Economic and Philosophic Manuscripts* [1844], in B. McLellan, *Karl Marx: Selected Writings* (Oxford, 1977), p. 82.

10. *Ibid.*, p. 82.

11. *Ibid.*, p. 82.

12. *Ibid.*, p. 82.

13. See, for example, Seigel, pp. 335–37.

14. McLellan, p. 156.

15. L. Easton and K. Guddhat, *Writings of the Young Marx on Philosophy* (Garden City, New York, 1967), p. 468.

16. McLellan, p. 84.

17. Easton and Guddhat, pp. 424–25.

18. McLellan, p. 568.

19. *Ibid.*, p. 567.

20. *Ibid.*, p. 567.

21. *Ibid.*, p. 569.

22. *Marx and Engels: Basic Writings on Politics and Society*, ed. L. Feuer (New York, 1959), p. 127.

23. McLellan, pp. 88–89.

24. A. Wood, "The Marxian Critique of Justice," *Philosophy and Public Affairs*, vol. 1, no. 3, 1972, pp. 281–82.

25. As will become clear in what follows, my claim that Marx's basic evaluative perspective shifts from the early evaluative concept of human nature as species being to a vision of communist society which purports to be more firmly anchored in the material-ist theory of history is *not* to be confused with Louis Althusser's well-known thesis that there is an "epistemological break" between an early "humanistic Marx" and a later "scientific Marx." For one thing, on my interpretation, Marx's later social theory still depends crucially upon evaluative elements—it is not in that sense strictly scientific. Also, the evaluative perspective which dominates Marx's later works is still humanistic insofar as it preserves much of the normative content of the earlier concept of species being. See L. Althusser, *For Marx* (New York, 1969), pp. 34–38, 51–86.

26. Easton and Guddhat, p. 419.

27. G. A. Cohen advances a similar interpretation in *Marx's Theory of History: A Defense* (Oxford, 1978), pp. 150–53. In labeling what I call the Protean core concept "Marx's concept of human nature (or essence)," I am not denying that an unexplicated use of this latter phrase, when applied to Marx's view, is misleading. It seems quite correct, however, once the difference between the Protean core concept and traditional notions of human nature or essence is understood, to refer to the former using the terms "human nature" or "human essense," because in *The German Ideology* Marx says that this capacity (or bundle of capacities) for changing ourselves through changing the ways we produce the means of life is universal to all men throughout history and differentiates us from other species. Nonetheless, other commentators, who appear to agree in substance with this interpretation I offer here, have been reluctant to say that the later Marx employed any concept of human nature or essence because they wished to avoid misleading connotations of the traditional notions Marx attacked. Consider, for example, William Leon McBride (*The Philosophy of Marx*, London, 1977, p. 86): "[I]t is highly paradoxical to use this expression ["human essence"] in discussing the later philosophy of Marx, for the reason that he made clear; 'essence'-talk has traditionally conjured up images of some fixed and changeless core, whereas human beings in Marx's world-view are capable, at least in groups, of drastically altering the patterns in accordance with which they act." Yet a few paragraphs later, McBride himself reverts to "essence"-talk, suggest-ing that there is nothing incorrect in saying *both* that Marx eschews traditional concep-tions of human essence or nature *and* that Marx subscribes to a (quite different) concep-

tion of human nature or essence! He says that, according to "Marx's view of human beings," they "are essentially fabricators, changers— 'shapers and fashioners.' " This passage strongly suggests that the disagreement is purely terminological and that McBride, too, recognizes that for Marx the capacity for changing ourselves through changing the ways we produce the means of life is human nature or essence in the sense of being that which is universal to, and distinctive of, our species throughout history. But to say that the later Marx does have a concept of human nature or essence in this sense is *not*, of course, to say that it plays in his theory the same roles which the traditional notions play in traditional ethical or psychological theories. As should be clear from what follows in my analysis, Marx's concept neither generates moral prescriptions nor provides illuminating explanations of any particular pattern of behavior. It lacks the normative content required for the former and is much too general for the latter.

28. Marx, *The Poverty of Philosophy* (New York: International Publishers, 1963), p. 147.
29. Marx, *Capital*, vol. I (New York, 1967), p. 609, note 2.
30. This example was suggested to me by Gordon Graham.
31. McLellan, p. 91–92.
32. For an extended discussion of this aspect of Marx's characterization of communism and an examination of several ways in which, for Marx, consciousness can be distorted, see Cohen, "Karl Marx and the Withering Away of Social Science," Appendix I, *Marx's Theory of History: A Defense*, pp. 326–44.
33. For what may be the most thorough and rigorous attempt to formulate and defend Marx's doctrine of historical materialism, see Cohen, *Marx's Theory of History: A Defense*.
34. J. Rawls, *A Theory of Justice* (Cambridge, Massachusetts, 1971), p. 408.
35. *Ibid.*, p. 417. How much it rules out depends upon how broadly "illusion" is interpreted.
36. Unfortunately, this important task would exceed the limitations of the present book.

Chapter 3

1. See, for example, S. Avineri, *The Social and Political Thought of Karl Marx* (Cambridge, 1968), especially pp. 96–177; and B. Ollman, *Alienation* (Cambridge, 1971).
2. See, for example, M. Blaug, *Economic Theory in Retrospect*, rev. ed. (Homewood, Ill., 1968), p. 245; P. Samuelson, *Economics*, 9th ed. (New York, 1973), pp. 542–43; and N. Holmstrom, "Exploitation," *Canadian Journal of Philosophy*, vol. VII, no. 2, 1977, pp. 353–69.
3. Holmstrom distinguishes between (a) and (b), but because she confines Marx's attack on exploitation to the labor process itself, she overlooks (c).
4. By "the labor process of capitalism" I mean the dominant or characteristic labor process, i.e., the wage-labor process of commodity production.
5. Marx uses the term "commodity" as a technical term to signal that the item in question is produced for exchange rather than for immediate consumption.
6. *Capital*, vol. 1 (New York, 1967), pp. 207–9.
7. Holmstrom, pp. 358–59.
8. My account here follows Holmstrom's but avoids the error of equating "exploitation" with "exploitation in the labor process."
9. *The German Ideology*, in D. McLellan, *Karl Marx: Selected Writings* (Oxford, 1977), pp. 185–86. Littrés' *Dictionaire de la Langue Française*, the standard multivolume French dictionary for the nineteenth century, includes the following entry under *"exploiter"* (to exploit):

Terme d'agriculture et d'industrie. Faire valoir, tirer le produit. Exploiter un brevet, un theatre. Par extension, tirer profit ou bon parti de quelque chose considere comme objet d'exploitation. . . . Il se dit aussi des personnes. Exploiter une dupe. Cet entrepreneur exploite ses ouvriers (Dictionaire de la Langue Française, Par E. Littré de l'Academie Française, Librairie Hatchette et Cie, Paris, 1873).

The part of this entry which defines "exploitation" as applied to persons is virtually identical with Marx's general characterization in *The German Ideology*. In *The German*

Ideology, Marx uses the term *"Exploitation"* more frequently than *"Ausbeutung,"* whereas in *Capital* the tendency is the reverse. Both words translate as "exploitation." So far as I can determine, Marx uses them interchangeably and there is no textual evidence for the hypothesis that his alternate usage marked any systematic distinction.

10. It is interesting to note that Holmstrom erroneously implies that Marx first introduced the term "exploitation" in *Capital,* vol. 1.

11. Marx, *Excerpt-Notes of 1844* in Easton and Guddhat, pp. 278–79.

12. Marx, *On the Jewish Question, Writings of the Young Marx on Philosophy and Society,* Easton and Guddhat (New York, 1967), pp. 245–48.

13. *The German Ideology,* p. 110.

14. Marx, *The Economic and Philosophic Manuscripts of 1844,* ed. by D. Struik (New York, 1973), pp. 150–51.

15. It is interesting to note that Marx contends that the bourgeois utilizes his wife by treating her as a mere instrument of production (*The Communist Manifesto, Marx and Engels: Basic Writings on Politics and Philosophy*) ed. L. Feuer (New York, 1959), p. 25.

16. See, for example, Avineri, pp. 51–52; R. Raico, "Classical Liberal Exploitation Theory," *Journal of Libertarian Studies,* 1 (1977), pp. 179–80; and R. Miliband, *Marxism and Politics* (Oxford, 1977), pp. 74–90.

17. *The Communist Manifesto,* in Feuer, p. 9.

18. Easton and Guddhat, pp. 177–90.

19. *Selected Works of Marx and Engels* (New York, 1972), pp. 170–71.

20. *Selected Works,* p. 171.

21. *Selected Works,* p. 293.

22. See *Capital,* vol. 1, p. 256, for example.

23. Though I will not argue the point, here, it also seems clear that even according to the view that the state is a tool of the bourgeoisie, the exploitative functions of the state are not confined to the labor process.

24. Holmstrom (p. 365) says that her account makes the connections between exploitation and alienation obvious. Unfortunately, this is not the case, since her account mistakenly confines exploitation to the labor process. This limits her to sketching a connection between the exploitation of the worker in the labor process and those forms of alienation which are present in that process.

25. Marx, *Precapitalist Economic Formations* (excerpted from the *Grundrisse*), ed. E. J. Hobsbawm (New York, 1975), pp. 104–8.

26. *On the Jewish Question,* in Easton and Guddhat, p. 248.

27. *Precapitalist Economic Formations,* p. 104.

28. *Excerpt-Notes of 1844,* in Easton and Guddhat, p. 269.

29. *Economic and Philosophic Manuscripts,* in Easton and Guddhat, pp. 287–89.

30. For a detailed account of Marx's use of the theory of alienation to describe the bureaucratic state, see Avineri, *The Social and Political Thought of Karl Marx,* pp. 17–24.

31. R. Nozick, *Anarchy, State, and Utopia* (New York, 1975), p. 253.

32. Blaug, p. 245; Samuelson, pp. 542–43. It may be that those who saddle Marx with this view do so because they erroneously assume that he holds some version of the labor theory of property, according to which one comes to have a property right in some object by producing it or as Locke puts it, by "mixing" one's labor with it. This theory, which Marx did not subscribe to, is quite distinct from the labor theory of *value.*

33. *Critique of the Gotha Program,* Feuer, pp. 116, 117.

34. Wood develops this aspect of Marx's polemic against conceptions of justice in considerable detail in "The Marxian Critique of Justice."

35. *Critique of the Gotha Program,* Feuer, p. 116.

36. Holmstrom's account seems to assume that Marx's concept of exploitation in the capitalist labor process and the labor theory of value are inextricably intertwined.

37. Nozick, p. 252.

38. *Capital,* vol. 1, p. 218.

39. After the appearance of the essay from which this chapter is adapted, G. A. Cohen published an interesting analysis of Marx's theory of exploitation which appears to agree with my earlier account in several important respects. On the basis of different, though

compatible arguments, Cohen concludes that Marx's theory of exploitation is independent of the labor theory of value. He also agrees that what I call the transhistorical
conception includes the condition that there is a surplus *product*, rather than the historically limited condition that there is surplus *value*, where this latter implies commodity
production. However, Cohen appears to have overlooked Marx's discussion in *The
Critique of the Gotha Program*, since his analysis implies, or at least strongly suggests, that
for Marx the fact that the worker does not get the full product of his labor constitutes
exploitation. Also Cohen asserts, without argument so far as I can tell, that exploitation
is a form of injustice, but does not attempt to explain how this claim can be squared with
Marx's derisive remarks about justice, which are considered in detail in the next chapter.
("The Labor Theory of Value and the Concept of Exploitation," *Philosophy and Public
Affairs*, vol. 8, no. 4, 1979, pp. 338–60.)

In "Freedom and Private Property in Marx" (*Philosophy and Public Affairs*, vol. 8, no. 2,
1979, pp. 122–147), George F. Brenkert argues that Marx's critique of capitalism is not a
juridical critique without considering the possibility of an internal juridical critique. He
then contends that Marx's basic evaluative perspective is "a principle of freedom." In his
analysis of freedom Brenkert emphasizes what I have referred to in
Chapter 2 as Marx's ideals of autonomy, community, and the all-round development of
the individual. He also stresses what I have referred to as the epistemic element—including the idea that the attainment of these ideals is possible only where social consciousness is no longer distorted. Brenkert and I also agree that it is a mistake to view Marx's
analysis of capitalism as purely scientific rather than evaluative or normative. Nonetheless, I believe it is more accurate to speak of communism (as the society in which this
concept of freedom is exemplified) as the basic evaluative perspective in order to
emphasize what I explained in Chapter 2 as the radical, but putatively nonutopian
character of Marx's criticisms of capitalism.

Chapter 4

1. John Rawls, *A Theory of Justice*, (Cambridge, Massachusetts, 1971), p. 3.

2. In "The Marxian Critique of Justice," Allen Wood argues that Marx rejects the
juridical model and that he does not criticize capitalism as being unjust. In the pages that
follow, I am quite critical of several key elements of Wood's interpretation of Marx, but it
will be clear, I hope, that I think Wood's article contains many important insights, raises
fundamental issues, and injects new life into recent work in Marx. (*Philosophy and Public
Affairs*, vol. 1, no. 3, 1972, p. 246.)

3. Rawls, pp. 177–82.

4. For some recent work relevant to this task, see S. Moore, "Marx and Lenin as
Historical Materialists," *Philosophy and Public Affairs*, vol. 4, no. 2, 1975, pp. 171–94; R.
Miller, "The Consistency of Historical Materialism," *Philosophy and Public Affairs*, vol. 4,
no. 4, 1975, pp. 390–409; and G. Young, "The Fundamental Contradiction of Capitalism," *Philosophy and Public Affairs*, vol. 5, no. 2, 1976, pp. 196–234.

5. *Karl Marx: Selected Writings*, edited by D. McLellan (Oxford, 1977), p. 389. This is
not to say, of course, that for Marx juridical concepts play *no* significant role in explaining
social phenomena in class-divided societies, it is only to say that they do not play the
fundamental role which Marx assigns to the concept of the material base of society.

6. R. C. Tucker, *The Marxian Revolutionary Idea* (New York, 1969), pp. 37–53.

7. The wide consensus that the Tucker-Wood view is basically correct has been
noted—and challenged—by W. L. McBride, "The Concept of Justice in Marx, Engels,
and Others," *Ethics*, vol. 85, 1975, p. 206.

8. See, for example, Tucker, pp. 27, 41, and 44, and Wood, pp. 254–55.

9. Wood, p. 265.

10. Wood, p. 259.

11. Wood, pp. 257–59.

12. *Capital*, vol. I (New York, 1967), p. 176.

13. McBride correctly points out that *"Unrecht"* can mean either "injustice" or "injury" ("harm") and then suggests that it is unwarranted for Wood to assume that the

former, rather than the latter, is the correct translation. This does not seem to me to be a telling criticism of Wood for the simple reason that the "injury" or "harm" translation seems implausible here, granted Marx's continual emphasis that by selling his labor-power to the capitalist the worker *does* suffer great injury, grievous harm, both mental and physical.

14. N. Holmstrom, "Exploitation," *Canadian Journal of Philosophy*, vol. VII, no. 2, 1977, pp. 353–69.

15. Holmstrom, pp. 366–67.

16. Holmstrom, p. 268.

17. *Capital*, vol. I, p. 271.

18. Both Wood's analysis and Holmstrom's criticism of it are hampered by a failure to distinguish between Marx's external and internal criticisms, though Holmstrom's remarks on p. 368 suggest that she believes Marx advances an external critique of capitalism from the perspective of communist justice. In *Marx's Social Ontology* (Cambridge, Massachusetts, 1978, p. 169, n. 4), Carol Gould explicitly asserts that Marx employs an external standard of justice in his critique of capitalism.

19. *Capital*, vol. I, pp. 713–14.

20. Holmstrom, p. 368.

21. A. Buchanan, "Exploitation, Alienation, and Injustice," *Canadian Journal of Philosophy*, vol. 9, no. 1, 1979.

22. McBride, pp. 204–5.

23. Wood, pp. 254–57, presents strong textual evidence for this basic point.

24. *Critique of the Gotha Program*, McLellan, p. 569.

25. McLellan, pp. 77–96.

26. McLellan, p. 569.

27. These are some of the many scattered passages in which Marx or Marx and Engels state or imply that scarcity will be greatly reduced in communism: *The German Ideology, Writings of the Young Marx on Philosophy and Society*, edited by L. Easton and K. Guddhat (Garden City, N.Y. 1967), p. 468; *Grundrisse*, edited by M. Nicolaus (New York, 1973), p. 705; McLellan, pp. 73, 381, 383–84; *Capital*, vol. III, p. 876; Avineri, *The Social and Political Thought of Karl Marx* (Cambridge, 1968), p. 147.

28. McLellan, p. 569.

29. Though his critics have often failed to notice it, Rawls' Difference Principle might be viewed as a principle of productive-distributive justice. Because what it distributes, strictly speaking, is prospects of primary goods, not material goods themselves, and because significant restructuring of the productive processes of a society may be needed to achieve the pattern of prospects it requires, the Difference Principle applies to the productive processes of society, not just to its distributive arrangements. Rawls acknowledges this when he notes that satisfaction of the Difference Principle might require public ownership of the means of production. (Rawls, p. 274).

30. See, for example, McLellan, pp. 77, 377, 381, 383–84; *Capital*, vol. III, p. 876; and *Karl Marx and Frederick Engels, Selected Works*, vol. II, (New York), pp. 93–94.

31. Engels, *Karl Marx and Frederick Engels: Selected Works in One Volume*, (New York, 1968), p. 430. In a recent article entitled "Marx on Distributive Justice," Z. Husami attacks the Tucker-Wood interpretation of Marx's views (*Philosophy and Public Affairs*, vol. 8, no. 1, 1978, pp. 27–64.) Husami quite correctly argues that Marx can consistently use conceptions (e.g., of human freedom and self-actualization) drawn from the nature of postcapitalist society as normative concepts with which to criticize capitalism. But he then makes the unwarranted claim that these concepts borrowed from the vision of postcapitalist society are not only normative, but *juridical* concepts. Further, Husami is right to point out that the Tucker-Wood line cannot explain passages in which Marx refers to the exploitation of the worker as "theft" or "robbery." But he is wrong in assuming that to account for these passages we must assume that Marx criticized wage-labor from the perspective of communist principles of *justice*. We need only maintain that Marx criticizes capitalism for failing to live up to its *own* conceptions of justice—that he advances *internal* juridical criticisms of capitalism. It appears that the texts Husami cites to support the claim that Marx criticizes capitalism as being unjust

from the perspective of communist justice can be accounted for as instances of Marx's internal juridical criticisms. My interpretation—unlike Husami's—squares with and even explains the three crucial data mentioned earlier: (i) Marx's refusal to refer to communism as a just society, (ii) his view that communism will abolish the circumstances of justice by diminishing scarcity and conflict, and (iii) his charge that talk about justice and rights is "obsolete verbal rubbish" and "ideological nonsense."

32. McLellan, pp. 51–52.
33. *Ibid.*, p. 54.
34. *Ibid.*, p. 54.
35. J. S. Mill, *On Liberty* (New York, 1956), p. 7.
36. McLellan, p. 56. The phrase *"so-called* rights of man" here requires explanation. Marx apparently uses it to reemphasize one of his most characteristic criticisms: the charge that the celebrants of these rights fail to realize the historically limited nature of these rights. Marx's point is that calling these rights the rights of *man* betrays the ahistorical blindness characteristic of all ideological thinking. The forms of activity which these rights are designed to protect are not forms of activity of human beings at all times and in all circumstances; they are activities of human beings *in capitalism.* There is no indication in the text that we are to understand the phrase "so-called" in such a way as to imply that there *are* rights which are rights of man as such and that Marx is only criticizing those who have improperly identified these universal rights.
37. *Ibid.*, p. 53.
38. *Ibid.*, p. 53.
39. N. Daniels argues that Rawls' theory cannot adequately cope with inequalities in the effectiveness of equal rights and that this defect signals a fundamental tension between Rawls' first and second principles of justice. Daniels' argument is one of the more promising criticisms of Rawls from a Marxian perspective. (N. Daniels, "Equal Liberty and Equal Worth of Liberty," in *Reading Rawls,* edited by N. Daniels (New York, 1975), pp. 253–81). For a different, though related approach to the problem of inequalities in the effectiveness in the exercise of equal rights, see my paper, "Deriving Welfare Rights from Libertarian Rights," in *Income Support* edited by P. Brown, C. Johnson, and P. Vernier of the Center for Philosophy and Public Policy, University of Maryland at College Park (Totowa, N.J.: Rowman and Littlefield, 1981).
40. McLellan, p. 57.
41. *Ibid.*, p. 35.
42. *Ibid.*, p. 568–69.
43. Tucker, pp. 51–52.
44. Rawls, p. 9.
45. In Chapter 3.
46. "The executive of the modern representative state is but a committee for managing the common affairs of the bourgeoisie." (McLellan, p. 223).
47. For an examination of the relevant texts, see A. Buchanan, "Exploitation, Alienation, and Injustice," pp. 121–39.
48. In the *Eighteenth Brumaire,* Marx's task was to explain how the government could play *both* roles simultaneously.
49. J. Murphy, "Marxism and Retribution," *Philosophy and Public Affairs,* vol. 2, no. 3, 1973, pp. 217–18.
50. H. Morris, "Persons and Punishment," *Monist,* vol. 52, no. 4, p. 500.
51. I examine Marx's theory of revolutionary motivation and argue that it is seriously defective in "Revolutionary Motivation and Rationality," *Philosophy and Public Affairs,* vol. 9, no. 1, 1979, pp. 59–82. See also, Chapter 5 of this book.
52. McLellan, p. 230.
53. *Ibid.*, p. 231.
54. *Ibid.*, p. 566.
55. If one assumes that the principle "To each according to his product" is offered by Marx as a principle of distributive justice that will be publicly recognized as such during a transitional stage preceding fully developed communism (see McLellan, p. 568), one might argue that it provides a significant instance of a positive, action-guiding use of a

juridical concept. The idea would be that appeal to this principle as a principle of justice motivates the proletariat to change society in such a way as to achieve the distribution it prescribes and that these efforts in turn lead to fully developed communist society—a society in which the circumstances of justice no longer obtain. The difficulty with assigning a significant motivational role to a transitional principle is that it forces us to reject his frequent declaration that successful proletarian revolution does not rely upon moral exhortation in general or on appeals to justice in particular. Further, it seems difficult to square such an interpretation with passages in which Marx advances a rather simple rational interest theory of revolutionary motivation which assigns no significant role to juridical concepts. Nonetheless, even if a juridical principle plays a significant role in the transitional period, it does not follow that it or any other juridical principle will be needed once the transition is completed.

56. Presumably Rawls and Dworkin would both wish to qualify this view so as to allow the possibility that, at least where the right in question is not one of the most basic ones or where the disutility of respecting the right-claim would be enormous, claims of right do not take precedence over considerations of utility. For a more detailed analysis of this conception of a right, see Chapter 7.

57. J. Feinberg, "The Nature and Value of Rights," in *Moral Problems in Medicine*, edited by S. Gorovitz, *et al.* (Englewood Cliffs, New Jersey, 1976), pp. 454–67.

58. My sketchy account of respect for persons as such owes much to S. L. Darwall's illuminating analysis in "Two Kinds of Respect," *Ethics*, vol. 88, no. 3, 1978, pp. 36–49.

59. Kant, *Groundwork of the Metaphysics of Morals*, translated by H. J. Paton (New York, 1964), p. 103 (*Akad*. 435).

60. Easton and Guddhat, pp. 269–70.

61. Nozick, p. 31.

62. See *The Holy Family*, p. 211, where Marx says that "punishment, coercion, is contrary to human conduct" (Moscow, 1956).

Chapter 5

1. See, for example, Marx's scathing criticism of the "true socialists' " conception of a republic based on the idea of humanity, in *Karl Marx: Selected Writings*, McLellan (Oxford, 1977) pp. 216–18. Note also Marx's admonition to the German socialists to cease their preoccupation with "obsolete verbal rubbish" about justice and right, p. 569.

2. In the Preface to the Second German Edition of *Capital* vol. I, Marx states that ". . . [bourgeois] political economy [could] remain a science only so long as the class struggle remains latent . . ." and that once it became overt—after 1830—bourgeois political economy became the trade of "hired prize fighters" who no longer asked "whether this theorem or that is true, but whether it was useful to capital . . ." *Capital*, vol I, New York, 1967, p. 15).

3. In the *Communist Manifesto*, Marx describes the proletarian revolution as the ". . . movement of the immense majority, in the interests of the immense majority" (McLellan, p. 230). The role of the communist party, Marx says on p. 231, is simply to make the proletariat aware that its interest lies in the overthrow of the system and to guide the resulting revolutionary action so as to maximize its efficacy. Additional textual evidence that Marx held what I shall call an interest theory of revolutionary motivation will be marshalled as my argument unfolds.

4. McLellan, p. 230. In *Capital*, vol. I, p. 269, Marx writes of "the depopulation of the human race" by capitalism.

5. McLellan, p. 569. See also p. 566: "What is 'a fair distribution' [*gerechte*, fair or just]? Do not the bourgeois assert that the present-day distribution is 'fair'? . . . Have not also the socialist secretarians the most varied notions of a 'fair' distribution?"

6. "A particular class can only vindicate for itself general supremacy in the name of the general rights of society." (McLellan, p. 71).

7. M. Olson in *The Logic of Collective Action* (Cambridge, Massachusetts, 1965), pp. 105–6, states very briefly the public goods objection I develop in detail in this essay.

Olson does not explore the relation between Marx's theory of revolutionary motivation and Marx's views on coercion and moral principles. Nor does he consider the problematic relationship between Marx's assumptions about proletarian cooperation and the failure to cooperate that Marx attributes to capitalists. Finally, Olson does not consider Marxian replies to the public goods objection. None of this is surprising, since Olson's reference to Marx is only a brief but suggestive digression on the application of Olson's general theory to Marx's views on revolution.

8. In Section VII, I respond to the charge that rationality is not to be identified either with individual or with group utility-maximization. Even if this charge is correct, the main points of my argument are unaffected.

9. My presentation of the concept of a public good and my analysis of the public goods problem borrow heavily from R. Sartorius's discussion in his paper, "The Limits of Libertarianism," in *Law and Liberty* (College Station, Texas, 1978).

10. Item (ii), jointness of supply, must be distinguished from (iii), nonexcludability. A good may be produced in joint supply, yet it still may be possible to exclude certain persons from partaking of it. "Nonexcludability," as I shall use it, is a dispositional term referring to the practical or political infeasibility of exclusion. "Jointness" is a manifest or nondispositional term referring to the way in which a good is in fact produced.

11. In *Sociologists, Economists, and Democracy* (London, 1970), B. Barry argues that the cases of the individual and the group utility-maximizer differ crucially. The difference, he thinks, is that the group utility-maximizer will not view his contribution as negligible because it will affect a large number of people. In "The Limits of Libertarianism," (p. 6), R. Sartorius points out that this will only be true where so-called *threshold effects* are not present. The idea is that in many of the more important public goods cases the likelihood of the individual's contribution occurring at the threshold of contribution which must be crossed if the good is to be produced is virtually nil. It seems clear that in the case of concerted revolutionary action a rational individual would regard the likelihood of his contribution occurring at a "threshold" as negligible. If this is so, then Barry's point is inapplicable and the public goods problem arises regardless of whether the proletarian maximizes individual or group utility. A Marxian who is still convinced that the cases are different and who wishes to argue that the public goods problem is avoided because each proletarian maximizes group utility would have to provide an account of how the proletarian comes to desire to maximize his class's interest rather than his own.

12. McLellan, p. 231.

13. Surplus value, for Marx, is the value the worker produces in excess of the value of the commodities needed for his subsistence as a worker (*Capital*, vol. I, pp. 177–98, 331). "The rate of surplus value is . . . an exact expression for the degree of exploitation of labour-power by capital or of the labourer by the capitalist" (*Capital*, vol. I, p. 218). Marx defines the rate of surplus value as the ratio of surplus value to the value of the commodities necessary for the workers' subsistence as a worker (*Capital*, Vol. I, pp. 218–19).

14. Though Marx's dominant view was that the proletarian revolution will be violent, he considered the possibility of peaceful revolution in certain countries under certain conditions. See Engels' Preface to the English translation of *Capital*, vol. I, p. 6.

15. McLellan, p. 565.

16. Though Lenin popularized the term "vanguard" in this connection, it fits Marx's conception of the role of the communist party accurately.

17. McLellan, p. 231.

18. This passage is cited and briefly discussed by S. Avineri (*The Social and Political Thought of Karl Marx*, Cambridge, 1971. p. 141).

19. *The German Ideology, Collected Works: Marx and Engels*, vol. 5 (New York, 1976), p. 75.

20. See, for example, *Economic and Philosophic Manuscripts*, pp. 87–96, and *Critique of the Gotha Program*, pp. 568–69, in McLellan.

21. Generalization principles include, for example, Kant's Universal Law Formula of the Categorical Imperative and the Principle of Utilitarian Generalization. The former states that one is to act only on that maxim one can at the same time will to be a universal

law. The latter requires one to do that action which is such that the consequences of everyone doing that kind of action in similar circumstances would maximize utility.

In Section 51 of *A Theory of Justice* (Cambridge, Massachusetts, 1971), Rawls proposes a principle requiring one to support just social institutions. Rawls' principle is not designed to solve what he calls the assurance problem: it operates where the individual can already count on the cooperation of others in supporting just institutions. A principle of justice capable of solving the public goods problem, therefore, would have to be stronger than Rawls' principle. Different degrees of strength are possible. The principle could require that one direct one's efforts to the establishment of just institutions, if one can do so without great inconvenience to oneself. A much stronger principle would exact such a duty even if its fulfillment meant one's own destruction.

22. Such a principle would be consistent with Marx's refusal to rely upon a conception of *justice* and is consonant with his vision of communism as a humane social order.

23. There may be still other alternatives. For instance, one might use the notion of leadership by example or rely upon the motivation of resentment. In the first case, one would develop a theory of revolutionary motivation that assigned a pivotal role to the ability of leaders to inspire the masses to emulate their personal example, without calculating costs and benefits. In the second case, the crucial motivating factor would be the resentment of the masses toward their oppressors. In this chapter, I shall not pursue either of these alternative solutions for two reasons. First, neither of them seems to be at all plausible as a Marxian solution, since Marx nowhere assigns a significant role to either factor. Second, unlike the three solutions I do consider, the theory of leadership by example and the theory of the motivation of resentment are not *rational solutions* to the proletariat's public goods problem. Instead, they remove the problem from the theory of rational decision and treat it exclusively as a problem of empirical psychological explanation.

24. For purposes of the argument I will assume that Marx intends his historicist views about concepts in general to apply to concept of rationality, while acknowledging that there may be no conclusive textual evidence to support this assumption.

25. The material base, for Marx, is the set of processes by which a society produces the material means of life—food, shelter, and so on (McLellan, p. 165).

26. In the Preface to *A Contribution to the Critique of Political Economy*, Marx distinguishes between "the material transformation of the economic conditions of production . . . and the legal, political, religious, aesthetic, or philosophic—in short, ideological forms in which men become conscious of this conflict and fight it out" (McLellan, pp. 389–390). The crucial point here is that even though men's interests and their consciousness of those interests depend upon conflicts in the material base, nonetheless men *do* "fight out" the conflict at the level of conscious purposive behavior.

27. It might be replied that Marx's point is that the proletarian does not ask, "What should *I* do to maximize my own or my class's utility?" Instead he identifies himself as a member of the proletariat and asks, 'What should *we* do?' He avoids the public goods problem by calculating the cost of *our* not participating relative to the benefits of *our* participating. The difficulty with this reply, however, is that it *assumes* what the Marxian must establish, namely, that inspite of the isolating, egoistic environment of capitalism, the proletarian can arrive at a new way of conceiving of his decisions which avoids the public goods problem. As I argue below, Marx assumes that this transformation will emerge within the capitalist factory, but he gives no account of how it does occur or even of what exactly it is.

28. McLellan, p. 236.

29. *Capital*, vol. I, pp. 329, 763.

30. For Marx's most extended discussion of the alienation of the worker from his fellows, see McLellan, pp. 75–112. For his account of the debilitating effects of factory work see Chapter 14, "Division of Labour and Manufacture," *Capital*, vol. I.

31. For some of these reasons see Sartorius, "The Limits of Libertarianism."

32. Rawls, *A Theory of Justice*, pp. 268–69.

33. Earlier versions of this chapter were presented at the University of Pittsburgh Philosophy Department and the University of North Carolina Philosophy Department. I

would like to thank Annette Baier, Kurt Baier, John Cooper, W. D. Falk, Richard Grandy, N. J. McClennan, Michael Resnik, and T. Seidenfeld for their helpful comments. I am also indebted to the Editors of *Philosophy and Public Affairs* for several helpful suggestions.

Chapter 6

1. Brian Barry, "Critical Notice of Wolff: *Understanding Rawls*," *Canadian Journal of Philosophy*, vol. VII, no. 4, 1979, p. 780.

2. John Rawls, *A Theory of Justice*, p. 7.

3. *Ibid.*, p. 7.

4. *Ibid.*, p. 62.

5. For a detailed development of this interpretation of Rawls' theory of primary goods, see my paper "Revisability and Rational Choice," *Canadian Journal of Philosophy*, vol. 5, no. 3, 1975, pp. 395–408.

6. Rawls, *A Theory of Justice*, p. 250.

7. *Ibid.*, pp. 302–3.

8. *Ibid.*, p. 61.

9. As we shall see later, the fact that the Difference Principle takes self-respect into account turns out to be very important for assessing Marxian criticisms of Rawls.

10. Rawls, *A Theory of Justice*, p. 98.

11. *Ibid.*, p. 87.

12. I have supplied these examples; they are not taken from Rawls' text.

13. Rawls adds a "Just Savings Principle" in his final formulation on p. 302 of *A Theory of Justice*.

14. Rawls, *A Theory of Justice*, p. 20.

15. *Ibid.*, p. 21.

16. *Ibid.*, p. 21.

17. *Ibid.*, p. 252.

18. Stephen Darwall has argued persuasively that some critics who deny the possibility of a consistent Kantian interpretation of Rawls' theory have confused this thesis with the quite different claim that in choosing Rawls' principles *the parties in the original position* are acting autonomously. (Darwall, "A Defense of the Kantian Interpretation," *Ethics*, vol. 86, 1976, no. 2, pp. 164–70) See also Darwall, "Is There a Kantian Foundation for Rawlsian Justice?" in *John Rawls' Theory of Social Justice*, edited by H. G. Blocker and E. Smith (Athens, Ohio, 1980), pp. 311–45.

19. See, especially the third part of the *Foundations of the Metaphysics of Morals* (translated by L. W. Beck, New York, 1959).

20. Rawls, *A Theory of Justice*, p. 11.

21. *Ibid.*, p. 15.

22. Many of Rawls' critics have erroneously assumed that Rawls characterizes the parties in the original position as rational egoists. On p. 127 of *A Theory of Justice*, Rawls distinguishes between (a) one's own conception of the good and (b) a conception of the good which is exclusively a conception of one's own good, and then characterizes the parties as having (a). This passage shows that it is false to characterize the parties as rational egoists and extremely misleading to say they are self-interested.

23. Rawls, *A Theory of Justice*, p. 12.

24. *Ibid.*, pp. 127–35.

25. *Ibid.*, p. 440.

26. *Ibid.*, p. 440.

27. Rawls' discussion lends itself to two different versions of the strains of commitment argument. According to one version, the parties include strains of commitment in their estimate of worst outcomes in following the maximin strategy. The other version does not invoke any formal decision principles. My discussion of the maximin argument covers the first version, so I will concentrate here only on the second.

28. Rawls, "Reply to Alexander and Musgrave," *Quarterly Journal of Economics*, November 1974, p. 653. See also, *A Theory of Justice*, pp, 175–76.

29. Rawls, *A Theory of Justice*, p. 145.

30. *Ibid.*, p. 278.

31. *Ibid.*, p. 278.

32. R. P. Wolff, *Understanding Rawls*, (Princeton, New Jersey, 1977), p. 210.

33. Barry ("Critical Notice of Wolff: *Understanding Rawls*," pp. 758–60) also criticizes Wolff's assumption that Rawls is concerned only with distribution.

34. See, for example, *The Hidden Injuries of Class*, R. Sennett and J. Cobb (New York, 1973), especially pp. 4–8, 18, 22, 28–29, 53.

35. Robert Nozick, *Anarchy, State and Utopia* (New York, 1974), pp. 160–63.

36. Stephen Darwall argues that any essentially Kantian moral theory, including Rawls', will require a theory of primary goods. (Darwall, "Is There a Kantian Foundation for Rawlsian Justice" in *John Rawls' Theory of Social Justice*.) For a related discussion of how a theory of the good would figure in a plausible Kantian theory of the right, see my critical review of Onora O'Neill's book *Acting on Principle*, *The Journal of Philosophy*, vol. LXXVI, no. 6, 1978, pp. 325–40.

37. Rawls, *A Theory of Justice*, p. 274.

38. I would like to thank Stephen Darwall for helping me clarify this objection.

39. C. B. Macpherson, *Democratic Theory: Essays in Retrieval* (London and New York, 1973), p. 87.

40. *Ibid.*, pp. 192–97.

41. Rawls, *A Theory of Justice*, p. 98.

42. Rawls, "The Basic Structure as Subject," in *Values and Morals*, edited by A. I. Goldman and J. Kim, Dordrecht, Holland: 1978, pp. 47–71. Note that this essay is a significant revision of a paper of the same title presented at the Pacific Division Meetings of the American Philosophical Association in 1977 and published in the *American Philosophical Quarterly*, 14 (April 1977). All subsequent references are to the revised version of "The Basic Structure as Subject."

43. For an excellent examination of the power and complexity of the notion of reflective equilibrium, see Norman Daniels' essay "Wide Reflective Equilibrium and Theory Acceptance in Ethics," *The Journal of Philosophy*, vol. LXXVI, no. 5, 1979, pp. 256–82.

44. Rawls, *A Theory of Justice*, p. 20.

45. In section 7 of Part III of this chapter, I examine the objection that Rawls lacks a theory of the transition from an unjust to a just society capable of showing that enough people in an unjust society will be sufficiently motivated to strive to implement his principles.

46. See especially sections 4, 5, and 6 of Part III of this chapter.

47. Macpherson, p. 94.

48. Rawls, "Reply to Alexander and Musgrave," p. 642, and "Fairness to Goodness," *Philosophical Review*, vol. LXXXIV, 1975, p. 543.

49. Brian Barry ("Critical Notice of Wolff: *Understanding Rawls*," p. 768) also notes that Wolff is guilty of this fundamental error.

50. None of Rawls' Marxian critics have, to my knowledge, broached the perplexing problem of how we can know that the Marxian conception of man is not also temporally parochial.

51. Rawls, *A Theory of Justice*, p. 127.

52. Rawls, "Fairness to Goodness," pp. 542–43.

53. Rawls, *A Theory of Justice*, pp. 522–23.

54. Rawls, "Reply to Alexander and Musgrave," p. 641.

55. In my dissertation, *Autonomy, Distribution, and the State*, University of North Carolina at Chapel Hill, 1975 (unpublished).

56. To emphasize this point, Rawls says, in "Reply to Alexander and Musgrave" (p. 642) and in "A Kantian Conception of Equality" (*The Cambridge Review*, February 1975, p. 97), that the index of primary goods is *not* a measure of satisfaction.

57. Rawls, *A Theory of Justice*, pp. 93–94 and p. 143; "Justice as Fairness," *Philosophical Review*, vol. LXVII, p. 170.

58. *Ibid.*, p. 207.

59. *Ibid.*, p. 254.

60. *Ibid.*, p. 255.

61. See also "The Basic Structure as Subject," p. 63.

62. Lecture IV, Stanford 1978, "Responsibility for Ends," unpublished.

63. The distinction between these two features of primary goods was drawn in my paper, "A Modification of Rawls' Theory," presented at the Western Division Meetings of the American Philosophical Association in 1974 and later in more detail in my essay "Revisability and Rational Choice" (See note 5, this chapter). In his most recent papers, especially "Responsibility for Ends," Rawls emphasizes the dual role of primary goods, drawing in part on my account in "Revisability and Rational Choice."

64. A. Schwartz, "Moral Neutrality and the Theory of Primary Goods," *Ethics*, vol. 83, p. 294, and M. Teitleman, "The Limits of Individualism," *Journal of Philosophy*, vol. LXIX, no. 18, 1972, pp. 545–56.

65. Rawls, "Fairness to Goodness," pp. 540–42.

66. In "Revisability and Rational Choice," I begin the task of arguing that an adequate theory of rationality will include what I call principles of critical revisability, and argue that such principles must be employed in Rawls' contractual arguments if the objections raised by Teitleman and Schwartz are to be successfully answered (See note 5, this chapter).

67. Richard Miller, "Rawls and Marxism," *Philosophy and Public Affairs*, vol. 3, no. 2, 1974, pp. 167–91.

68. *Ibid.*, p. 225.

69. *Ibid.*, p. 228.

70. Wolff, *Understanding Rawls*, pp. 204–5.

71. *Writings of the Young Marx on Philosophy and Society*, Easton and Guddhat (Garden City, New York, 1967), p. 192.

72. Norman Daniels, "Equal Liberty and Equal Worth of Liberty," in *Reading Rawls*, edited by Norman Daniels (New York, 1975, pp. 253–81).

73. *Ibid.*, p. 259.

74. Rawls, *A Theory of Justice*, p. 204.

75. Daniels, "Equal Liberty and Equal Worth of Liberty," p. 259.

76. *Ibid.*, p. 259.

77. Rawls, *A Theory of Justice*, pp. 151–52.

78. *Ibid.*, p. 277.

79. See, for example, *A Theory of Justice*, pp. 20–21.

80. See *A Theory of Justice*, pp. 251–57 and p. 587.

81. Teitleman, p. 551.

82. Rawls, "Fairness to Goodness," p. 540.

83. Rawls, *A Theory of Justice*, p. 3.

84. With the possible exception of the "utopianism" objection explored earlier in this chapter.

85. Nozick has suggested a quite different objection that the Difference Principle permits or even requires the exploitation of the better-off by the worst-off (*Anarchy, State, and Utopia*, p. 33).

86. Rawls' most comprehensive account of the notion of the basic structure is found in "The Basic Structure as Subject" (revised version); see note 42 of this chapter.

87. Rawls, "The Basic Structure as Subject," p. 55.

88. Nozick, *Anarchy, State and Utopia*, pp. 150–62.

89. *Ibid.*, p. 178.

90. *Ibid.*, p. 151.

91. Rawls, "The Basic Structure as Subject," p. 51.

92. *Ibid.*, p. 53.

93. It can be argued that Marx's scattered discussions of colonialism and of the exploitative character of international relations in a world dominated by capitalism provide the basis for another important Marxian criticism of Rawls. Though I believe that Rawls' attempt to provide a theory of justice for the nation state without examining problems of justice in international relations cannot ultimately succeed, I must reserve consideration of this enormously complex issue for another occasion.

Chapter 7

1. I. Kant, "On the Old Saw: That May Be Right in Theory But It Won't Work in Practice," translated by E. B. Ashton (Philadelphia, 1974), p. 60.

2. See, for example, *Capital*, vol. I (New York, 1967), p. 529.

3. See F. Miller and R. Sartorius, "Population Policy and Public Goods," *Philosophy and Public Affairs*, vol. 8, no. 2, 1979, pp. 148–74.

4. One of the best guides to this literature is D. Mueller's *Public Choice* (Cambridge, 1979), pp. 148–74.

5. Marx, *The Civil War in France*, in *Karl Marx and Frederick Engels: Selected Works* (New York, 1972), p. 291.

6. *Ibid.*, p. 294.

7. *Ibid.*, p. 294.

8. *Ibid.*, p. 294.

9. A classic presentation of some of the more important obstacles to efficient planned allocation, as well as bibliographical references to theories of planned allocation that purport to deal with these difficulties, can be found in F. A. Hayek, *Individualism and the Economic Order* (Chicago, 1948), pp. 119–208.

10. One of the most influential contemporary analytical works on bureaucracy is that of W. Niskanen: *Bureaucracy and Representative Government* (Chicago, 1971) and "Bureaucrats and Politicians," *Journal of Law and Economics*, December 1975, pp. 617–53. See also Mueller, pp. 148–70.

Bibliography

Althusser, L. *For Marx* (New York, 1969).
Avineri, S. *Hegel's Theory of the Modern State* (Cambridge, 1972).
———. *The Social and Political Thought of Karl Marx* (Cambridge, 1968).
Barry, Brian. "Critical Notice of Wolff: *Understanding Rawls,*" *Canadian Journal of Philosophy*, Vol. VII, No. 4, 1979, p. 780.
———. *Sociologists, Economists, and Democracy* (London 1970).
Blaug, M. *Economic Theory in Retrospect*, revised edition (Homewood, Ill., 1968).
Brenkert, George F. "Freedom and Private Property in Marx," *Philosophy and Public Affairs*, Vol. 8, No. 2, 1979, pp. 122–147.
Buchanan, Allen E. *Autonomy, Distribution, and the State*, University of North Carolina at Chapel Hill, 1975 (unpublished doctoral dissertation).
———. "Exploitation, Alienation, and Injustice," *Canadian Journal of Philosophy*, Vol. 9, No. 1, 1979, p. 121.
———. "Deriving Welfare Rights from Libertarian Rights," in *Income Support*, edited by P. Brown, C. Johnson, and P. Vernier of the Center for Philosophy and Public Policy, University of Maryland at College Park (Totowa, N.J., 1981).
———. review of Onora O'Neill's *Acting on Principle*, *Journal of Philosophy*, Vol. LXXV, No. 6, 1978, pp. 325–40.
———. "Revisability and Rational Choice," *Canadian Journal of Philosophy*, Vol. 5, No. 3, 1975, pp. 395–408.
———. "Revolutionary Motivation and Rationality," *Philosophy and Public Affairs*, Vol. 9, No. 1, 1979, pp. 59–82.
Cohen, G. A. "The Labor Theory of Value and the Concept of Exploitation," *Philosophy and Public Affairs*, Vol. 8, No. 4, 1979, pp. 338–60.
———, *Marx's Theory of History: A Defense* (Oxford, 1978).
Daniels, Norman A. "Wide Reflective Equilibrium and Theory Acceptance in Ethics," *The Journal of Philosophy*, Vol. LXXVI, No. 5, 1979, pp. 256–82.
———. (ed.) *Reading Rawls*, (New York, 1975).
Darwall, Stephen. "A Defense of the Kantian Interpretation," *Ethics*, Vol. 86, No. 2, 1976, pp. 164–70.
———. "Is There a Kantian Foundation for Rawlsian Justice?" in *John Rawls' Theory of Social Justice*, edited by H. G. Blocker and E. Smith, (Athens, Ohio, 1980) pp. 311–45.
———. "Two Kinds of Respect," *Ethics*, Vol. 88, No. 3, 1978, pp. 36–49.
Easton, L. and Guddhat, K. (eds.) *The German Ideology, Writings of the Young Marx on Philosophy and Society*, (Garden City, New York, 1967).
Feuer, L. *The Communist Manifesto, Marx and Engels: Basic Writings on Politics and Philosophy*, (New York, 1959).
Feinberg, Joel. "The Nature and Value of Rights," in *Moral Problems in Medicine*, edited by S. Gorovitz, *et al.* (Engelwood Cliffs, New Jersey, 1976), pp. 454–67.
Gauthier, D. "The Social Contract as Ideology," *Philosophy and Public Affairs*, Vol. 6, No. 2, 1978, pp. 130–64.
Gould, Carol. *Marx's Social Ontology* (Cambridge, Massachusetts, 1978).

197

Hayek, F. A. *Individualism and the Economic Order* (Chicago, 1948).

Hegel, G. W. F. *The Philosophy of Right,* edited by T. M. Knox (London, 1973).

Holmstrom, N. "Exploitation," *Canadian Journal of Philosophy,* Vol. VII, No. 2, 1977, pp. 353–69.

Husami, Z. "Marx on Distributive Justice," *Philosophy and Public Affairs,* Vol. 8, No. 1, 1978, pp. 27–64.

Kant, Immanuel. *Foundations of the Metaphysics of Morals,* translated by L. W. Beck, (New York, 1959).

———. *Groundwork of the Metaphysics of Morals,* translated by H. J. Paton, (New York, 1964).

———. "On the Old Saw: That May Be Right in Theory But It Won't Work in Practice," translated by E. B. Ashton (Philadelphia, 1974).

Littré, E. *Dictionnaire de la Langue Française* (Paris, L'Académie Française: Libraire Hatchette et Cie., 1873).

Lowenberg, J. (ed.) *Hegel: Selections* (New York, 1957).

Lukács, G. "Reification and the Consciousness of the Proletariat," in *History and Class Consciousness,* translated by R. Livingstone (Cambridge, Massachusetts, 1971), pp. 83–222.

Macpherson, C. B. *Democratic Theory: Essays in Retrieval* (London and New York, 1973).

McBride, W. L. "The Concept of Justice in Marx, Engels, and Others," *Ethics,* Vol. 85, 1975, p. 206.

———. *The Philosophy of Marx* (London, 1977).

McLellan, D. *Karl Marx: Selected Writings* (Oxford, 1977).

Marx, Karl. *Capital* (New York, 1967).

———. *The Economic and Philosophic Manuscripts of 1844,* edited by D. Struik, translated by M. Milligan, (New York, 1964).

———. *Grundrisse,* translated by M. Nicolaus (New York, 1973).

———. *The Poverty of Philosophy* (New York, 1963).

———. *Precapitalist Economic Formations,* edited by E. J. Hobsbawm (New York, 1975).

Marx, Karl and Engels, Frederick. *The Holy Family* (Moscow, 1956).

Miliband, R. *Marxism and Politics* (Oxford, 1977).

Mill, John Stuart. *On Liberty,* edited by Currin V. Shields (New York, 1956).

Miller, F. and Sartorius, R. "Population Policy and Public Goods," *Philosophy and Public Affairs,* Vol. 8, No. 2, 1979, pp. 148–74.

Miller, R. "The Consistency of Historical Materialism," *Philosophy and Public Affairs,* Vol. 4, No. 4, 1975, pp. 390–409.

Miller, Richard. "Rawls and Marxism," *Philosophy and Public Affairs,* Vol. 3, No. 2, 1974.

Moore, S. "Marx and Lenin as Historical Materialists," *Philosophy and Public Affairs,* Vol. 4, No. 2, 1975, pp. 171–94.

Morris, Herbert, "Persons and Punishment," *Monist,* Vol. 52, No. 4, p. 500.

Mueller, D. *Public Choice* (Cambridge, 1979).

Murphy, J. "Marxism and Retribution," *Philosophy and Public Affairs,* Vol. 2, No. 3, 1973, pp. 217–18.

Niskanen, W. *Bureaucracy and Representative Government* (Chicago, 1971).

———. "Bureaucrats and Politicians," *Journal of Law and Economics,* December, 1975, pp. 617–53.

Nozick, R. *Anarchy, State, and Utopia* (New York, 1975).

Ollman, B. *Alienation: Marx's Conception of Man in Capitalist Society* (Cambridge, 1971).

Olson, M. *The Logic of Collective Action* (Cambridge, Massachusetts, 1965).

Raico, R. "Classical Liberal Exploitation Theory," *Journal of Libertarian Studies,* Volume 1, 1977, pp. 179-80.

Rawls, John. "The Basic Structure as Subject," in *Values and Morals,* edited by A. I. Goldman and J. Kim (Dordrecht, Holland, 1978). pp. 47–71.

———. "Fairness to Goodness," *Philosophical Review,* Vol. LXXXIV, 1975, p. 543.

———. "Justice as Fairness," *Philosophical Review,* Vol. LXVII, p. 170.

———. "A Kantian Conception of Equality," *The Cambridge Review,* February, 1975, p. 97.

———. "Reply to Alexander and Musgrave," *Quarterly Journal of Economics,* November, 1974, p. 653.

——. "Responsibility for Ends," Lecture IV, Stanford University (unpublished), 1978.
——. *A Theory of Justice* (Cambridge, Massachusetts, 1971).
Ryazanskaya, S. W. (ed.) *Marx and Engels: Selected Correspondence*, translated by I. Lasker (Moscow, 1975).
Samuelson, P. *Economics*, 9th ed. (New York, 1973).
Sartorius, Rolf. "The Limits of Libertarianism," *Law and Liberty* (College Station, Texas, 1978).
Schwartz, A. "Moral Neutrality and the Theory of Primary Goods," *Ethics*, Vol. 83, 1973, p. 294.
Seigel, J. "Alienation," *History and Theory*, Vol. XII, No. 3, 1973, pp. 329–42.
Sennett, R. and Cobb, J. *The Hidden Injuries of Class* (New York, 1973).
Taylor, Charles. *Hegel* (London, 1978).
Teitleman, M. "The Limits of Individualism," *Journal of Philosophy*, Vol. LXIX, No. 18, 1972, pp. 545–556.
Tucker, R. C. *The Marxian Revolutionary Idea* (New York, 1969).
Wolff, R. P. *Understanding Rawls* (Princeton, New Jersey, 1977).
Wood, Allen. "The Marxian Critique of Justice," *Philosophy and Public Affairs*, Vol. 1, No. 3, 1972, p. 246.
Young, G. "The Fundamental Contradiction of Capitalism," *Philosophy and Public Affairs*, Vol. 5, No. 2, 1976, pp. 196–234.
Anonymous (ed.). *The German Ideology, Collected Works: Marx and Engels*, Volume 5 (New York, 1976).
——. *Karl Marx and Frederick Engels, Selected Works* (New York, 1972).
——. *Karl Marx and Frederick Engels, Selected Works in One Volume* (New York, 1968).
——. *Selected Works of Marx and Engels* (New York, 1972).

Index

Utilization, 38, 42, 43, 46, 48, 135, 136, 137–40
Utopianism, 48

Veil of ignorance, 113, 116, 117, 145, 148
Vergegenständlichung, 16, 17

Wage-labor, 37–38, 40, 43–47, 48, 54
"War of each against all," 7, 10

Wealth, 142, 150, 155; *see also* Class divisions
Welfare benefits, 71
Welfare state, 88, 92, 125
Willing, 3, 4–5, 6
Wolff, Robert Paul, 122–23, 124, 135
Wood, Allen, 26, 52–54, 55, 56, 60, 80
World market, 7
Worst-off (*see* Representative worst-off man)